LOON

Loon

Memory, Meaning, and Reality
in a Northern Dene Community

HENRY S. SHARP

University of Nebraska Press | Lincoln and London

LIBRARY OF CONGRESS
CATALOGING-IN-PUBLICATION DATA
Sharp, Henry S.
Loon: memory, meaning, and reality in a northern
Dene community / Henry S. Sharp. p. cm.
Includes bibliographical references and index.
ISBN 0-8032-4292-1 (cloth: alk. paper)
1. Chipewyan philosophy. 2. Chipewyan mythology.
3. Chipewyan Indians—Social life and customs.
4. Northwest Territories—Social life and customs.
I. Title.
E99.C56 S53   2001   305.897′2—dc21   2001017447

Dr. Timothy L. Pruett Jr.
Ms. Nancy Bolton, RN
Dr. Peter Lobo
and the entire medical
and support staff of the
University of Virginia
Multi-Organ Transplant
Program.

Dr. Fred B. Westervelt
Jefferson Nephrology Ltd.

*For the dedication, knowl-
edge, effort, and caring
it took to make the magic
work for my daughter.*

But now I had to face an elemental question, as an anthropologist of course, but even more so as a person who had always been deeply involved with nature: Is there not a single reality in the natural world, an absolute and universal reality? Apparently the answer to this question is no.

RICHARD K. NELSON, *Make Prayers to the Raven*

CONTENTS

PREFACE

For more than thirty years The People of Mission have allowed me to come among them and have shared with me the experience of their lives. That experience has been beyond price and has shaped the course of my life. No book could encompass all they have shared with me, but I hope this one will aid those who have never experienced the North to appreciate The People and their world as it existed between 1969 and 1992.

I wish to express my sincere thanks to the staff of the University of Nebraska Press. Editing is a difficult and often unappreciated task. I wish to thank the copyeditor, Maureen Creamer Bemko. I owe a particular debt of gratitude to Gary Dunham for his sustained interest in this work as it evolved from a concatenation of original essays and reprinted articles into an integrated narrative ethnography.

The University of Nebraska Press arranged for two sets of reviewers for the manuscript. Of the anonymous first set, one provided an extensive and detailed review that engaged the ideas in this work and was extremely valuable to me in refining and reformulating the arguments. The other established that they did not like it, me, the topic, the working title, the writing, or much else about the work. The comments of both reviews were quite useful in developing the arguments and their presentation, although they were useful in rather different ways. The reviewers of the penultimate draft, each of whom chose not to remain anonymous, were Robert Jarvenpa (SUNY–Albany) and David M. Smith (University of Minnesota–Duluth). Both Bob and Dave provided insightful comments and advice, most of which I have taken.

As the manuscript has developed over the years it has benefited from the insights and encouragement of Professors David M. Smith, Robert Jarvenpa, Edith L. Turner (University of Virginia), Roy Wagner (University of Virginia), Margaret Huber (Mary Washington College), Peter Huber (P. B. Huber Inc.), and Phillip Moore (Curtin University). Edie, Bob, Dave, and Phil have all committed the time and effort to read the entire manuscript at one stage or another of its development. I thank them for their patience, their insights, and their advice. The faults of the book are mine, but many of its virtues are theirs.

The University of Virginia is supportive of local scholars. I wish to thank it for providing, through the Department of Anthropology, e-mail, access to the Internet, and the use of its libraries.

Ethnology is still an expression of relationships between people, and so much that is of value in those relationships cannot be marked by reference to publications. Northern Athapaskanists are rare critters. Most of us are forced to live our professional lives with only intermittent contact with others who share our interest in Northern Athapaskan peoples and cultures. What contacts we do have, largely at conferences and by e-mail, are precious. The references within the text do not begin to reflect that influence. I particularly value the decades long exchange of ideas about the Chipewyan and the nature of power in Chipewyan culture that I have had with David M. Smith. The influence those exchanges have had upon my understanding of the Chipewyan is immense.

"Experience" as an analytical subject is something to which I have come but lately and only with hesitation and uncertainty. I remain to be convinced that experience is either a subject that can be successfully explored or a viable analytic category as the ascendancy of reductionism seems an almost inevitable consequence of the interpretive pursuit of experience. Yet, during the nearly fifteen years I have participated in Edie Turner's seminar, I have been impressed by her constant search for the limits of the anthropology of experience and the range of issues she has been able to bring under anthropological examination. If I am not yet convinced of the validity of an anthropology of experience, I have become convinced that the range of otherwise unexaminable topics demands exploration of the limits of what a focus upon experience can bring to ethnological analysis.

Anthropology has a limited interest to nonacademics, so I especially thank Kelvin McDaniel, Roman Locke, Harold Burton, John Wilkinson, Ed Thomas, Robert Hall, Gilbert Gough, Frances Winegar, Jack Messina, Patti Vineyard, and Jeff Peck for coping with my attempts to explain the arguments advanced in the book while I was trying to formulate them. Kelvin and Roman especially deserve my thanks for their patient willingness to listen to the abstractness of anthropology when we were supposed to be working on other things.

I owe particular thanks to the people of Mission. I cannot name them all here, but I wish to thank all of them for their kindness, tolerance, and patience. I especially wish to thank Thomas and Louise Disain, Louie and Mary Louise Disain, Boniface and Mary Disain, Joe Bigeye, Alphonse Disain, Irene Maynard, Mary MacDonald, Victor Disain, Johnny and Florence Mercredi, Mr. and Mrs. Abraham Artchie, Bernadette Disain-Sharp, Campet Medal, Pierre Robillard, Noel Bouvier, Napoleon MacKenzie, Peter Disain, Simon Robillard, Lena Carter, Mr. and Mrs. Willie Broussie, Germane Dadzene, John Laban, Jimmy Laban, Toby Laban, Louie Toutsaint, Fred Toutsaint, Louis Ditheda, Pierre Catholic, Ben Toutsaint, William Bouvier, Oliver Bouvier, Martin Robillard, Mary Yooya, Artchie Disain, Moise Yooya, Mary Jane Yooya, Mr. and Mrs. Mike MacKenzie, Alex Black Lake, Edwin Mercredi, Gilbert Mercredi, Boniface Mercredi, Modest Bigeye, John Louie Bigeye, Moise and Victoria Eckodh, Billy Sandypoint, John Sayazie, and Ben Adam.

Because the world of white Northerners is so small and each individual is so readily identifiable with a particular place and time, I have chosen not to name any of the white population of Mission or Discha. Many of them were helpful and supportive during my fieldwork, especially during my first few months at Mission. The presence of an American student committed to living entirely within the confines of the First Nation community was perplexing—and sometimes disquieting—to a white Canadian population facing uncertainty about its own future. Inevitably, my presence became an issue in local white politics and social relationships, yet even those who found my presence most disconcerting were consistently polite and helpful.

At some point ethnography has an obligation to provide privacy to the people who are its subjects. The names of all persons, other than anthropologists whose assistance or work is being acknowledged, are pseudonyms. The individual names that appear in this work are consistent with those that

I have used in other writings over the last fifteen years. Place names near Mission are disguised, usually by using a local name for them, but I have generally used the real names of places within the region unless I am following an author who has used a pseudonym for a place name.

I should especially like to thank my aunt and uncle, Paul Miller and Jacquie Miller, for their sustained caring, encouragement, and interest in my daughters' lives and dreams.

Writing is a time-consuming process. Thinking about the data and experience to formulate what is to be written can usually be accomplished—except for capricious moments of intense concentration—while engaged in other activities. The writing itself means hour after hour at the keyboard to the neglect of other obligations and duties. Both my daughters had left home by the time I began intensive work on the manuscript, but I wish to thank my children, Karyn and Catherine, and my mother, Catharine M. Sharp, for their patience and their toleration of the neglect the writing of this book has caused.

ON WORDS

The Chipewyan of Mission refer to themselves as Dene, Chipewyan, or "The People of Mission." "The People" is another translation of the word Dene. I use them interchangeably. The word Chipewyan is not Dene in origin and is one of those words that, to the disgust of every proofreader (and the occasional manuscript reviewer) I have ever dealt with, does not take a plural form. Chipewyan is Chipewyan. I have never heard the plural form used by any Chipewyan or by any of the local white population. Only in written English is this usage sometimes ignored.

I use the word "white" to refer to the non-Indian Canadian (and sometimes American) society—past and present—and its members. Within the context of Mission, white refers to a group defined by culture, values, and social position rather than by skin color. The Dene recognize as well as anyone else the differences in skin color and physical characteristics whites use to categorize individuals into races. They categorize members of other Native American cultures as Indian, but they conceive of African-American tourist fishermen or Canadians of non-European extraction as white because of their values, behavior, and social position. Theirs is a sensible position, and I have chosen to follow it here.

Blood plays a series of roles as metaphors of family and kinship among the Chipewyan, but Indian status in Canada is determined by inclusion on a treaty list prepared by each recognized band rather than by ideas of blood. The rules for inclusion or exclusion change through time, but the actual number of First Nation individuals always exceeds the number on the treaty list. Customary practice in anthropological writing calls for the use of the term "status" to designate those individuals recognized as belonging to a First Nations group. I have followed the lead of the English-speaking population at Mission—white and First Nations—that uses the word "treaty" to make this distinction. The word "status" is presumed to be less offensive than the word "treaty," but the only people I have ever encountered who found the term offensive were white male anthropologists.

In common with many First Nations cultures, the Mission Chipewyan refer to animals in the singular. This usage often seems glaringly incorrect in English, but wolf is wolf, not the wolf, the wolves, a wolf, or wolves. The reasons for this are explored in chapter 9. I have tried to follow this usage whenever the issue of number is relevant in the use of the name of an animal or would lead to a statement that I regard as less than accurate.

There are places in the text where I capitalize whole words, for example, DOG, WOMAN, or MAN for the specific purpose of indicating that the word refers to a category. I prefer capitalization to indicate precisely that I am referring to a category and to eliminate the possibility of confusing the category designator with a proper noun.

At places the word "know" is capitalized. This word refers specifically to having power/knowledge (*inkoze*) and is capitalized to prevent any chance of error in its meaning.

The Royal Canadian Mounted Police are customarily called the RCMP (each initial spoken individually). This practice is followed in Mission, in all the parts of Saskatchewan where I have spent any time, and in British Columbia, where I lived for eleven years. I follow that usage here.

Mission is a small place of recent origin. The name is used to provide some degree of privacy to its inhabitants, but it is one of the names the Dene themselves use to refer to their home. Chipewyan culture varies considerably from place to place, and I presume this book to refer specifically to the Mission Chipewyan.

There are a number of places in the text where words are given meanings that deviate from their customary usage. Sometimes this simply reflects local usage at Mission. In other cases, where I have not been able to find an effective substitute, quotation marks have been placed around them to alert the reader that the ordinary English usage of the word may convey meanings not applicable to the specific case of the Chipewyan. This is reasonably obvious in the case of words like "spirit" or "soul." Sometimes it is necessary to use a word in a special sense ("event" is the most obvious case) before the reader has been exposed to a later argument about its meaning. The quotation marks serve no purpose other than to alert the reader to interpret the word judiciously because of a following argument.

INTRODUCTION

The Central Canadian Subarctic home of the Chipewyan is a place of perpetual enigma. Within it, human life is constructed by the discord between
beauty, seclusion, abundance, and scarcity. It is framed by the extremes of a
climate given to sheer brutality. The People themselves are marvelously
enigmatic, yet their understanding of themselves, their land, and their relationships to it and its other inhabitants expresses a subtle and penetrating
wisdom.

There comes a point after living among them, trying hard to understand
them by paying careful attention to what they do and what they say, that it is
possible to explain in familiar terms almost everything they do and say. On
rare occasions there occur circumstances whose explanation defies the familiar reality of Western thought. This work is focused upon a few of those
unusual circumstances that I have found to be critical to understanding the
Chipewyan and appreciating the differences between them and ourselves.

Northern Athapaskan ethnography has always been a bit out of phase with
the ethnography of the rest of Native North America. Since the publication
of Cornelius Osgood's *Winter* in 1953, there have always been a few good
books on Northern Athapaskan cultures that have transcended regional
ethnography. Joel Savishinsky's *The Trail of the Hare* (1974) and Bob Jarvenpa's excellent *Northern Apprenticeship* (1998) are good examples of works
on Central Canadian Subarctic cultures that have broad appeal. This is true
for Northern Athapaskan cultures in other areas, as Richard Nelson's somewhat controversial *Make Prayers to the Raven* (1983) illustrates. A few, nota-

bly Hugh Brody's *Maps and Dreams* (1983), are widely read and have been influential outside anthropology. Some very few, like Julie Cruikshank's *Life Lived Like a Story* (1990), have altogether transcended specialized ethnography and have had a substantial influence on a wide range of academic disciplines.

Notwithstanding the broad appeal of a few works, the heart of Northern Athapaskan ethnography has always been the journal article and the technical monograph. Developing the ethnography of Northern Athapaskans through technical publications directed first to specialists and only secondarily to other interested souls has had its benefits. If few of anthropology's hot issues are resolved through the use of Northern Athapaskan material, distance from that more heated world of disciplinary passion has allowed the development of a literature rich in ethnographic detail and generally quite thorough in its appreciation of theoretical issues.

It has also produced a literature seemingly quite civilized in its conduct. It is rare for Northern Athapaskanists to call each other names or directly challenge each other. The polemics of even the most fractious debates among us pale before those in areas that attract greater attention. This is partly due to the different ways Northern Athapaskan cultures seem to be seen by those who actively conduct fieldwork among them and by those who deal with them through the literature. The latter seem to see Northern Athapaskans as more uniform than do fieldworkers, and it is my experience that they are far more willing to make comparisons between cultures.

Chipewyan culture varies quite significantly from village to village. Most Northern Athapaskan ethnography—this work included—is very much directed inward toward a single group of people in a particular set of circumstances at a specified time and place. This characteristic is marked by a lack of comparison between cultures and a lack of reference to the work of ethnographers dealing with other Northern Athapaskan cultures. It is not that we do not read each other's work but that we are acutely aware of the differences between the cultures and are intensely suspicious of comparisons between peoples often living many hundreds of miles apart who are separated from each other by intervening languages and cultures and who exist in different historical, ecological, and social circumstances. Comparison is a deeply desired goal in Northern Athapaskan ethnography, but I think most of us feel that the depth of the existing ethnography is not yet sufficient to allow very much of it. That time will come, but for the present Jean-Guy

Goulet's *Ways of Knowing* (1998) (on the Dene Tha) is about the only ethnography that strikes me as effectively using comparison in the analysis of a
Northern Athapaskan culture. Yet even there I think the differences between
the Dene Tha and the Chipewyan are underdrawn.

This does not mean Northern Athapaskan ethnography is bland or without conflict. Rather, much as among the peoples themselves, conflict is
indirect and subtle. Over the years I have taken to reading Northern Athapaskan ethnography much as I would go about trying to uncover the social
context of a medicine fight. Many of the most important statements in the
Northern Athapaskan literature are made through acts of omission rather
than through acts of commission. Disagreement or lack of confidence in the
work of others is not expressed directly but is shown through odd juxtaposi-
tions of sources and references, strangely elliptical footnotes or comments,
or lack of reliance upon apparently obvious sources.

At a time when uncontextualized snippets of tape-recorded speech have too
often become substitutes for sustained fieldwork, I have based this work on
the traditional methodology of ethnographic analysis: participant observation. For an anthropologist of my generation, this meant living among the
people and, as much as I could, dressing as they did, obtaining my food as
they did, and going hungry when they did. This approach to ethnology
demands total immersion in Dene life: day after day, week after week, month
after month, field trip after field trip. In the field and out of the field,
the data—the notes, the experiences, the emotions, the photographs, the
memories—are continuously examined and reexamined, interpreted and
reinterpreted. My emerging understandings of The People were carried back
among them to be checked and rechecked, examined and reexamined, tested
and retested, in what has become a continuous process of seeking the mean-
ing(s) of my experiences in order to increase my understanding of the Dene.

I quickly learned that the Chipewyan would not tolerate questioning or
formal interviews. The People did not intend to teach me (see Goulet 1998:
3–8 for the manner in which the Dene Tha controlled his education among
them); instead they expected me to learn from participation. They did not
mind my taking and keeping notes as long as I took them in private. They
would not accept my taking them in the course of interaction with them.
They did not tolerate tape recordings but were quite fond of photographs.

Since Jean-Guy Goulet has raised the issue of methodology in Northern

Athapaskan ethnography with his call for "radical participation" (Goulet 1998: 25–28), it seems appropriate to comment upon the nature of my own fieldwork. I entered the field in December 1969, having flown to Discha via commercial air service. Before departing I had made contact with the Chief—Denegothera (see chapter 13)—and received his permission to come. He offered to rent me his cabin, and I accepted that arrangement. In 1969, Mission did not have the status of a reserve so there was no legal authority to grant or refuse me permission. My entry was not a community project, and there was no community-wide involvement with my coming. I was simply offered a rental and told I could come. Everything else was up to me.

The fieldwork part of my research was conducted between December 1969 and August 1992 and involved sustained interaction with a sample of the Mission Dene that constituted nearly 10 percent of the total population. I had less regular interaction with nearly one-third of the adult population and irregular interaction with virtually the entire adult population.

My position in the community was always a curious one. I was there because of the relationships of friendship and affinity that I developed, but there was never any illusion that I was part of the community or one of The People. I was always myself, and The People were always themselves. While I was there, I was expected to live among them and take part in their lives, but neither of us had any intention of turning into other than what we were. By temperament, I am not a particularly outgoing individual. I dislike intruding upon others and truly disdain pushing myself into situations, relationships, or circumstances where I am not welcome. This aspect of my personality fit well with the manner in which the Chipewyan conduct themselves. We became a feature of each other's lives. Our mutual presence was accepted for what it was, and we all got on with the business of getting along and living our lives in each other's company.

In time I developed a series of strong relationships among The People that became the basis for my return visits. After a few years I found that the constraints that came with accepting research funds interfered with the conduct of my research. Since 1977, I have not sought research funding and have gone to the field without it. I discovered within the first year of my research that my interests lay in bush life rather than in village life. I spent December 1969 to June 1970 and August 1972 to January 1973 living in the village. The rest of my time among the Chipewyan has been spent in the bush, usually 150 or more air miles from the village along the forest-tundra interface.

As my experience of the Chipewyan grew, I learned not to try to direct my research but to learn from our experience of the "events" of our lives together. I enjoy teasing out the chains of causality that have produced the social interactions I have observed or participated in, and the focus of my research has been primarily upon the microanalysis of specific "events" and circumstances.

I have known many of the individuals who appear in this book for more than thirty years and have been able to follow the changes in their lives on a continuing basis. I have had that thirty years to think back upon "events," to talk about them with Chipewyan involved in them, to follow how they have produced changes in their lives, and to see how those changes reflected—and were embedded within—what they did at the time. If I was not following a specific research method or program such as Goulet advocates with radical participation, my approach better suited my circumstances and interests, and I think its benefits have more than offset its drawbacks.

This book is an exploration of some of the ways the Chipewyan create and order the shared reality of their culture.[1] I have written it to explain an encounter two Chipewyan men and I shared with a "spirit" that appeared to us in the form of a loon. I intend this task in the spirit, as Rodney Needham once said, of "a plea for getting on with the job, and this means for the most part making sense of particular things done by human beings in society" (Needham 1962: vii). Even for Northern Athapaskan ethnography, a focus upon an encounter with a "spirit" is a bit unusual, although Richard Nelson skirts around the issue and Dave Smith has written on it several times (Nelson 1983; D. M. Smith 1993, 1994, 1997, 1998). I have found it necessary to develop a series of unusual analytical metaphors in order to explain the context and meaning of that encounter with a spirit.

There are two distinct aspects to this: how I have come to understand the Chipewyan and how I have chosen to explain that understanding to those who have not shared the experience of interacting with them. My understanding of the Chipewyan is derived from personal experience, a type of knowledge the Chipewyan regard as the most valid of all forms of knowledge (Goulet 1998: 27–59). It is not something I can share directly, and I make no attempt to explain the processes by which I have arrived at that understanding. In the phrase normally reserved for context-bound humor that has failed, "you had to be there."

I began this work out of a sense of frustration at my inability to explain the encounter (and certain of my other fieldwork experiences) in a way that was meaningful to students. To explain these particular "events" I adopt, as I have in the past (Sharp 1988a), the role of a storyteller. I follow Western conventions in that instead of simply telling of the "events" as the Chipewyan would, I provide analysis, interpretation, and context to make the meaning of the stories intelligible. In a sense, the entire book is an exercise in explaining the deficiencies of a simple logical Western explanation of the encounter (see chapter 6). All of the chapters following the account of the encounter with the loon are intended to develop the concepts and cultural context that I think are needed to understand it.

Not the least of the problems in attempting to explain an encounter with a "spirit" is the general acceptance by academics of a model of physical reality in which spirits do not appear in ordinary life. Anthropologists know that we cannot apply unexamined Western cultural categories and values to the interpretation of other cultures. We are less aware that the unexamined use of cultural categories interpreting physical reality is also problematic (Sharp 1996). In ethnological analysis as in ethnographic writing, there is no absolute physical constancy we can safely carry unexamined from our own experience to the experience of the cultural other.

The explanatory metaphors that I have found to be the most effective way to explain these aspects of Chipewyan reality are developed in the text rather than in the introduction. This allows me to introduce many of them through ethnographic data and near where they need to be applied. (It also avoids an excessively long introduction!) These metaphors are neither physics nor philosophy but mechanisms to explain how Chipewyan culture works. As cultural beings bound within a particular social context we presume our folk physics to be the true condition of physical reality just as we assume that the categories of our culture that refer to social life and values represent the truth of human social life. My concern with this came from my recognition that a Western understanding of the nature of physical reality is inadequate to interpret Dene reality (Sharp 1996).

Culture continues through time in such a way that structure and process are but different aspects of that temporal continuity. Regrettably, writing ethnography is a three-dimensional process in which structure and process must be disassociated. This enigma, this need to represent a four-dimensional phenomenon within the confines of a written page bound to three dimensions, is perhaps unresolvable.

I have adopted as the central premise of this work that reality is socially constructed. This proposition is as simple to state as its implications are difficult to comprehend. Consistency with the premise demands that reality be seen as an analytical variable rather than an analytical constant. I further interpret the meaning of the premise as to have a corollary: that social phenomena are indeterminate. By this I intend a direct analogy to quantum mechanics. The nature of social phenomena is not a given, and it is not inherent in the phenomena themselves. The nature of social phenomena is a product of the means by which they are observed/measured and, in human culture, the means of observation and measurement is the shared assignment of meaning to them.

Approaching culture as an indeterminate phenomenon is no easy task. It is extraordinarily difficult to set aside the reality created by one's own culture and attempt to conceive of a reality constructed upon different premises (Roscoe 1995). Culture is the ultimate reality, but it is also the ultimate illusion (see chapter 15). To use culture as an explanatory device in this manner dictates that, for all its indeterminate nature, culture be treated as a real and existent phenomenon—as real as gravity, Permian glaciations, and the carbon cycle. Culture is a "thing" (Durkheim 1951, 1964), a causal force that produces effects in both the social and the physical worlds.

One of the areas where the differences in the conceptualization of physical reality between the Dene and ourselves is most apparent is the cultural treatment of time. The subject of time has received extensive treatment in two well-known works: Johannes Fabian's *Time and the Other* (1983) and Alfred Gell's *The Anthropology of Time* (1992). Fabian's book, which would have made a nice article, is directed more toward issues in anthropological writing than it is to issues in anthropological analysis. It has no relevance to this work. Gell's book, which I did not read until after I had completed this analysis, is more substantive and more relevant. *Loon* quite merrily falls within the Durkheimian paradigm by accepting "that collective representations of time do not passively reflect time, but actually *create* time as a phenomenon apprehended by sentient human beings" (Gell 1992: 4).

I do not presume this work to rise to the level of discovering Kantian "categories" or determining "the categories, the basic framework of all thinking and experience" (Gell 1992: 6), but whether philosophically sound or not, these aspects of Dene time usage exist. Confronting them is a necessary aspect of understanding Dene cultural reality.

Where this work diverges from Gell's concerns is in regard to the nature of time itself. His argument hangs upon his acceptance of a philosophical distinction between A time, in which time is seen as a flow from past to present, and B time, in which it is possible only to determine that one event has preceded another event (Gell 1992: 149–65). The Chipewyan use both A time and B time (along with other forms of time), but they also use it in a manner that corresponds to—and is reducible to—neither.

This usage of time, which I generally refer to as nondirectional time or mark by the analogy of time to place, I do not intend to raise to the level of C time, but within this pattern of time usage there is neither the arrow of time characteristic of A time nor the ability to state that one event came before another as in B time. In this usage of time, there is no direction in time.[2]

I take it as the obligation of ethnography to take into consideration individual variation and individual histories as well as the variations and histories of groups as both appear within a set of processes and dynamics capable of explaining those variations and histories. Explanation must be privileged over prediction. The heart of anthropology lies in individual ethnographers' attempts to transform their understanding of their experience of the "other" into terms intelligible to their readers. Dene reality—their thought, their perceptions, their means of explanation, their ideas of causality, their means of weighing and testing evidence, their ideas of time—has not been constrained or conditioned either by the postulates of Western science or by the presuppositions of our white folk physics. Their reality is different. The elements we share in our disparate realities lie in our common humanity and experience of each other. The differences in our disparate realities reflect the different natures and histories of our cultures.

1

LOON *The Story*

By late August 1975 the small hunting camp in which I was staying at Fox-holm Lake in the Northwest Territories had completed its initial harvest of caribou (Sharp 1998a: xxii). The intensity of the hunting had slacked off considerably, but hunting is a more or less continuous activity, and the men still went out to take fresh meat and survey the country. Most of the meat they had already taken had been sun-dried, but it was too warm to store untreated meat. Dry meat is wonderful stuff that can be stored for months if it is kept dry, but we all knew that we would quickly eat what we had. Still, the men did not foresee the need to resume serious hunting until tempera-tures had dropped enough to cache their winter meat supply.

Caribou remained plentiful around the lake, and the men thought they would remain at the edge of the forest until the first significant snows of late September. By then the small lakes should have begun to freeze, and the caribou would begin to move south into the forest.

Foxholm Lake is less a single lake than a lake chain forming a nearly closed circle about sixty miles in circumference. It is not a small lake by the stan-dards of the country, but neither is it a particularly large one. Less than two-thirds of a mile across the portage from our camp is a small side lake that is about five miles long by a half to three-quarters of a mile wide. This lake, the northernmost extension of Foxholm Lake, joins the main body of the lake through a narrows that is less than 150 feet across. East of there, Foxholm Lake widens out like a sideways V. The lake is widest at its southern margins where it connects to an inflowing river and lake chain that extends west by northwest to complete a nearly full circle. This lake chain terminates on the small oval lake where we had our cabins.

The people in our camp had radioed back to Mission that caribou were plentiful. That news had caused a party to fly out to hunt. They had only a few days before they had to return, so joined by several of the men of our camp they began immediately. The visiting hunters stayed in our camp, but caribou were far more plentiful on the north shore of Foxholm Lake than they were near camp. Our only boat was my small wooden canoe, and courtesy demanded offering its use. There were too many visitors for me to haul all of them to the north shore of Foxholm Lake, so each day they walked to the narrows to be ferried across. This was much safer than venturing out on the larger lake in what would have been an overloaded canoe. As the water of Foxholm Lake is very cold, they always chose to be ferried over the narrows.

The first party to visit us included the new chief and several of the councillors from the Mission Band (see chapter 13; Sharp 1986: 262–63). The chief from Birchtown and several other men from there had also come along. Theirs was a reconnaissance trip, paid for by the two bands, to see if enough caribou had come to Foxholm Lake for other Dene to risk the cost of making the trip. They were here to get meat for people in the villages who were unable to hunt on their own as well as to take meat for their own use.

Once I had ferried them over the narrows they would fan out and look for caribou. They broke into pairs or small groups that later dispersed. Most of the work—hunting, butchering, packing meat to the shore where it could be picked up from the lake—was done individually, although men sometimes received assistance from others in their own group.

I usually returned to the main camp until it was time to pick them up, but solitude is such a rare event in fieldwork that I could not resist the charms of one particularly lovely afternoon and remained on the north shore of Foxholm Lake to await their return.

After several hours, Phil returned early from his own hunt and joined me. The youngest son of Paul and May, the couple around whom the camp I was attached to was formed, he had just arrived to spend the fall with us (Sharp 1988a: 47–49, 14–16; 1977: 380–84, 385–87). He had been hunting in the company of a married man in his mid-thirties from Birchtown. This man was *seri* (same-sex sibling-in-law) to the chief from Birchtown (Sharp 1975: 75). Neither had had a particularly successful hunt, but they had heard others shoot and were curious about how they had fared. None of us was in any rush to return to camp. We sprawled on a small sand ridge near the end of the point, facing west to enjoy the afternoon sun while we talked about caribou. We were relaxing there when I saw a common loon (*dadzene*) swimming in the narrows a short distance from us.

Loons are prized as food as well as for their hide and feathers. They are normally hunted with rifles (like large game) rather than with .22s or shotguns (like small game). When Dene shoot at them they aim at their necks rather at than their bodies. Phil had been hunting with a 30–30, along with the military surplus .303 Enfield, the most common rifle then in use. The neck of a loon swimming quietly 150 feet away is not an easy target, but it is not beyond the range the Chipewyan think reasonable to gamble a shell. As soon as they had seen the loon, Phil took out his rifle and began to shoot at it.

Phil's first shot barely missed the loon's neck, the bullet striking the water just beyond where the loon was floating on the narrows. It seemed stunned by the noise and the force of the bullet's impact. It rose up and flapped its wings, gave off a characteristically indescribable loon cry, and dove beneath the surface of the lake. Although Phil kept his rifle in hand as we watched and waited, we were all convinced—and talked about it—that the loon would swim away underwater and not resurface until it was well out of range.

To our surprise, the loon surfaced in the main part of the lake just beyond the sand ridge on which we were now sitting alertly. It was even closer than it had been at Phil's first shot. Phil fired again, once more barely missing its neck. Again the loon acted stunned, swimming in circles, crying, and rearing up to flap its wings before diving beneath the water. Again we waited, expecting the loon to swim out of range or surface where we could not see it. Once more the loon surfaced within fifty yards of us. Phil shot again, again barely missing its neck. Once again, the loon rose up, flapped its wings, gave forth a cry, and slipped beneath the lake.

Seventeen more times the loon rose from the lake to rest on its surface well within rifle range. Seventeen more times Phil fired at the loon. Seventeen more times he barely missed its neck. Seventeen more times the loon cried, flapped, swam in circles, and either dove or gently slipped beneath the lake. It swam back and forth in front of us, moving underwater into the narrow passage then back out onto the main lake, back and forth, again and again. Phil fired an entire box of rifle shells—twenty shots—at that loon. The then customary estimate of the number of rifle shells required to hunt for a full family for an entire fall season—from August to December—was only ten boxes of shells. One-tenth of an entire season's worth of shells Phil fired at that loon before he put his rifle down and quit. The loon remained within close rifle range the entire time, and when Phil ceased firing it rested quietly on the lake instead of moving away from us.

Phil was a teenager, still inexperienced and not yet expected to be able to care for himself or others. Our companion was an adult, the head of a household, an experienced hunter and trapper who had a family to care for. When Phil finished shooting, the other hunter took up his rifle. The loon rested quietly on the lake until he fired at it. His first shot also just missed the loon's neck. The loon once more flapped its wings, cried, and slipped beneath the lake. Again we watched and waited, sure the loon would finally swim away underwater. Once again the loon choose not to escape and surfaced close to us. Again our companion fired and narrowly missed. Again the loon cried, flapped, and slipped under the water. Eight more times he fired, and eight more times the loon cried, flapped, and slipped underwater only to surface a short distance away. After his tenth shot, the man put down his rifle and turned away from the lake and the loon resting quietly in front of us.[1]

All three of us turned to face the afternoon sun. I copied the actions of the other two and put my rifle by my side and said nothing as we morosely ignored the loon and refused to talk. At some point as we sat facing away from where we had last seen it, the loon quietly took its leave of us. We remained like this until our own silence became uncomfortable and we tried to reassert normality by beginning to talk again of caribou and to speculate on the hunts still in progress.

Over the next few hours the remainder of the men completed their work and returned to where we awaited them. They had heard our fire and were curious why there had been so much. As each came in, he asked about the firing from the point. Each time the question was asked, the man from Birchtown responded by saying that it was "just Phil shooting at a loon." No further explanation was offered. Phil said nothing about the incident, and no further questions were asked of us. I ferried the men over the narrows and took the canoe back to camp while they walked in.

2

MISSION *The People*

The people who were camped for the fall at Foxholm Lake belonged to the Mission Band of Chipewyan. Their village, far to the south in Saskatchewan, was founded in the early 1950s by the local white priest. In the early 1950s the Mission Dene numbered barely 250 souls, and at its founding Mission housed but a small part of that population. By the winter of 1970, the band list contained the names of 548 treaty Indians.

The village faces a medium-sized lake roughly thirty miles long by one to four miles wide. The lake lies at the junction of two distinct types of forest: the transitional zone of the Boreal Forest to the north and the Boreal Forest to the south. The area around Mission is one of discontinuous permafrost dominated to the south and west by limestone overlaying the granite of the Pre-Cambrian Shield. To the north, the bare granite of the shield is exposed and heavily scarred by the retreat of the last remnants of the Laurentide Ice Sheet. The land of The People is harsh and rugged but low in relief. Its physical landscape is lake and muskeg ruptured by outcrops of striated granite bedrock, boulder fields, and moraines grieving the vanished glaciers.

In Western terms, The People arrived in their homeland about 2500 B.P. Athapaskan speakers, they were wanderers over North America from Mexico to Alaska and heirs to uncounted thousands of years of knowledge of life in the cold. They displaced those who had come before them to claim the land during one of the larger interglacial declines in solar energy brought on by the Milankovitch cycle. The First Nations people who comprise the Mission population are a Northern Athapaskan people. Known to whites and other outsiders as Chipewyan, they call themselves Dene (whose various English meanings include "a person," "a human being," a "man," or "The People").

All Northern Athapaskans call themselves Dene although they pronounce and spell the word differently in each of their languages. Dene has a number of meanings that serve to distinguish the Dene from other forms of being— human or otherwise. In some contexts it makes a statement of gender, distinguishing male from female. In others it distinguishes the human from the not-quite human. Dene form the bulk of the First Nations' population between Hudson Bay and the interior of Alaska. They range, at the extreme, from the Great Plains to within sight of the Arctic Ocean. Dene peoples also live along the Pacific Coast and in the Southwest, the most widely known of these being the Navajo and Apache of the American Southwest.

For two generations now the majority of the Dene have lived as village dwellers. Village life has become the normative experience of Dene children as in each birth cohort over the last fifty years, fewer and fewer Dene children have found in the bush their formative experiences as Dene, but there are some in each birth cohort who learn in the bush to be Dene. The knowledge and traditions of Dene bush experience are replicated and carried on in each birth cohort, but that ancient wisdom now exists alongside other, more cosmopolitan, bodies of wisdom. Even as their economy comes to depend more and more upon a melding of wages and government payments, these outside resources remain insufficient to support the Dene. Even in modern times the Dene are not able to isolate themselves from the harsh immenseness of the bush that surrounds them. Always, it is necessary to seek subsistence by hunting and fishing within the vast harsh land and brutal climate that surround and contain their lives.

For thousands of years the Dene Nations have successfully secured themselves, their economies, and their homelands against all intruders. The great strength of Dene culture is its ability to graft new knowledge into its very structure without ceasing to be Dene. For millennia the Dene have responded to changing environmental and political contingencies in a harsh and unyielding environment without surrendering the core of meaning and praxis that makes them Dene. Dene thought is synergistic and syncretic. The Dene have drawn upon the knowledge and technology of whites for centuries, incorporating from white culture what they chose and responding to the circumstances the presence of whites created.

They still maintain their identity as a people and protect themselves from being swamped by the force of contemporary Canadian civilization.

The effectiveness with which the Dene Nations have protected themselves is paradoxical to Western thought, most particularly to Western political and legal thought. The Dene Nations were stateless, acephalous nations devoid of the formal institutions of statehood and power so cherished in Western thought as markers of the emergence of civilization. The political methods of the Dene have worked for thousands of years. What brought them into village life was not politics but a change in the caribou herds upon which they depended for food.

Caribou herds are subject to periodic crashes in their numbers, and one of these occurred near the end of World War II. What caused the crash will never be known, but white influence was a factor. After World War I too many white trappers moved into the Dene homeland. Too many whites who killed caribou as if their numbers were limitless. Too many whites with dog teams to feed. Too many whites to scatter much too much poison bait for wolves and disrupt the relationship between human, wolf, and caribou. By the end of the 1940s, the crash of the caribou herds had made the risks of a subsistence life too great. This crash was different than any other one in Dene history in that, for the first time, the Dene had an alternative set of resources adequate to see them through the crisis.

The Chipewyan have been in direct trade with whites since 1715 and perhaps in indirect trade with them via the Eskimo since the time of the Viking settlements in Greenland. The seeds of a white presence in the Mission Dene homeland began with the establishment of a trading post on Lake Athabasca in the first decade of the nineteenth century. The Chipewyan using that post were not particularly pleased by its policies and operating procedures and burned it out within a few years, but its establishment signaled the advantages of a trading post on Lake Athabasca. In time, another post was opened, and The People who were to become the Mission Dene directed their trade to it.

Reaching the store from the eastern and northern parts of their homeland involved a journey down to Mission lake, along the river to Lake Athabasca, then on to the trading post. The trip between Mission Lake and Lake Athabasca is a difficult one requiring the portage of several impassible rapids. Journeying Dene prefer to complete a portage before stopping to make camp, and this preference combined with the topography of the land along the river to create a few favored camping sites. One of these sites was just above the first impassible rapids inland from Lake Athabasca. Traveling Dene parties could stop and visit kin living nearby before continuing their trip to the trading post. Travelers returning home from the post could rest and visit before starting their journey north. As trade with the Dene intensified in the twentieth century, free traders began to compete with the Hudson's Bay Company store on Lake Athabasca by moving out away from the store to trade.

By the 1920s, the presence of the free traders had drawn many Dene into the area—Discha—for the summers. Summer is often a boring time removed from the reality of life that begins in the North with the caribou migration and, near Discha, with the first snows of fall. The traders offered entertainment, the opportunity to visit and socialize, occasional opportunities for wage labor, and a market for Dene products. By the late 1920s, the presence of the free traders and the Dene had prompted the Hudson's Bay Company to establish a store at Discha. The site was accessible by barge, so supply was easy. Prices were comparable with other stores and held low by competition with the free traders. Spared the longer trip to the other store, the Dene made Discha their central point of trade, and a small village began to grow up.

The Chipewyan and the whites segregated themselves. The Dene camped above the rapids on a small lake that had excellent fishing. The whites settled below the rapids, closer to the stores of the traders. Over the next two decades the Dene settlement at Discha grew steadily. It was a convenient place for those physically unsuited for life in the bush as well as a source of wage labor and social amenities for those so inclined. Many Dene who wintered in the bush in Saskatchewan found it convenient to build cabins there.

With the crash of the caribou herds after World War II, the Dene drew in upon Discha as a refuge from the scarcity of food in the bush. Those who trapped and hunted in Saskatchewan found it easy to use Discha as a base. Some men began to leave the women and children of their families at Discha while they went off into the bush to hunt and trap alone or in small parties. Dene who hunted and trapped farther away from Discha, particularly those who went into the Northwest Territories, were slower to take to Discha as a permanent base, but many began to build cabins there for use in summer and at Christmas and Easter. As the caribou herds continued to decline, and the credit and cash flow of the Dene were reduced by a declining fur market, more and more Dene moved into Discha and stayed there for longer and longer periods of time.

The post–World War II period brought the Dene their first resident priest to staff the church that had been built years before. A resident priest was a major attraction to the Dene. The post–World War II period also brought an increase in government services, regular civilian air service at the wartime airstrip, a nursing station, and an influx of administrative personnel belonging to a variety of governmental agencies. There was also an influx of miners and mining exploration companies. The natural resources of the Canadian North have long been a beacon to southern Canada. Tapping that mystic wealth is still sometimes seen as the panacea for Canada's economic problems.

Although gold always has its role to play in drawing miners, it was uranium that brought a serious governmental presence and corporate money into the homeland of the Mission Dene. There are so many uranium deposits in the homeland of the Mission Chipewyan that it is a wonder the local wildlife does not glow in the dark. In 1970, the local white folklore was uncertain. Was it "one hundred minable deposits within a fifty-mile radius" of Mission or was it only "fifty in a twenty-mile radius"? In the emerging nuclear age and cold war that followed the cataclysm of World War II, Mission Dene country became impossible for Canada to ignore. Issues of ownership of resources and sovereignty over the land had to be settled by an active Canadian presence, and a major means of demonstrating control over the land (and its mineral resources) was through the delivery of social services to the inhabitants of the land.

The Dene, facing a crisis with the caribou, turned to the resources offered by white Canada and made use of them. The nursing station founded at Discha had a particularly powerful appeal as infant mortality dropped and deaths from infectious disease declined as antibiotics became available. The rate of death in childbirth declined markedly. The village of Discha continued to grow, but the Chipewyan population was slower to grow, an after-effect of the 1948 measles epidemic that had killed nearly fifty Dene, most of them children.

In the early 1950s, the priest became convinced that the social environment at Discha was harmful to his congregation. He made plans to relocate the church to the shore of Mission Lake. A rough road had been cut from Discha to Mission Lake, where a small uranium mine had been opened in the late 1940s, and two small fly-in fishing camps had been started shortly thereafter.[1] The docks for the mine and the fish camps were situated on a bay where a river flows out of Mission Lake, past Discha, then into Lake Athabasca. Over the course of a few years the priest built a church on Mission Lake and cut services at Discha to only once a month. With the best location occupied by the loading dock and the fish camps, the priest selected what he felt to be the second-best location on the lake. A hand-cut, often corduroy secondary road joined the church to the main road. The priest chose a sand esker (hill) covered with patches of burned and intact forest. He considered the burned areas to be good sources of firewood. Initially, there was ample firewood close by while the lake water was clean and the fishing was good.

This was a period when the number of government administrators who came to live among the Dene began to increase greatly. The traditional administrators of the North, the priests and the Royal Canadian Mounted Police (RCMP) found many of their powers taken away from them and many of their links with The People severed. To the distress of the local constables, the RCMP were forced to abandon the long winter patrols that had taken them out into the bush among The People and had kept them aware of their concerns and their beliefs. The length of RCMP's tours of duty in the North were shortened, and their personnel became increasingly transient. No longer could RCMP officers spend most of their careers in the same place so they could come to know and understand the people they were there to administer and police.

Throughout the 1950s, the Dene slowly abandoned Discha and moved to Mission. Even the more determined bush families in the Northwest Territories were compelled by still declining caribou herds, continuing low fur prices, and rising costs at the store to spend at least part of the year in Saskatchewan, where they had access to the resources of the Canadian government due them as part of their treaty rights. They chose to build their cabins at Mission rather than at Discha. The Dene settlement on the lake above the town of Discha slowly withered while Mission grew. The first major crisis in determining the future of Mission came in the mid- to late 1950s.

The Hudson's Bay Company did not wish to undertake the cost of building a new store at Mission, but it was losing business by being so far from the Mission population. The federal and provincial governments were reluctant to commit the funds necessary to build a school and administrative offices or to provide services for what they regarded as a temporary settlement. After a great deal of political maneuvering, the priest was able to get commitments for a school at Mission, prompting its construction and the building of a store. In governmental eyes this established Mission as a viable community and ensured its continued existence.

The church and store, along with their associated residences and outbuildings, and the somewhat later construction of a new school with teachers' residences, defined the physical layout of Mission. The store faced the lake, running parallel to it. The church occupied a fenced area to the right of the store, facing the lake but running perpendicular to it. Between these two complexes, the road from Discha terminated near a small dock for floatplanes and boats—a physical marker of a decades-long political division between church and store. A hundred yards behind the store and about the same distance (though on a diagonal) from the church lay the two-room frame and clapboard school. The ground between these institutions, save within the fences that marked off the church and the residence of the store's white manager and clerk, was bare sand devoid of vegetation. This open space and its cornering buildings defined the center of Mission and the power of the white agents who lived there.

The Dene who settled at Mission did so on their own terms and through their own efforts. They constructed small log cabins that were crowded but easy to heat with stoves made locally out of half a fifty-gallon oil drum. There are not enough hardwoods near Mission to burn for firewood, so spruce and jackpine fueled the stoves for cooking and heat. The Dene built their log cabins where they chose, always avoiding intruding on the central space of the village. By preference, they built their cabins close beside those of their kin. Mission quickly became a clustering of cabins expressing the social ties between its residents and the social and economic alliances they had formed among themselves.

Unfortunately, nothing the size of Mission that draws public money can be allowed to exist in an unplanned state. Somewhere, sometime, a town plan based on a linear grid system had been drawn up to facilitate planning the efficient delivery of public services.[2] Small individual lots were marked off for each of the nonexistent houses, all following good Canadian suburban land-use practice for high-density developments of single-family dwellings. Dene cabins were not marked on the maps or included in the planning.

By 1965, a housing program was under way at Mission. Initially, eight new houses were constructed each year and, according to the plan, laid out to form one of the streets marked on the map. The Chipewyan thought highly of these houses. They were larger than Dene cabins and had three bedrooms, a kitchen, a nonfunctional bathroom, and a small living room. As the housing program continued through the years, two- and three-bedroom layouts became available. The houses were prefabricated frame constructions that followed a standard design used throughout western Canada. Quite functional in the lower mainland of British Columbia, they were cold and drafty in the climatic conditions prevalent at Mission. Most of the people still living in log cabins were those who spent long periods of time in the bush away from the community.

These new houses were sought by the Dene for their space and their prestige. Through the first fifteen years of the housing program, the new houses wreaked havoc on the social arrangements of the Mission Dene. Where the new houses were built was determined by the town plan and convenience of construction. The completed houses were allocated by the band in accordance with federally established regulations that took account of need, family size, number of small children, and other factors.[3] The difficulty came in the placement of the houses to be allocated. For a Mission resident to refuse to take a house when at the top of the list ensured a delay of several years before having another chance to obtain one. Taking a house when it was completed also meant the new owner would have to move away from the cluster of kin that lived around the site of their old cabin. Individual Dene tried—without much success—a number of creative ways to solve this problem, including trading houses or having the residents of several cabins move into a single house. It was not until the Dene themselves gained control of the administration of the housing program and began to build the houses where people wanted them that the problem vanished.

Mission is an isolated place. Its neighboring communities lie 80 miles to the southeast and 250 miles to the south, with Discha twelve miles to the west. To the north there are at best a few straggling Inuit settlements between Mission and the Arctic Ocean and Russia. In January 1970, Mission was a study in off-white: snow-covered, wind-blown, and cold. Its smell was clean, crisp, and dangerous if too deeply inhaled. Its sound was the clarity of footsteps on crystalline snow singing with the cold. Mission Lake was covered with snow, its ice already frozen to a depth of four feet. The surrounding forest, recovered from its freshly burned state into an almost impenetrable scrub of young spruce, lay deep in snow. The boundaries between land, lake, forest, and town existed only in human plans and on maps. Outside, in the world of experience, these boundaries were beyond the visual imagery of human perception. The reflectivity of the snow dominated the landscape. It is never truly dark once the snow comes. Light comes from everywhere, as often from the ground as from the sky. Grey-white and shades of washed-out blues and purple dominate Mission at night. By day, all half-dozen hours of it, the colors of Mission were controlled by the cloud cover. When the sun shone, Mission exploded into whites, shallow blues, and brilliant flashes of red and green among the refracting snow's uncountable mirrors and prisms in an intensity of brightness and color that quickly brought fatigue and tears to one's eyes. When it was cloudy, Mission took on brighter grey-whites in the half-light. Day and night flowed between each other without any clear distinction between them.

Within these indeterminate boundaries marked at best by nuances of snow reflectivity, Mission sat as a sea of narrow trails connecting scattered clusters of cabins to the rows of new houses and the central buildings of white occupation. The single road designed for the passage of cars, alien and intrusive, entered Mission from the hill atop the village. Passing in front of the new school and the row of townhouses used by the teachers, the road looked like a lost and confused refugee from the outskirts of Regina before it died in front of the store. Human traffic, the lifeblood of the town, flowed over the spider-like network of trails connecting cabins and houses to each other and in turn to the buildings of white occupation. These hard-packed trails were narrow, their width determined by the passage of dog team and toboggan. The edges were sharply bounded. A single step off a packed trail left one leg-down and crotch-deep in snow. Over these narrow trails moved the Dene, following the dictates of their lives and the conduct of their business. The trails, packed and maintained only by Dene use, would have been a social psychologist's dream, a perfect physical expression of the direction and density of the social ties in Dene lives.

Within this web of human movement, the houses of Mission sat like nunataks protruding from a glacial ice sheet; each dwelling was an island of life and activity. Although close to half the Dene lived in new houses, the spacing of Mission was still dominated by the clustering of cabins located according to Dene preference. Away from central cluster of the village, Mission did not seem like a town so much as an outcropping of life in a surf of snow and forest. Dwellings were often hundreds of feet apart. Looking around the village made the surrounding forest and frozen lake a visually intimate part of a daily life through which the Dene flowed, each human a significant presence through their very movement and purpose of action.

Surrounding Dene homes and Dene lives were the dogs. Ideally, there were six dogs on each team, a team to each hunter. Sometimes there were several teams around a house. The dogs of Mission outnumbered The People of Mission by a half. The dogs were virtually all male. Each was tied to a stake, each stake clustered near others of the team. Their stake was the favored place for each dog's urination and scent marking. Throughout the winter each dog built a large ovoid of frozen urine on its stake, a visible marker of its presence even as the dog itself lurked within its house or its hole within the snow. Each short chain defined a dog's domain. The chains were only about five feet long, and the stake that anchored each chain was placed to separate one dog from another and prevent contact and conflict within the team. Heaven help the stranger, animal or human, wandering between them. Within the diameter defined by its chain each dog packed the snow from its pacing. At the edges of its packed domain were deposited the debris of its meals and its accumulated defecation. The dogs of Mission defined a different world of boundaries and patterns. Related to the human patterns within the snow that surrounded them all but yet a world distinct: one that was necessary but dependent and threatening.

The sound of Mission was the sound of dogs. Its dogs rarely barked except in threat to intrusion. It was their preference to howl. They had not the range, harmony, sophistication, or individual virtuosity found in wolves, but there were sometimes more than 750 of them. They did not howl in isolation. Team answered team as sound flowed over Mission. Day and night sound rose and fell, ebbing and surging to the whim of those captives upon whom life depended. Through the village flitted the community's vacuum cleaner and garbage control system of feral dogs. Abandoned cripples sought to survive yet another winter, truly feral animals beyond human interest and control; escaped dogs sought food wherever they could find it. Females in estrus sought food and sex in a short but elemental struggle before their receptivity passed and they returned to the chain of their owner.

Life was hard for Dene dogs (see Sharp 1976). Few feral dogs survived a year, and in winter all were but a hair's breadth away from starvation. They will eat anything they can find. Even at forty below zero they will thoroughly lick the inside of the tin cans tossed outside; they try to dig into the outhouses in midwinter to reach the feces inside; they kill and eat smaller and weaker dogs; they eat the remains of dogs that have died and been placed upon the lake for disposal; they prey upon any small animal they can catch— cats had short lives at Mission—and some of them are a threat to children.

That winter of 1970 found Mission poised upon a threshold of increasing physical and social change. That summer, electrical service was installed throughout the village.[4] The new electrical supply allowed the repair and enlargement of a community freezer house, alleviating many of the food storage problems that came from Dene dependence upon seasonal access to wild game and fish as their major food resource. Eight new houses were constructed in the housing program. Residential telephone service, via a microwave relay station, was extended to the community, breaking the hold the Hudson's Bay Company Ltd. and the school had had on long distance communication.[5]

Most of the Dene were accepting of the changes in their physical environment and the effects of those changes on their well-being. Because so much of their food came from the land, they were in the position of being thoroughly impoverished but still having housing, food, and an occasionally significant disposable income. They had more material possessions than at any previous time in their history. Medical services had greatly improved. The birth of a child in the bush or the loss of a woman in childbirth had become a rarity. Infant mortality seemed greatly lower, and people began to expect that their newborns would live to adulthood. The fear of starvation, that ancient specter of the Arctic and Subarctic whose very shadow confounds analysis and rational thought in Western writings, was nearly eliminated.

These changes were not without social and emotional cost. By 1970, the first generation for whom the village was the only home it had known was reaching maturity. The prospect of a generation of Dene who did not know the bush and lacked the skills to live from the land was disconcerting. Many of the residents, particularly the elderly and middle-aged, found village life boring and pointless. Wresting a living from a harsh land had been the central challenge of their lives, and they did not know how to replace the sense of purpose that it had given them. The cultural mechanisms that the Dene had developed for their own survival were geared to a scattered population. Their lives had been constructed around the almost continuous presence of small groups of kin, and they were accustomed to roles and tasks clearly defined by that scattered life. Living in a village, always in the presence of hundreds of fellow Dene, was both distraction and challenge that called for adjustments the Dene had not yet created.

There were problems that came from the physical environment and the new pattern of land use determined by white practice and ideas about property. To the Dene the land is ownerless. Talk of "mother earth" is not Dene, but they think of the land almost as a living being. The idea of owning the land is intrinsically without meaning in Dene culture. The land is there for everyone. If owned, it is owned by everyone. The Dene moved freely throughout their homeland, never staying long in a single place. To spend an entire winter in a single dwelling is a recent idea. To spend a year in the same place was unthinkable a generation ago. The land of the Dene accepts this practice comfortably. It does not accept living in one place comfortably. Local food resources quickly vanish and wood supplies are overwhelmed. Growth and decay are slow in this place. It can take more than a century for the soil cover to regenerate from but an afternoon's usage, and a simple overnight winter camp may leave scars visible for decades. Small patches of forest may take generations to regenerate and accumulate dry deadwood after harvesting. Fish grow slowly in the cold waters and may live more than a century. The lakes are large, and the water in them is clean. The fauna and flora flourish, but they cannot stand sustained use at a single point. Human activities must be spread out over large areas or the local consequence is dramatic ecological alteration or outright devastation.

The right of private property may be a cornerstone in Western ideology, but someone forgot to explain its importance to the Subarctic's lakes, lichens, spirits, and growing things. To build a permanent settlement may not be to court disaster, but there will be a price to be paid. Because the bay by the river flowing out of Mission Lake was occupied by the fish camps and the loading dock for the uranium mine when the priest sought to found Mission, he was forced to choose a lesser place. Mission is in an old permafrost area, perhaps more properly in a forming permafrost area. The ground, even in sand, freezes early and thaws late. The water table is close to the surface, and meltwater from the spring runoff flows rapidly though the sand into the lake. Since the first attempts at settlement in 1951, the village site has had more and more construction. People stayed at Mission for longer and longer periods of time, and they stayed in greater and greater numbers. The new construction planned by the whites compressed the village, causing more and more people to live closer together for longer and longer periods of time.

Every fall the ground freezes at Mission. As the ground freezes, it traps the human waste within the pits of the outhouses. The entrapped waste rarely freezes, but it is trapped by the frozen ground until the rains of April begin. When the spring melt-off comes and the ground begins to thaw, the ground-water flows under the sand and through the pits. Snow cover four or more feet deep melts and flows through the sand into Mission Lake.

Even using the most conservative figures, the several hundred humans at Mission had, over twenty years, deposited several hundred tons of feces and several hundred thousand gallons of urine into the sand of Mission. The dogs, which far outnumbered the humans, had deposited more than one hundred tons of feces and well over one hundred thousand gallons of urine into that same sand. Besides all this biological waste, Mission Lake has been a major dump for the village of Mission. Along its shore, or just off its shore, have been dumped dead dogs, oil, trash, offal, and other garbage. All of these in addition to the natural contaminants of a living lake. Even here where so many biological processes are slow, a lake thirty miles long has a powerful capacity to clean itself. A sand hill is a very effective filter medium but even a sand hill—like a living lake—can be overpowered. None of this might matter very much were it not that Mission Lake is the source of Mission's drinking water.

This has not been particularly auspicious for Dene health. In 1970, as in the previous decades, drinking water was taken from along the shore when the ice was gone and from but a few yards offshore when ice covered the lake. The water of Mission Lake is so polluted that, even after flowing through two intervening lakes and a many-miles-long trip down an often violently aerated river to Discha, the river there is still so polluted that it is unfit for human consumption. The river is the source of Discha's drinking water.

Had Mission been located on the bay, where the river leaves Mission Lake, it is probable the current flowing though the bay would have prevented the pollution buildup in Mission Lake. Discha would not have been helped, but Mission would have been. The traditional wisdom of Northern peoples, particularly their wisdom about their environment and climate, is something they have acquired painfully by careful and intense observation of the

world in which they live. It is experience that has been obtained at the cost of
many human lives. To take not heed of that wisdom for reasons of ideology,
economics, or accounting methods will extract a price in human life.

The revolution in Dene life that had just begun to get started in 1970 was well
under way by 1972. Driven both by changes in electronics and communication technology and the expression of Canada's economic growth in an
increasing presence in the North, the pace of change began to acceler-
ate. New short-wave radios using state-of-the-art technology could now be
rented for use on the traplines. For the first time, trappers and hunters
dozens of miles away from Mission were able to keep in touch with news in
their world and with their families in town. Physically, Mission had acquired
another sixteen new houses. The spacing of dwellings within the community
had begun to take on that which had been envisioned by the white planners.
Homes were closer together, and the village was more crowded. The crowd-
ing and the increasing population aggravated the problems of trash and
garbage disposal. Telephone and power lines ran throughout the village,
giving it a cluttered look and feel. Potable drinking water remained a serious
problem.

One marker of change was the presence at Mission of a half dozen Dene-
owned snowmobiles. The presence of these expensive machines was a har-
binger of dramatic changes in the way the Dene related to their land.

Economically, these were curious times. Inflation began for the Mission Dene before it began in southern Canada and the rest of the world.
The increased governmental presence in Mission and Discha brought jobs.
Where Mission had offered no more than four full-time jobs to its residents
in 1970, there were a wide variety available in 1972. The Canadian federal
agencies responsible for immigration and manpower were undertaking deliberate programs to upgrade the quality of the work force in northern
Saskatchewan, and these programs were proving to be of benefit to Mission.
While the programs did result in some improvement in English-language
skills, their most significant benefit was their openness to female applicants.
For the first time, Mission women had access to income-producing activities
for which remuneration equaled what men could earn and did not involve
domestic skills, sexual services, or the production of handicrafts. The ability to generate an income had widespread effects in altering the marriage

system away from the traditional arranged marriages toward marriages in which the partners were self-selected.

It had been impossible to maintain a bush life, one dependent upon subsistence hunting and trapping, since the end of World War II. By 1972, a purely subsistence lifestyle was no longer acceptable to the Dene and absolutely intolerable to the Canadian and provincial governments. It is difficult to speak of governmental motivations, but one factor underlying governmental opposition to the Dene leading a subsistence life was fear that a substantial portion of them might abandon Mission for a more productive location. That would leave behind a large capital investment devoid of Indians to administer.

The 1975 camp at Foxholm Lake reflected many of these changes. Before this time the use of aircraft to hunt was largely limited to short excursions in search of moose. The cost of air charter was so high—and the distances so great—that people did not fly out to hunt caribou unless they came close to the village. The visiting hunters (granted they were using band funds) were a marker of an increasingly cash-based economy, some of whose participants were able to afford to fly out on lengthy trips in search of caribou or to pay the cost of the multiple charters that would drop off and then pick up hunters several days later.

The trends of 1970–72 continued throughout the 1970s. Between my field research in 1975 and that in 1977, some of the changes at Mission were dramatic. Throughout this period of rapid development of what J. G. E. Smith has called the "micro-urban village" (J. G. E. Smith 1978), the housing program at Mission continued unabated. Dene population growth was slower than governmental construction, so the increase in the supply of new houses temporarily outstripped the supply of eligible families. By 1977, the program was converted to focus upon the repair of existing houses. Other buildings were added, and new services were introduced. A new nursing station and nurse's residence were built at Mission, but it proved impossible to find a nurse able to face the social and professional demands of living and working at Mission, so a nurse commuted from Discha. The school was expanded and new teachers' residences built. A new loop was cut from the rerouted Discha road, one that made a loop through Mission rather than dead-ending there. The store was remodeled and expanded. Television service came to Mission. Mission settled some of its treaty claims and formally became an Indian reserve, settling into assuming its own administration and learning to manage its own affairs within the governmental structure.

Because my visits to Mission were spread throughout the 1970s, the changes at Mission may have seemed greater to me than they did to the Dene who were there to live through them. Snowmobiles provide a good example.[6] By 1977 there were more snowmobiles at Mission than I could accurately count. There were at least fifty Dene-owned machines compared to the half dozen of 1972 and the single broken machine of 1970. Concomitant to the increase in snowmobiles came an increase in the number of Dene-owned cars, trucks, and vans. Where in 1970 taxi traffic between Mission and Discha was a sideline controlled by resident whites, in 1977 there were several competing Dene taxi services. Technology catches the eye and points to the changing economic position of the Dene, but there were more subtle indicators of the rate of change and the Dene skill at adjusting to them and refashioning them in their own style.

All those snowmobiles and vehicles did not just mean that the Dene had more money; they meant that the Dene were undergoing a dramatic reinterpretation of their relationship with their land. Within the village, the spider's web of toboggan trails was gone. In its place were roads forged by the constant traffic of vehicles and an even wider maze of snowmobile trails. In 1970 people moved at their mile-eating rapid walk, but in 1977 traffic moved at the breakneck speed of the snowmobiles and the ponderous determination of the wheeled vehicles. Pedestrians moved by day at some risk. At night, foot travel was downright dangerous. Snowmobiles are fast. Many can exceed 60 MPH, and those speeds were sometimes reached within the confines of Mission. Not only was the town denser in population and more concentrated in buildings, but the noise of the snowmobiles continued day and night. The People complained constantly of the noise of the snowmobiles and the recklessness with which they were driven.

Mission was noisier not just because there was more noise, but because the kind of noise had changed. The dogs of Mission were gone, reduced to a few teams kept for racing or by the determined constancy of a few conservatives. The howling of the dogs and their footsteps upon the resonating snow had been replaced by the gnashing and gnarling of two-cycle engines bent for speed. It might not seem like much, this replacing of dog teams by snowmobiles, but it is a good symbol of other things that were happening in

Dene lives. The People complained of the noise, the speed, and the recklessness not because they were opposed to change or just distressed by the noise
but because these things were metaphors for the kinds of changes that were
occurring in their lives.

To live a life in the bush of the Canadian North was to live a life seeking
the meaning of small sounds dominated by the silence and clarity of the
snow and the cold, by the shifting and the movement of ice, by the shards of
pattern carried by the wind. There are Dene, many Dene, who claim they
can hear the northern lights. That life demanded—demands—a special attention to the nuances of natural sound. To have this world cast aside in but
a few years is a major change. This example is defined by but a single sensory
channel, but equivalent changes were occurring in all aspects of Dene lives.

If the changes in the noises of Mission are an indicator of the changes in
Dene lives, those changes were far reaching, and it was the less conspicuous
aspects of those changes that produced real effects upon the Dene. Snowmobiles are fast. Snowmobiles are showy. Young Dene men are convinced
that snowmobiles impress young Dene women. Young Dene women deny
this, but it is apparent that snowmobiles do impress other young Dene men.
Mostly, snowmobiles are toys for the young and the wanna-be young. But
they are fast. Speed is intoxicating, particularly to a people whose only other
choices to move through the deep snow and cold of a subarctic winter are to
walk or to go by dog team. Trips of thirty or forty miles that used to take one
or two days became trips of only a few hours. The speed and mobility of the
snowmobile opened areas within forty or fifty miles of Mission to almost
everyone. Fill the tank and go. Out and back in a day. Fishing on the lake
improved because people could move rapidly to nets on its most distant
parts. The harvest of moose within forty or fifty miles of Mission increased
because people could get out more quickly and more often. People who had
not trapped for years put out small traplines. Wood for Mission's insatiable
winter fires was gathered more quickly and easily from better stands of
timber farther away. Water, still a deadly issue, could be taken from points
on the lake farther removed from Mission's pollution. When the caribou
came within range of Mission, hunters could descend upon them in mass.[7]

For trips up to forty or fifty miles the snowmobile is a godsend. Out and
back in a day. Camp out if you need more time. Plenty of power to haul back
any meat you have killed. Walk back if the snowmobile breaks down and you
cannot repair it or if you run out of gas. But only for forty or fifty miles. It

becomes difficult to walk back forty or fifty miles if the snowmobile breaks down. The logistics of using a snowmobile become very different with distance. Oil and gas are not products of the bush and they are expensive, nearly five dollars a gallon in 1992 and proportionately so in 1977, 1975, 1972, and 1970. Gas must be cached in advance or hauled along, greatly reducing the payload that can be hauled in or out. Using a snowmobile, other than in a mass exodus of snowmobiles going to the same place so that assistance is available, calls for planning and preparation. Beyond forty to fifty miles out from Mission, the advantages of the snowmobile rapidly diminish. By the mid-1980s many of the hunters who went out the farthest each year had abandoned the use of snowmobiles in their hunting areas except for hauling, to exploit game passing by on the lakes, or to play with. Dog teams began to make a comeback.

The snowmobile was not a cause; it was an effect. The Mission Dene took to the snowmobile because they were prepared to change the way they related to the land. They were prepared to change the way they related to the land because so many of them had become village people. Permanent bush life began to change with the crash of the caribou herds in the 1940s. Before then, life had been marked by periodic visits to the store. With permanent village life after the crash, life came to be marked by periodic visits to the bush. The new life had reached a stage where the new toy was useful.

Snowmobiles were available to the Mission Dene long before they adopted them. The change in technology did not produce a change in the Mission Dene; the Mission Dene adopted the new technology when it suited changes that had occurred in their lives for other reasons.

The Chipewyan had been in direct contact with European culture for more than 250 years by the time I began my fieldwork among them. Throughout that time the Dene have consistently displayed the ability to maintain themselves as a separate cultural entity capable of extracting social and technological innovation from white culture without being swamped by it. Cultures exist in a perpetual state of change. The continuity of culture comes from the process of sharing and transmitting symbols and values rather than from the specificity of the values and symbols themselves. For the Dene, the 1970s were an acceleration point in a process of change in attitude toward life in the bush that had been under way for decades. It was that change that opened the door to other social changes in Dene life. The 1980s and the early 1990s were so outwardly marked by changes in the technology of communication that it is all too easy to focus upon them to the exclusion of other changes that were in progress. The same statement can be made about the larger culture of Canada and America that surround the Dene, and, as truly for the Dene as for ourselves, the Chipewyan managed to adapt those changes to what they intended for their lives. We are as Canadian or American now as we were in 1880 in spite of the changes in our dress, technology, speech, and the ethnic composition of our nations precisely because that flow of sharing and transmission of symbols and values remains unbroken. Just as we have managed to remain Canadian or American in spite of the changes in the nature of our lives, the Chipewyan have managed to remain Chipewyan in spite of the changes in their lives, for the flow of transmission in symbols and values among them also remains unbroken.

Beginning in the 1970s, income levels began to rise dramatically. In 1975, employment was available almost on demand, and younger Dene men fluent in English could afford to turn up their noses at jobs paying a thousand dollars a month. Through the 1980s and early 1990s, wages rose to levels commensurate with those of white Canadians working in the North, and the availability of jobs was still high. The Mission Band itself had become the largest employer at Mission. Because housing costs were still low, the Mission Dene retained their curious mixture of apparent poverty coupled with a substantial disposable income. The Dene explored entrepreneurial activities during the 1980s. Individuals opened businesses involving air transport and fish camps as well as a hotel and numerous taxi services. The band itself became involved with a store and other commercial activities.

Mission had grown explosively as the children of those whose lives had been saved in the 1940s and 1950s reached the age of marriage and childbearing. In 1992, Mission had more than twelve hundred souls and was crowded. There was only one log cabin still standing at Mission, and it was unoccupied. Some of the Dene had come to feel that it should be retained as a monument to Mission past.[8] Many houses had fences around them. Fences had previously been a sign of white occupancy, and the practice had had no more than two Dene adopt it in 1969. In 1992, fences were no longer a marker of ethnicity or a striving for status but a necessity to protect both children and adults from the excesses of traffic in both winter and summer. Informal roads and paths ran everywhere without apparent rhyme or reason. Sanitation and trash removal were improved but not yet adequate. A pipe had been run deep into the lake, providing year-round water that, while not safe, was safer. The water at Discha remained polluted, and no alternative to the river water had been devised. Running water was to be installed in Mission's homes the summer of 1994, but the only source for the water that was to be piped to the individual homes was Mission Lake.

Public buildings have proliferated in the village. The central area of Mission, the old barren court defined by the two-room school, the church, and the store, has almost vanished under the new construction. Mission is unmistakably an Indian village because of its architecture, but it has the feel of a once modest housing development that has gone to pot. The houses were never equal to the demands of the climate, and the effects of decades of wear show on them. The repairs that have been made are patchwork. Different colors and combinations of colors were used in each year of construction, and matching materials are not to be had. Bare plywood has had to replace colored siding. Glass windows break easily in this climate, and they are difficult to keep intact. Sheet plastic, one of the great bush luxuries of the 1960s, still covers many windows. The ground cover remains stark and barren, and at times Mission is overwhelmed by mud, blowing sand, or wet trash emerging from the winter's snow. The sand will not support grass, and the native lichens have no chance of growth in such a heavily disturbed area.

Inside the houses, the effects of electronic technology and rising levels of disposable income are marked by the presence of decent furniture, televisions, vcrs, camcorders, and appliances. Refrigerators and home freezers are particularly useful and in most every home. A large number of homes are still heated by wood—fuel oil is as disproportionately expensive as gasoline—but the stoves are of a much higher quality and efficiency than were those made from surplus oil drums. From the beginning, all the new houses at Mission have been constructed with bathrooms. Sewer service is still not available and may never be available in this environment. Chemical toilets have become available and are in widespread use. This represents no small improvement during the winter, although it means the loss of the art of using in the dark an outhouse whose seat is ringed by an inch of solid yellow ice.

The changes in technology and physical surroundings reflect the changes in Dene lives that have come from their increased commitment to a sedentary life in the village. As the population of Mission has increased, the flow of Mission Dene into the outside world to live and seek their livelihoods has increased. Technological change has rarely come as a shock to the Chipewyan. They have always been travelers. Individuals have always penetrated the cultures that surrounded them and brought back word of change. Just as they knew through these travels of TV and movies long before they became a part of their daily experience, so those Chipewyan who move out and live within the larger framework of Canada still serve as a buffer between Mission and the rest of the world—a buffer that both introduces technological and social change and moderates its influence by allowing the Chipewyan to know what they want from that change long before it arrives on their doorsteps.

The changes that have occurred over a single lifetime have been dramatic (as they have been among ourselves). Individuals who were born in cabins hundreds of miles from a store and saw neither a store nor a white Canadian until they were in their teens ended their days in the intensive care units of urban hospitals more than half a thousand miles away from where they were born. Many who never heard English until they were nearly adult have lived to see some of their grandchildren fail to learn to speak the Chipewyan language and spend more time watching *Sesame Street* than listening to the stories of the "old days." Education has become a major vehicle for mediating relationships between the Mission People and the outside world. Where the new chief of 1972 used his broken English as a positive campaign issue, the current chief has an MBA degree. The poorly regarded elderly have been converted through the flow of ideas, values, and pension checks from the outside into the respected elders that are so prized in white Canadian conceptualizations of First Nations' cultures (Sharp 1979, 1981a).

If it is in our nature as whites to see these changes in Chipewyan lives as signs of the loss of their identity and authenticity as Native Americans, let it be noted that with those changes there has been a burgeoning of talent and artistic expression in the new circumstances of Mission lives. Young Mickey as a grown man has come to make his living maintaining computers for one of the uranium mines (Sharp 1988a: 46, 92–93). The band he formed as a young man had become good enough to travel all over northern Saskatchewan and was invited to perform at the Grand Ole Opry. The traditional market for Chipewyan beadwork still exists, but now there are Mission Chipewyan who sell their paintings to the outside world. Art objects that bridge the line between the artistic and the spiritual move out from Mission to the larger world of Canada. If many adult Chipewyan make their living at jobs undreamed of a generation ago and all are involved in technological processes that in their childhoods would have seemed beyond fantasy, the same can be said for us, and if we do not question our own authenticity as Canadians or Americans, how can we question the authenticity of the Chipewyan as Chipewyan?

It is easier to see changes in the physical environment than it is to see changes in the social environment, but between 1950 and the present, the most significant changes in Dene life have been cultural rather than physical or technological.

The most significant change is the way the Dene have come to relate to the land now that they are largely village dwellers rather than bush dwellers. This change did not come easily, and ties to the bush have not been totally surrendered. In the late 1970s the caribou herds were beginning to show signs of recovery from the crash of the 1940s. By this time, Dene expectations, economics, and subsistence were so thoroughly intertwined with those of white Canada that a return to bush life was not possible. One legacy of the worldwide inflation of the 1970s was to drive the costs of goods and services far beyond the levels that could be met by income derived from trapping. Transportation needs and charter air costs alone had escalated so greatly that where in 1970 it cost several hundred dollars to go to and from the trapline, in the 1990s it could easily cost five thousand dollars just to go.[9] One way the Dene preserved their ties to the bush, a way that was emerging in the mid-1970s, was for hunting and trapping to become an occupational specialty rather than the occupational norm. Extended kin groups, with ties to wage labor, would contribute to the costs of sending a family into the bush for a season of hunting and trapping. Often it was grandparents or kin unable or unwilling to adapt to village life that were supported in their bush life. In return, the bush family would send fresh and dried caribou meat back to the village. This was never a rational economic choice. Little meat was returned to the village kin, and its price per pound often exceeded that of the most exotic foods in the outside world. Caribou meat, particularly dried caribou meat, is valued so highly that economic considerations simply do not apply. In 1992 Mission still depended heavily upon the bush for its food, but that food was being produced by a decreasing percentage of the Dene. There were now families two generations deep in adults who have never known bush life and who do not have the skills to survive in the bush.

Another major area of change came from the Chipewyan response to the Canadian imposition of an ideological agenda about the family and the role of the individual. The ideological agenda of white Canada rarely came from conscious intent; it was an agenda imposed by operating procedure. The ideology of the culture was so thoroughly embedded in the matrix of Canadian culture that it was never thought about and never seen as an imposition of social change upon the Dene. The allocation of new houses, the issuance of Family Allowance checks to the mother of a child,[10] the allocation of the economic assistance—Rations—that were a Dene treaty right often of critical economic importance, the payment of welfare, the calculations of Old Age Pension benefits, determining who was responsible for ensuring children attended school, in program after program the federal and provincial governments assumed the Dene lived in nuclear families. Assumed that the economic ties among the Dene corresponded to those in white Canadian culture. Assumed the Dene have only a single residence. Assumed that Dene children did not live with their aunts, uncles, grandparents, or other kin as readily as they lived with their biological parents. In situation after situation, the practice and ideology of The People was ignored and the ideology and assumptions of Canadian culture about relations between kin and obligations between individuals were imposed as operating procedure.

In time, the Dene began to respond to this pressure, adopting Canadian cultural practice in order to receive necessary services and benefits. For most of the Dene, these practices were a nuisance they had to appear to conform to, at least in their dealings with "the government." They still lived by the old ways, still tried to practice the old sense of responsibility for kin and affines, but it became harder and harder to do so as the village grew. It is one thing to know that the meat of a moose should be shared willingly throughout a camp. It is another to try and share the meat of a moose among twelve hundred people. The Dene tried, but the scale of Dene life and the intrusion of government programs was too great. Kinship nets contracted. The kin ties were still recognized, but the sense of obligation had begun to evaporate. Kin ties alone were no longer sufficient. It now takes other ties—residence, past cooperation, friendship—in addition to kinship to make the ties social and economic ones. The children of the Dene grew up in a world where the old ties were held up as the ideal, but what they observed was the world of contracted ties and obligations and it was this pattern they carried into adulthood and applied in their own lives.

Mission has not yet become like the outside world. While elderly people complain that there are so many children at Mission that they do not even know who all of them are, they have done that at least since 1969. People are still interdependent to an extent unthinkable in the rest of urbanized Canada and United States. The pressures of scale remain, indeed intensify, as Mission continues to grow, but ideas about kinship and family are remarkably stubborn.

Beyond Mission still sets the bush. The cold and the harshness remain. This is still an easy land in which to die, and all that makes human life possible is knowledge and the help of other people. The unyielding nature of the bush continues to exert its force on the Mission Dene, even those Dene who are purely town dwellers, as they experiment with social arrangements, forms of economic alliance, and forms of family.

The challenges to the old ways do not cease. In 1998, over the strident objections of its inhabitants, the final construction of a road link between Mission and the outside was begun. The increased traffic in souls, tourists, drugs, disease, vices, and ideas this road will bring will force the pace of the experimentation from which will ultimately emerge a uniquely Dene adaptation to presence of modern Canada.

The old life, even the mid-twentieth-century version of bush life, was taxing. It placed great demands upon body and soul. The struggle to survive and achieve some security placed a premium upon knowledge, endurance, and constant effort. The harsher conditions were, the more challenging mere survival was, the more bush life engaged the body, mind, and soul of those who lived it and filled them with purpose. With that life came a fine appreciation for the competence it generated in those who survived it. The loss of that clear and precise definition of the purpose of life is the most frightening change the Dene must face with the abandonment of bush life.

The transition to a settled village life has provided no single focus to replace that sense of purpose and valuation of competence. There may be no single thing that ever can replace it. The rewards of Canadian culture are marked by material things, but the Dene have never valued things over relationships. Nothing in modern Canadian culture seems able to replace what the Dene have lost. Finding a substitute for that all-engaging sense of purpose may be the greatest challenge they face in preserving their unity as a people as they adapt themselves to the twenty-first century.

3

INDETERMINACY

Indeterminacy is a maddeningly simple concept. In its minimal application it means that the outcome of an event is influenced by the way in which the event is measured or observed. The presence of an observer creates an interaction between the event and the observer that, through the very act of observing/measuring, alters the nature of the event. In its more complex manifestations indeterminacy means that the outcome of an event does not become determinate until the measurement of that outcome has taken place. At the extremes, indeterminacy means that the outcome of an event is determined by the observation/measurement of the event even though the event may occur before or after the observation/measurement has taken place.

Indeterminacy is customarily assumed to be applicable only at the scale of subatomic particles. The ordinary universe of human experience is presumed to operate in a nicely determinate manner that can be explained by the application of Newtonian physics. In most of science, indeterminacy (and its implications) seems to have as little relevance as it does in ordinary experience. Psychology and sociology avoid indeterminacy as an aspect of human social life. History, which cannot escape the implications of indeterminacy, relies on the presumed rigor of its methodology to avoid confronting it.[1]

In this work I presume that human social behavior, like the behavior of subatomic particles, is indeterminate. As with the applicability of quantum mechanics and Newtonian mechanics, the use of indeterminacy is rarely necessary in the analysis of human behavior. For most of this analysis we can ignore indeterminacy. However, where conditions are right and indeterminacy does apply, its use is imperative. In those circumstances, it is impossible to separate an event in human social life from the means by which it is observed and measured. As the events of human social life are measured by the meaning ascribed to them, there is no possible way to separate an event from the interpretation(s) of that event. In this analytical framework the classic paradigm of a determinate universe does not apply to human social behavior. If one is human, if one is a social being, objectivity and absolute truth are impossible.

The inseparability of an event from the means by which it is measured can be illustrated by thinking about an archaeological site. We regard an archaeological site as part of the natural world. In the folk physics of our culture, an archaeological site has, like a mineral deposit, a reality of its own. It is a natural object whose properties and nature are fixed by physical laws independent of humanity and whose boundaries are determined by the distribution of the objects within it. It exists whether we know of it or not. If we know of it, we can investigate it, ignore it, destroy it, interpret—or misinterpret—it, but none of that alters the nature or the boundaries of the site. We are good positivists. We believe that reality exists, that an archaeological site has an existence we can attempt to understand but whose nature we cannot alter.

Robert R. Janes (1983: 1), before he begins his demonstration that uncovering such a site among the Northern Dene is a virtual impossibility, cites Robert Ascher's lucid statement of this position: "[I]n time every community will become first a 'ghost' town, then a cube below ground. The problem of the pre-historian is to reconstruct the community from the cube. Since the connection between the archaeological present and the ethnographic past lies along the route of increasing disorder, the advancement of interpretation depends upon knowing what happens along that route" (Ascher 1968: 52).

From this perspective, objects—regardless of their origin and the factors that led to their initial placement—have passed from the human world to the natural world. The pattern of their deposition and the extent of their decay or preservation is purely the result of the operation of natural laws upon them.

From the perspective that social behavior is an indeterminate phenomenon, the reality known to humans does not exist independently of them. The word more commonly encountered in ethnographic writing to deal with this issue, *interpretation,* is not used here because it implies that events are real and determinate beyond the meaning humans give to them. Indeterminacy is used here precisely to make the point that events do not exist beyond the meaning humans give to them. Interpretation is a question of different understandings of a common reality. Indeterminacy is a question of the creation of a common reality from the chaotic and variable raw data of experience.

From the perspective of indeterminacy, an archaeological site has no existence beyond the *meaning* that humans place upon it. This does not mean that objects are not in the ground any more than it means that humans do not die or that mountains are not indifferent to human meaning. It does mean that the existence, nature, and boundaries of an archaeological site are determined by the nature of the human interest in the site.

In a site that is fully excavated, the excavation will extend into areas where there are no artifacts, so the absence of artifacts does not mark the boundaries of a site. In a site that is not fully excavated, artifacts will remain in situ, so neither the presence nor absence of artifacts marks the boundaries of a site. The site cannot be defined even by the presence or absence of previous human action. Part of any good excavation will focus upon objects that have no relationship to past human activity. Pollen may be gathered from the remains of long-vanished lakes far removed from any artifacts left by humans, and those lakes themselves become part of the site. The investigation may include the collecting of fossils, and a good investigation may extend to collecting the fossil remains of insect life. An archaeological site merges imperceptibly into a paleontological site. Insects are ubiquitous, and where there is soil there also are their fossils. The presence of fossil insect remains may tell much about the lives of the people who left the artifacts, but it cannot mark the boundaries of a site that merges imperceptibly through pollen and insect remains into the whole of the earth itself.

Archaeological sites are not found in nature; they are found in the activities of humans. An unknown archaeological site has no existence at all. Without human interest—without the site coming within a culturally generated field of meaning—it is but part of the earth itself and indistinguishable from it.

The notion of indeterminacy as an analytical construct is applicable to all humans (and to some animal species). It is a social rather than a psychological construct. Analytically, meaning is the source of determinacy, and meaning is a property of socialness. There is an obvious analogy with language.

Even though it is only individuals who speak, only individuals who generate speech acts, language is a product of the interaction between individuals. It is a product of the sharing of speech and speech acts rather than a product of the individuals or the individual speech acts themselves.

I have found one of the best ways to appreciate the issue of indeterminacy is by thinking about the effects of differences in scale in the determination of reality. We presume human scale and create a reality consonant with that scale. Thinking about the same phenomena from the standpoint of different scales can begin to hint at the appearance of indeterminacy at a human scale.

Some examples are obvious: the smoothness of the surface of a wall from a human perspective contrasted with the texture of the same wall from the perspective of a fly. It takes little effort to understand how what is smooth to a human is rough to a fly, yet the example is significant. Not only does the roughness of the wall allow a fly to climb it but it also allows the fly to walk upside down upon the ceiling in apparent defiance of gravity. What gravity is may not change mathematically, but the effect of gravity clearly depends upon scale.

Thinking of the contrast between a microscopic and a human scale is more difficult but productive. As humans, we have a clear idea of the boundaries of each person's body to support our conceptualization of what constitutes a person. From the scale of a microbe—let alone a virus—the boundary between the body of a person and the surrounding world is indistinct at best. Indeed, at a viral level I doubt if it is at all possible to maintain that a person is in fact a discernible aspect of reality. What can be more easily seen through thinking of differences in scale at smaller levels aids in seeing how complex phenomena are created from the sharing of meaning to order the indeterminate mass of experience that reaches each individual social being.

The Dene are not great teachers.[2] They communicate their knowledge from generation to generation in their myths and their stories but above all through their social practice. Knowledge is in the stories. It is there for the understanding of all who will listen to the stories and think about them, but the responsibility to listen and to understand rests with each individual Dene. They expect those who do not know to learn through observation, through the examples others provide, and through their own experience of attempting to do.

Indeterminacy is not an overt Dene concept or part of an overt Dene model of reality. Nevertheless, Dene culture is one that recognizes the indeterminacy of social phenomena. The indeterminacy of social phenomena emerges through the sharing of interpretations and representations of experiences rather than from the experiences themselves (Sharp 1988a: 67–69). It is the *sharing* of representations of individual experience that give meaning to experience and order to reality.

There are two distinct aspects to indeterminacy to be dealt with here.[3] The first is the Chipewyan usage of indeterminacy in their construction of their own culture and their use of it in their social life. Its usage in their culture will begin to be apparent in their relationship to their land and its inhabitants and is most clearly focused in the story of the encounter with the loon. The reality they have constructed involves far more interaction with the land and its inhabitants than does the white relationship to the land and those of its inhabitants whites realize exist within it (see Nelson 1983: 14–23). In Chipewyan reality, many nonhuman inhabitants—and perhaps the land itself—are self-aware and play an active role in their interaction with the Dene, while in the white reality that exists within the same geographical bounds, those inhabitants are not self-aware, are inactive, or are not even present.

As other aspects of the contextual and interpretive material create a matrix of meaning around the "events" of the story, indeterminacy will begin to show in wider contexts, particularly in how the Dene conceptualize and use time and in what constitutes an explanation for "events" within Dene social life.

The second aspect of indeterminacy, its analytical usage as a means of explaining the "events" upon which this work is focused, initially will be less obvious than will its role in Dene culture. As an analytical concept, indeterminacy cannot be separated from the role of meaning in constructing reality, and it is premature to try to explore that now.

4

FOXHOLM LAKE *The Place*

The village of Mission is a phenomenon of the second half of the twentieth century, but even the epic and escalating changes in the lives of The People that began with the young adulthood of the first generation of the twentieth century pale before the continuing experience of the millennia during which Chipewyan shaped—and were shaped by—their land. The Chipewyan are not separable from their land. There is no hope of appreciating them without a tenacious sensitivity to the harshness and beauty of their homeland and the transcendental ballet of predation that has existed between Dene, Wolf, and Caribou since time immemorial.

For more than two thousand years the Dene have made their living as predators upon the wildlife of this land. This wildlife, upon which they depended entirely, is scarce. At any given time, most animal species are dispersed widely and unevenly. Through time—and time may be but a very few seasons—there are drastic changes in the mix of species as well as in the geographical distribution of individual species within the Dene homeland. Many of the most important prey species are migratory. Even in the best of circumstances these migratory species are available in only some places, and even then they are available only seasonally. Not only are prey species geographically variable but the population dynamics of all the subarctic and arctic fish, bird, and animal populations upon which the Dene live are erratic. The number of individuals of each species fluctuates dramatically through time, and the Dene have many times experienced these risings and fallings of the animal populations on which they live. Knowing how to deal with these variations is a major part of their survival knowledge (see Burch 1972; 1977: 142; J. G. E. Smith 1978).

The caribou, even more than the Dene, are creatures of movement. From their calving grounds in June, they sweep along the barrens to the edge of the forest. Some never leave the tundra or winter at its fringes, but most of the caribou move into the transitional forest between August and October. Within a month they may be a hundred miles into the transitional zone of the Boreal Forest and may yet venture hundreds of miles deeper into the Boreal Forest itself. Those that enter the forest usually, but never predictably as to when or where, winter within it. By March, the cows feel the pangs of future birth rising and begin moving toward the calving lakes. In less than a month they may be back along treeline, awaiting their plunge onto the barren grounds to deliver a new generation of their species.

The scale of caribou movements is staggering. The direct line from their calving grounds to their wintering areas may exceed five hundred miles; their round trip often exceeds a thousand miles. Caribou do not travel in straight lines but wander over the landscape. We can observe that they, who lose several gallons of blood to mosquitoes, black flies, and other biting insects each summer, respond to insects, snow, temperature, vegetation, storms, wind direction, or predators; to the shape of the land and its form and texture; to the size, shape, and depth of the lakes. Environmental conditions are not sufficient to explain their movements. Caribou move for reasons known only to themselves, and they are never still. They wander constantly, circling, moving, coming, going, back and forth, hither and yon. One day they are here, the next gone beyond finding. The specificity of their movements is beyond human prediction.

It was upon their knowledge of the caribou and the nature of caribou movements that the ancestral Dene built their lives: to find the caribou, to hunt the caribou, to prepare its flesh for food, to prepare its hides for clothing and shelter. The twenty-five hundred years of experience during which the Dene shaped and were shaped by their land may not compare with the forty thousand to sixty thousand years' experience the Aborigines have of shaping and being shaped by Australia (Flannery 1994), but it represents a depth of knowledge and experience inconceivable in European history. That twenty-five hundred years of experience of surviving through predation on the barren-ground caribou has given the Dene a depth of knowledge and wisdom about this land, its climatic cycles, and its wildlife that is the abstract capital of Dene existence.

The tie between the Chipewyan and their land has been mediated through the caribou from whom they have drawn their sustenance and their identity. Behind all of the complex and multifaceted perspectives the Dene have upon this land—from aesthetics to luck, wonder, and fear—lies always the shadow of the absence of caribou. Life in this place has always been the search for caribou. In the failure of that search for caribou, Dene life cannot be sustained.

As the Chipewyan conceptualize the land, it is not quite right to think of Foxholm Lake as a lake. The Dene name things in a different manner than do those speaking English. The names of places are not names in the formal sense of an English name where the name becomes a fixed designator for a specific location. The Chipewyan tendency is to refer to areas and to do so by using descriptive phrases that reflect past events, human activities, or inhabitants. Foxholm Lake is a designator not just of the lake itself but of the region around it as well. The best English translations of the Dene name for Foxholm Lake are "wolves den there" or "the lake and area around which large numbers of wolves make their dens."

For the extended family group camped at Foxholm Lake in 1975, the camp was located at the westernmost end of the range that Paul had used throughout his life. But a few miles west of the lake, where the forest thickens and extends northward for hundreds of miles, the land is hunted and trapped by Dene from Birchtown. There are no boundaries between the two groups of Dene, merely a declining presence of the Dene from Mission—some of whom prefer the forest-tundra interface—and an increasing presence of Dene from Birchtown—who prefer the forest proper.

Foxholm Lake is a special place to those of the camp in which I was staying when we encountered the loon that August afternoon. On Paul's side of the family their ties to this place are at least four generations deep. Paul himself was born on Adeker Lake, the next large lake to the south of Foxholm Lake.[1] Paul's father had hunted this area throughout his life, and as Paul matured, he focused his activities eastward toward South Lake (Sharp 1988a, 1996). Paul had married May in the mid-1930s. She had grown up far to the south along the Churchill River among the Southern Chipewyan and had few ties to this land before her marriage to Paul. May did have an excellent command of English, as did all those of her brothers and sisters who had moved to the Mission area in their youth (Sharp 1975: 73). During the 1930s and 1940s, their skill in English allowed them to form effective partnerships with white trappers working out of Discha. Paul and May frequently ventured far out on the barren grounds in the company of her siblings and various white trapping partners. Indeed, far out upon the tundra are two small lakes named on the maps: Sid's Lake and Merry's Lake, one for the husband of one of May's sisters, the other for another of her sisters who drowned there after becoming entangled in a fishnet she was checking.

These alliances with white trappers drew Paul and May far north of the range his father had used, but Paul preferred the environs of Foxholm Lake and the next lake to its south where he had been born. Although he and May spent many seasons in a variety of locations between Mission Lake and the deep tundra, their time was concentrated within a forty-mile-by-forty-mile rectangle centered on the southern part of Foxholm Lake. Most of their children had been born within this area—two at Foxholm Lake itself—and two who had died in infancy were buried on an esker overlooking the river alongside which Paul had been born.

The ties of Paul and May to this place continued in their children's generation. Two of their sons still make their livings within this area while two other ones frequently wintered within it. The locations of their daughters' lives have been more scattered by their choice of husbands and the diversity of their affinal ties, but at least two return to that forty-by-forty block with some regularity. Nearly ten of Paul and May's grandchildren have spent large parts of each year of their childhood within it. A pattern of attachment to a fairly small core area with the spreading out of children and grandchildren is the common pattern of Chipewyan family history, but within this one extended kin group is also visible the Chipewyan tendency to explore and sample large and diverse areas outside the core area.

The use of the land is tied to knowledge of the land. A great deal of nonsense (e.g., Yerbury 1986) has been written about the need for hunters to know a territory, with that need controlling their movements and dictating marriage patterns, kinship systems, and rules of postmarital residence. Here, in this part of the Subarctic, it is necessary to reiterate that this is nonsense. The people do come to know some areas of land intensely, often in a detail staggering to those raised in more densely settled areas, but that is not the issue. Knowing a territory is not remembering where every rock is placed or where every species of plant grows; it is having a sound understanding of the nature of the animate beings within the land and how those beings relate to each other and to particular kinds of local environments.

This knowledge is portable. Time and again I have watched Paul explain the land to others less familiar with it than he was. For a journey, younger, less experienced men might receive a detailed verbal or hand-drawn map, sometimes a map so detailed that he drew out from memory both shores of the streams along which they would travel.[2] More experienced men often were told merely sequences of landmarks (usually eskers) and directions to travel from or toward them. Once I saw him explain where he thought a brother-in-law (seri) spending his first winter this close to the tundra should set his trapline. The advice was brief, little more than suggesting a river line to follow that Paul thought should be productive of fur and that ran through good caribou-hunting territory. This man was Paul's age and as experienced as Paul. He had heard of these places even though he had never been far enough north to have seen them before. He found the information Paul gave him sufficient for him to carry out a successful season of hunting and trapping.

The Dene could not have survived through a detailed knowledge of place within a dynamic and constantly changing environment but have survived through a detailed understanding of how animate life relates to other forms of animate life and interacts with climate and environment. Knowing a territory is not memorizing where things are but understanding how things relate to each other.

The specificity of Dene knowledge of local landscapes can be staggering in its detail. Simple movement within their land is dangerous at all seasons of the year. At some seasons, especially during the transitions between the seasons, it can be extremely dangerous. The land itself is dynamic. Ice jams and floods alter the physical shape of the land. Small lakes freeze, thaw, and flood, and these actions can tear up the surrounding land and vegetation. Shorelines move constantly while passages between lakes open and close on an irregular basis. What one year was a deep-water passage allowing free movement of a heavily laden canoe may the next year be a shallow passage riven by jagged rocks waiting to tear the bottom out of the same canoe. The texture of the muskegs varies from season to season, and this month's dry pathway may be next month's foot-wetting damp place. Vegetation, in the absence of fire—which is rare this close to the tundra—does not change so quickly, but usable stages of growth—for example, dry wood or deadfall—remembered from past seasons may well be absent the next time people pass through.

On top of the normal dynamics of the land are the seasonal changes within it. Routes of travel are largely dictated by weather, snow accumulation, ground freezing, and ice formation. While people prefer high and dry routes in summer, they must seek lower routes sheltered from the wind in winter, yet those routes must also be dry for wetness is the great killer in this land. In the decision making people must go through in order to move safely, there must be awareness of the continuous interplay between the state of freezing of ground and lakes, wind, snow depth, open water, distance, usable resources, food supply, and a host of other variables. Always, storms remain the wild card. Thunderstorms can produce in minutes waves that will overturn a canoe while sustained wind storms can make the larger lakes impassible for weeks. Snow storms can sweep in in hours, leaving dogs immobilized. Wind can take visibility to nothing within a matter of seconds, creating whiteout conditions that leave even the most experienced travelers totally without visual reference.

The People represent their cognitive maps of the terrain in a variety of ways. Physical descriptions of the land are rare. The form of the land is normally tied to the specific context of particular human activities or abstracted to ties between the land and the animal/persons who inhabit it—for example, "Foxholm Lake always has lots of caribou"—although on occasion comments may refer to the physical aspects of the land—such as, "East of Snowbird Lake it is really wet ground." The normal manner of describing the land is by reference to eskers, lakes, and watercourses. I have rarely heard this method used to describe the land between landmarks—for example, "between these four hills"—and virtually always in the context of directions of how to get somewhere or identify a particular area—as in a stream course—to trap, hunt, fish, or seek safe passage.

The extent to which this knowledge of the land can result in detailed "maps" was brought home to me in the summer of 1992, when I was on a hunting trip with Phil. We had camped on Foxholm Lake, about a mile east of where we had encountered the loon in 1975, near the base camp George had used the last few years. Phil had put the most effort into searching for caribou (Sharp 1998: 67–68), and it was returning by boat from one of his hunting trips that produced the display of detailed knowledge that has impressed me the most of all that I have seen. As we traveled along the north shore of Foxholm Lake, Phil began to express concern for George's eldest son's (Phil's *saze*, the "infant son" of Sharp 1988a) lack of knowledge of the bush and his persistent refusal to follow basic safety precautions when he was out in the boat. His expression of concern led him to tell me about the dangers of traveling during times of reduced visibility (especially during fog) or changing weather conditions (especially during the first snows of fall). His train of thought led him to start citing examples of the kinds of things his saze did not know or did not act upon if he did know. Using the effects of snowfall during fog as his worst-case scenario, he began a running monologue, systematically linking conditions under the lake where we were traveling to the distance we had to keep from the shore to the shape of the shoreline and to landmarks a bit farther back that one could hope to see during times of reduced visibility. For several miles of our travel along the lake he pointed out—sometimes every ten or fifteen yards—rock piles inboard or outboard of our route of travel, systematically linking them (this without looking!) to land forms (e.g., shore shape, rock piles, single standing trees, or boulders) along the shore and matching them with landmarks (e.g., rock formations, patches of timber, cracks in rock walls,) a bit farther inland.

Within a few miles Phil had gone through scores of obstacles in the lake and the markers that indicated safe passage around them. Each time he indicated which marker would be more useful with fresh snowfall on the ground, which would be hidden by new snowfall, and which would be useful in fog. The most staggering aspect of this display was that we were in an area miles away from the primary areas within which he hunted, trapped, and fished, an area within which he had much less experience of the lake and land than he had of those areas he used on a more regular basis.

Above all, The People order their land through their experience of the "events" of their history and their interaction with those other persons with whom they share the land. The lives of Dene distant past are immediate in the marks and artifacts they have left upon the land. Because most of the Mission Dene homeland is frozen and still rebounding upward from the weight of the glaciers, human cultural debris—particularly stone artifacts—tend to remain at or near the surface. Away from wet places the ground cover is nearly always but a thin coating of lichen, and it takes an interminably long time for it to cover objects dropped on the ground. The effect is to make many of the dry places, particularly dry places used as hunting camps or lookouts, carpets of lithic debris left by the "Old Ones." Stone chips and flakes are almost as common as berries, and in places they carpet the land even more conspicuously than do the berries.

Besides the general clutter of human debris are those rarer but more precious places where the marks of human antiquity are indicative of determinable human activities. Tipi rings often mark the land by the hundreds (Sharp 1996), and near concentrations of tipi rings are the scars of the small lodges individual Dene built for interaction with the spiritual. These places, while it would be inappropriate to place upon them all the baggage that travels with the English word "sacred," are noted by the Dene and treated with respect for the power/knowledge that has flowed between human and nonhuman within them. Sometimes upon the wind-blown tops of the high eskers are stone rings, usually filled to overflowing with verdant growth, that flag the site of larger constructions that served the spiritual needs of larger numbers of Dene. The specificity of their purpose forgotten, these rare sites are learned by The People as they gain familiarity with an area, and the sites sometimes serve not merely the mundane purpose of lookouts or resting places for hunters but as the loci of worship and communion with the sources of power/knowledge that animate this land.

If the marks of the unnamed human past are everywhere within the land, the marks of the named human past are less plentiful but play an even greater role in specifying the meaning of place and the nature of the land itself. Before the Dene began to concentrate at Discha and Mission they lived scattered throughout their land (Sharp 1977, 1978). From the time of our earliest records of contact with the Chipewyan until well into the 1980s, The People have alternated residence between isolated bush camps, rarely containing twenty persons, and large villages that sometimes housed upwards of several hundred people (Helm 1993; Sharp 1988a: 20–21). These villages were seasonal aggregations made possible by Dene sensitivity to caribou movements and their skill as hunters. The normal arrangement of life was the small camp of kin and affines disposed ten or twelve miles from each other. Foxholm Lake, within the memory of Paul and May, supported two or three such groups each year until the crash of the caribou herds.

The form of the land is shaped by the memory of these camps and their occupants. Stretches of apparently empty terrain are not voids in an unexplored landscape but the places where persons-remembered lived, worked, and died as well as places where the events of one's own life have been played out. The land is not just *is*. The land is the living memory of all that has gone before in the living experience of each Dene who sojourns here as well as being the received memory of the stories and experiences of each of those known to them *and* the setting of all that is to come to and for The People.

5

THE WHITES' LAND

The land of The People is a vastly different place for Mission's white population than it is for the Chipewyan. The European settlement of North America was largely restricted to places suitable for some form or another of agriculture. From the beginning, it was obvious that the land of The People was not suitable for farming. As a direct result, the land of The People has never had a large white population and The People have never had to yield occupancy of their land. The cost and difficulty of transport were and continue to be so great that even rich mineral deposits have had to go undeveloped. Even in the most recent period only a few of the more southern of the region's extensive uranium deposits have become commercially viable.

From its earliest encounters with this place, white Canada has viewed this land with fear and loathing as a wasteland inhabitable only at the constant risk of death, accident, or starvation. This Canadian view of the land is not unique to the land of The People. Margaret Atwood has brilliantly demonstrated the pervasiveness of this perspective on its environment in Canadian literature, and this is a case where literature accurately reflects the belief of the larger Canadian culture (Atwood 1972, 1995).

The white population of Mission is heir to this tradition. What is home to The People is something very different to Mission's white population. A few of the older generation of whites who had come to the North to spend their active lives there still remained when I began fieldwork in 1969, but most of the whites of Discha and Mission are transients who serve but a year or two before moving on. Those with seasonal work, like the teachers, usually leave the North during the parts of the year they are not working, and most vanish for lengthy holidays every chance they get. Throughout the 1960s, 1970s, and

1980s, the local whites have had neither the knowledge nor the equipment that would have allowed them to move freely through the bush surrounding Mission. For most of them, the only exposure they get to the wilderness that surrounds them is the occasional summer day-trip picnic in a borrowed boat or a short fishing trip to where the river can be reached by well-established tourist trails. Few walk even a few hundred yards into the surrounding forest to watch birds, hunt small game, or simply explore. For most of the white population, the land of the Dene is a harsh and fearsome guardian of a prison to which they have confined themselves.

6

LOON II

The Western explanation of this encounter with a loon is simple. The hunters shot at the loon and missed it. The appearance of a loon that afternoon was simple happenstance. They failed to kill it because they did not shoot well enough to hit it. Had the shot been more difficult, then Western culture might make reference to "luck," that is, to a condition external to the hunter's skills. Hitting a loon at that range was within the parameters of their previously demonstrated skill, so their failure to hit it is explicable as a failure in the exercise of skills presumed to rest upon the physiological functioning of each hunter. If forced to push our own mode of explanation as to why they missed the loon, we would offer—since they had the skill to hit it—explanations that reflect their temporary physiological condition (e.g., they were tired, or they were not feeling well). Our folk physics explains by making reference to unknown, but presumably demonstrable, conditions of physiological impairment or other deviation from normal biological functioning in a mechanical universe of cause and effect.

This mode of explanation, while satisfying to us, is patently spurious. The explanations we assume to be empirically sound and scientifically valid expressions of the true nature of physical reality are in fact no more than presumptions about the nature of physical reality and the nature of causality within it. This is no more than an elementary teaching point of introductory anthropology courses: that members of a culture presume (generally without reflection) that the categories given by their culture depict reality.

The explanations offered in ordinary Western life that are based upon the physiological states of the actor are only presumably based upon the physiological states of the actor. These explanations are not demonstrable in ordinary life, and they are not subject to testing or other empirical measures.

Our cultural values frown upon the autopsy and pathological examination of living human beings—which is what would be required to demonstrate that the hunters missed their target because they were suffering from physiological deficiencies. In the absence of such an examination, the validity of our explanations lies in their assertion rather than in their demonstration.

The Chipewyan explain events like this in a very different manner. Their mode of explanation is also part of a general theory of causality, but it is one that is demonstrable in daily life. If their mode of explanation would seem tautological and inaccurate to us, our mode of explanation would seem incomplete and tentative to them. Both modes explain equally well, but the Chipewyan mode of explanation is more complete in what it explains (Levy-Bruhl 1967, 1979).

The myth about the seven kinds of men is one I find pivotal to understanding Dene thought (Sharp 1979: 42; 1994b: 257–59). In outline, the myth goes something like this: The God organized a contest between the seven kinds of men. As a result of this contest between the kinds of men, the God would give to each their unique talents and powers. The contest took the form of a race. A race that the Dene won. The white man was unhappy with the result of this fair contest and went to the God and lied to Him, tricking Him into believing that the race had been fixed. The God believed the white man and declared that there was to be another race. A race the white man won. Because the white man won this unfairly called second race he was given the first prize: the control of "things." Control of the material world through the means of physical causality. The Dene, who came in second in this second race, received second prize: the use of *inkoze* as a means to live in the world.[1]

All was well while the white man and the Chipewyan lived apart from each other. Life was hard for the Dene, but it was complete. The Dene lived in the realm of inkoze and lived "like the animals." The Dene spoke no human language, using instead the common tongue of the realm of inkoze whose knowledge they shared with the animals. They knew no human marriage regulations and married among themselves without regard to the prohibitions of incest. This world of inkoze in which they lived was one in which the separation of human and animal was not complete. Dene could and did intermarry with the animals, and their offspring were sometimes animal, sometimes human. During this time, the great culture heroes of the

Dene were among them, and both men and women knew the inkoze necessary to accomplish their tasks in the world.

The People, for whom birth into the human realm now separates them
from the realm of inkoze, survive because the animals give them knowledge
of inkoze in dreams, visions, and fortuitous encounters. This time of living
in the realm of inkoze lasted until the white man came among them, bringing their knowledge of "things." When the priests came, then also came
knowledge of human marriage rules. The Dene language instantly appeared
and the people now spoke their own language instead of the common
tongue of inkoze and the animals.[2] The time of inkoze was passing. The time
in which the Dene now live is a time in which the influence of inkoze is
diminishing. A time when the beings of inkoze are withdrawing from contact with the Dene and old men choose to take their power/knowledge to
their graves. What remains of the relationship between the beings of inkoze
and the Dene is maintained most strongly in the paradigm of the hunt
(Sharp 1988a, 1988b, 1994b).

The most immediate difference between white and Dene modes of explanation is the whites' exclusion of the loon from active participation in the
events. To us the loon is passive and mechanical, merely a target. The reasons
these two men failed to hit the loon lay in a deficiency of their internal
systems, deficiencies of the actor that resulted in a failure in their performance. The results in the external world are, even if only indirectly, a product of the internal world of the actor. Conversely, Dene assume the competence of the actor and of the actor's ability to shoot well enough hit the loon.
Their explanation for the events involves the loon as an active participant in
the process. The reason for their failure to kill the loon is that the loon chose
not to die for them, an explanation that is external to the actor and that lies
in the nature of the relationships existing between the actors and the loon.
Since, in Dene thought, all animal/persons *know* more than humans and are
more powerful than humans, for a human to kill an animal requires the
animal's consent. Dene life is predicated upon the willingness of animal/
persons to sacrifice themselves for the benefit of the Dene, but in any given
encounter, that presumption always has an air of uncertainty about it (Sharp
1988a, 1994b).

Since animals are more powerful beings than are humans, the death of an
animal at the hands of a hunter forms a sacrificial paradigm in which a being

of superior power gives itself to the Dene in order to bind the Chipewyan to the realm of inkoze.[3] Killing an animal that sacrifices itself to the Dene maintains the Dene conjunction with the realm of inkoze. As long as the Dene hunt, their separation from inkoze is not final.

The reason so many shots were fired at this loon lies in its behavior and the fact that animals are persons existing—to white and some other cultures—simultaneously in two dichotomous realms. It is more useful—and more accurate—to recognize that in Dene thought animals are an indeterminate phenomenon. In a practical sense, measurement is the response of the animal to the actions or observation of the Dene. The nature of any unknown animal the Dene encounter, other than a dog, can only be determined from the actions taken by the animal after the encounter begins. Reality is not determined beforehand or even at the time of the "events" but after the fact of the "events" when the meaning of the "events" has been made known. The arrow of time is not operating in Dene encounters with animals (Gould 1987; Gribbin 1984: 177–213; Hawking 1988). It is only through an after-the-fact reasoning, parallel to the differentiation of kinds of animals from humans in Chipewyan myth that the order of the world can be known (Sharp 1986: 258–59). As it is only possible to determine whether a person in a myth is an animal or a human after the consequences of their actions and choices have come to unfold, so it is only possible to tell whether a loon is a bird or something else by the consequences of Dene interaction with that loon. The loon we encountered might have been the one that appeared to warn the young orphan to flee his camp because the caribou swimming up the lake were in fact a Cree raiding party disguised by magic. It could have been the being that came to a Chipewyan camp only to destroy it and all its inhabitants because The People insulted it. In terms of the conceptions of time built into English grammar, what is happening now is not determinable until the future has come to be.

That a spirit should take the form of a loon and appear to three ordinary persons at Foxholm Lake is not surprising, for the land of The People is home to many persons and beings unknown to white Canada.

7

WILD THINGS

Within the reality created by Chipewyan culture are many beings whose existence is concealed from transient visitors and whites. Among those beings whose home is within the land of the Dene, there be giants. They are beings that whites, if they come to hear of them, regard as superstition or delusion.

Giant beings are a worldwide facet of human experience, one widely reported by Native American cultures (e.g., Turner 1996: 20, 42–43, 84–86; Nelson 1983: 74). Chipewyan reality is created by the sharing of the process of assigning meaning to Chipewyan experience, but that process serves to create an intelligible shared reality rather than a systematic natural history of reality. Chipewyan reality is one that understands mystery even while applying empirical knowledge to deal with it. The Dene toleration of mystery, itself a recognition of the indeterminacy that lies at the core of human culture, was evident in their reaction to the discovery of a fuzzy giant brown creature on the east shore of Discha Lake. That lake has been traversed, explored, camped along, and fished for hundreds if not thousands of years. It is as well known to the Dene as any area can be known to a human population, yet twice within the last three generations of the twentieth century unknown beings of inkoze have been discovered along its shores.

In the 1920s, some of the Dene chose to construct cabins along the western shore of Discha Lake rather than to stay there in tents. Cabins are easy to build from the light soft woods that dominate the area. It is, however, difficult to seal the gaps between the logs used in construction and very difficult to make roofs that do not leak. In most of the places Dene build cabins they are forced to rely upon moss to chink the gaps between the logs.

In some places there are deposits of clays that are superior to mosses for chinking cabins. The Dene use these clays when they are available. Discha Lake has such a deposit at the base of a small ridge just off its northern shore. The Dene have known of this deposit for generations and have regularly used its clay to chink their cabins. Gathering clay required a boat trip across Discha Lake, but the deposit was far enough above the river egress and rapids at the northwest end of the lake that there was little danger from water currents. Parties of women often went by themselves to gather clay from pits that had been dug into the hillside.

The discovery of the giant brown fuzzy creature occurred when a party of women made a boat trip over the lake to gather clay. They went to a favorite clay pit whose long history of usage was implied by the depth to which it had been sunk into the hill. One of the women had gone down into the pit (only one person could work in it at a time) and begun to dig when she noticed a small patch of long brown hair in the clay. She was perplexed by the fur and called the rest of the women's attention to it. They gathered around the pit and looked into it to see what she had found. They called to her to try and dig it out.

Uncertain what she had found, she carefully began to excavate the fur. She, and the remainder of the women standing there watching and listening to her commentary on the excavation of the fur, at first thought she had found a bear. They were puzzled. Aside from the question of why a bear would be buried in a clay pit, the fur was far too long to belong to any bear they had ever seen or heard of. The woman continued her cautious excavation of the fur until she had cleared a piece nearly a yard square. At this point, the women realized the fur was moving in a gently rhythmic manner that made it seem like part of a breathing animal. When they realized the fur was still attached to an animal that seemed to be alive, they debated what to do before deciding to gently cover it up, fill in the pit with brush, and return home.

My time among the Dene began many years after this encounter, but people still sometimes reflected on the incident. There seemed to be a general consensus that the fur was part of a giant animal, probably some form of bear, that lived beneath (inside) the ridge. As far as I could determine, the clay pit was abandoned and there has been no attempt to investigate what the women had found. Whatever it was, The People had decided that it was best for all concerned if it were left undisturbed.

Now that the Dene knew the beast was there, they were content to speculate about its nature. They felt no need to disturb the being or try to find out
precisely what it was. This lack of systematic investigation into what was a
significant puzzle might seem odd, but often the most prudent course of
action when faced with a being of inkoze that has chosen not to interfere in
human lives is simply to withdraw and not disturb it. The Dene had already
gathered the relevant information about the beast. They knew in general
that it was a being of inkoze, for no ordinary bear could have been that big or
would have been in that place. They also now knew where it was and how to
avoid it. Its presence had caused them no previous harm. There was no
reason for them to expect that it would now cause them harm if they
respected its presence and left it alone. Western and Chipewyan approaches
to this creature might be different, but the Dene approach quickly isolated
those aspects of the being that were relevant to their own lives and, unlike
ourselves, they had the discipline and wisdom to let it be.

Inkoze is a greater realm that contains human life and experience within it.
Its nature is dynamic, convoluted, and beyond human understanding. To be
human, to be Dene, is to seek inkoze power within that greater realm and to
live in harmony as a participant within a realm that humans cannot control.
The Chipewyan know they do not possess a comprehensive natural history
of the beings of inkoze with whom they share reality. They neither seek such
a natural history nor feel intimidated by its absence. Their approach to these
beings is respectful but empirical. However, the empirical knowledge of
generations past is not formulated into a systematic typology, and the discovery of new beings of inkoze does not always lead to further exploration of
that new awareness.

Beings of inkoze exist and act toward each other for reasons generally beyond human knowledge or understanding. In their interactions with each
other, humans are at best bystanders and sometimes naught but casualties of
their actions. Relationships between the beings of inkoze are often far from
amicable. They sometimes kill each other.

The two forms of giant beings Dene run the greatest risk of encountering
are giant fish and giant otters. These creatures are of an ambiguous nature.
Some are benign or indifferent to humans while others are hostile to them.
As beings of inkoze, giant beings are not bound by human rules or human

morality. They move throughout the Dene homeland according to their own rules and whims. The locations they inhabit change through time, and it seems that their numbers change over time as well. The Dene know that they do not know their total numbers or all of the locations where they dwell. The Dene do have a sufficiently sound understanding of the preferences these beings have for particular kinds of locations to be able to guess with some accuracy as to where giant beings are likely to be found.

For at least several human generations, three giant otters and one giant fish have been known to live in/under Mission Lake. The Dene know the locations they frequent, and these have not changed within living memory. Mission Lake's giant fish, which in Western terms may have its origin in the sighting of transient waterspouts common to large lakes subject to high winds (Kenny 1981, 1982, and personal communication), is an exceptionally large one even by the standards of giant beings. The only part of it that Dene have seen are the fins upon its back. The fish rarely swims, but it only becomes visible when it does and its fins project out of the lake.

It is fortunate Mission Lake's giant fish rarely moves about because it is so large that it produces earth tremors when it does move. Few Mission Chipewyan have had the opportunity to see its fins moving on the lake. Most of them know the beast only from these tremors. I have met individuals who inferred, from the distance between the spines supporting its dorsal fin, that the fish must be at least a mile in length, but most Dene thought that rather excessive. It was generally thought to be between one hundred and three hundred feet in length.

I have not encountered a species designation for giant fish. Most max out at about one hundred feet in length with a width of ten to twelve feet. The Dene have encountered the remains of giant fish but, to my knowledge, never in a fresh enough condition for them to consume them. The most recent discovery of the remains of a giant fish occurred "not too long ago."[1] This giant fish lived under a particularly nasty set of rapids it had created for itself several dozens of miles eastward along an otherwise smooth part of the river system connecting Mission Lake to Wollaston Lake. These rapids were an aggravation to Dene who traveled along this river link between the two lakes as they were far too violent to freeze in winter or to be traversed by boat. Travelers had to make a difficult portage of several miles that required them to climb and descend a ridge before they could continue their journey along the river.

In common with other giant beings, the giant fish did not live in the water itself but had created for itself a subterranean home beneath the land underneath the water. Because of the rapids it had created, the Dene considered this particular giant fish hostile and avoided the stretch of river where it lived.

The death of the giant fish was discovered by a man from Wollaston Lake who had been visiting Mission and was taking his family back home. They were canoeing along the river and had neared the head of the portage when they noticed hundreds of screeching sea gulls and bald eagles circling over the rapids. Eagles are scarce in this land. Congregations of gulls and eagles are very rare, and one this large was disconcerting. Cautious about what such an aggregation might mean but curious as to why so many birds were circling, they beached their canoe at the head of the portage and moved vigilantly up and over the portage trail. As they reached the apex of the trail on the ridge crest, they were able to see down to the spot the birds were circling. From their vantage point they could see the giant fish lying dead along the shore with a mass of birds gathered around to feed upon it.

The river flowed smoothly past the remains of the giant fish; all traces of the rapids vanished from the river. Realizing there was no longer any need to make the portage, they returned to their canoe and continued their journey along the river. They passed close by the remains of the giant fish but apparently did not get out of the canoe to examine the carcass. They did observe it carefully as they passed by and noticed that the land around the remains of the giant fish was heavily scarred by lightning strikes. There was some sign that the lightning strikes had caused a small forest fire.

Dinosaurs are a much less clearly defined kind of giant being than are giant fish, and knowledge of them might be much more recent in origin. Some of the people I talked to were convinced that dinosaurs were not a traditional belief of the Mission People but a recent introduction by a then still living Discha resident who had learned about them while he had been a patient in a tuberculosis sanatorium in Alberta. I know no Dene who have direct personal experience of an adult dinosaur, but a woman who used to live there has seen a baby dinosaur in the reeds alongside Discha Lake. The Dene told me that they did not know whites knew about dinosaurs until they were featured on the cards enclosed in packages of Red Rose Tea. It was from talking with whites about those cards that the Dene learned the English word "dinosaur."At the time there was talk of dinosaurs—I have not heard them spoken of since 1980—there was a strongly renewed interest in the Alberta oil sands and extensive exploration of them. Some of this exploration was based from Uranium City. The Mission Dene knew of these explorations and knew people who had worked on them, but as far as I know none of the Mission Chipewyan had worked on them. Descriptions of the oil sands that the Dene had picked up from whites that placed their origins in the remains of once living plants and animals fit comfortably with Chipewyan ideas about the subterranean dwellings of beings of inkoze. Most of the Dene, unfamiliar with Western ideas about geology, geological processes, and geological time, applied Chipewyan ideas about the nature of time within the realm of inkoze to these descriptions and came to conceptualize the oil sands as a still living subterranean desert located somewhere across Lake Athabasca from Uranium City. Many of The People presumed dinosaurs to be natural inhabitants of this hidden desert although other life forms, particularly snakes, played a greater role in their conceptualization of it (Sharp 1987: 228).

In spite of the presence of the baby dinosaur on Discha Lake, adult giant beings live beneath the ground beneath water or in the air above the clouds. This is a double dichotomy of structural relationships. It is probably safe to make an association between thunderstorms—themselves living beings—and eagles, but the eagle is not the true form of the being of inkoze that calls the thunderstorm.[2] Thunderstorms are above ground, and the being of inkoze that calls forth the thunderstorm is normally found above the clouds of the storm.

There is an above-ground-above-cloud:below-ground-below-water opposition that characterizes the relationship between beings of inkoze. The surface of the earth is the focal point or mediator between the opposition—below-ground-below-water:above-ground-above-cloud. This opposition is between two aspects of the "spiritual" while the mediator—the surface of the earth—is the mundane realm of ordinary human life. However, inkoze is the containing realm of all existence and its power/knowledge permeates all existence. The effect is to leave the commonplace surface of the earth permeated by power/knowledge that may, at any moment, express itself in interaction with human life.

This below-ground-below-water:above-ground-above-cloud opposition also applies to other creatures of inkoze whose epistemological status and origin are less certain and whose appearance among humans may be even more unpredictable.

Trying to order the geometry of Dene space-time by binary oppositions is a useful and revealing approach, but its usage may create a false image of the geometry of Dene reality. The traditional reliance upon discrete and distinctly bounded categories implicit in Western logic expressed in these oppositions leads us to presume that Dene cosmology is structured into a series of planes or levels. This presumption, aggravated by the interpretation of the surface of the earth as a mediator between them, enters through the almost automatic assumption that the realms below-ground or above-cloud are linked into a single realm; that all the homes/portals of beings of inkoze that dwell under-ground-under-water open into or are part of a single unified plane existing in opposition to a single unified plane above-ground-above-cloud. In turn, the default assumption is that both above-ground-above-cloud and below-water-below-ground exist as a single realm (inkoze) in opposition to the earth's surface (mundane existence).

This interpretation is a conclusion about the nature of Chipewyan reality derived from an application of Western dualism. In fact, there is no evidence in this material that these dwellings/portals open into a unified realm rather than into separate or only tenuously connected realms. We, in effect, presume a Euclidean geometry of planes, of opposed levels, where Dene reality seems to assume a non-Euclidean geometry in which these separate dwellings/portals may, or may not, link. If there is a unity within these realms, it is of such a topological nature that it cannot be represented through binary processes or through any structural model either the Dene or I have been able to create.[3]

When giant beings emerge from the water and come onto land, their emergence often prompts the formation of a thunderstorm and an ensuing conflict with the being of inkoze that called the thunderstorm. For reasons unknown to the Dene, or at least unknown to the Dene I knew, the creatures of inkoze that call the living thunderstorm are implacably hostile to many of the giant creatures. The emergence of these giant beings onto the surface often provokes a battle that usually ends with the giant-being being driven back beneath the water although, as with the giant fish, these battles can lead to death. Dene rarely see these interactions between giant beings and the beings that call the thunderstorm to attack them. Their knowledge of these events is derived largely from their experience as trackers. When they find where such an encounter has taken place, they inspect and interpret the scars on the land, the burns of lightning strikes, the shattering of the ice on the lakes, the tearing up of the ground cover, the bending of the trees, the tracks on the ground, and any other clues they can find to make their interpretation. The sign left behind where dinosaurs have emerged from the water is particularly easy to interpret because, in addition to the scars, lightning burns, and torn ground cover, there is often a distinct trail left behind by the dinosaur's tail dragging on the ground.

In common with most of their Northern Athapaskan brethren, the Chipewyan of Mission regard knowledge gained through personal experience as the most certain of all forms of knowledge (D. M. Smith 1973; 1994: 72; m.s.; Goulet 1982, 1992, 1998; Rushforth 1992). Dene interpretations of the physical evidence of these encounters between beings of inkoze are taken for exactly what they are: interpretations of physical evidence. The Dene vary among themselves as much as we vary among ourselves, and if we sometimes forget this, the Dene are well aware of it. Some individuals are always more ready to believe new things or accept gossip and stories than are other people. Some are downright gullible, and their credibility is judged accordingly. The reliability and skill of each individual Dene at observing and reporting what each has observed is generally a known quantity that is based upon each individual's earlier performances. The interpretations each individual offers are judged according to the individual's reputation. Interpretation is a more open question than is reporting direct observation, but from even the most respected source an interpretation is only an interpretation. It is not accorded the same validity as that which comes from an individual's own personal experience.

The most frequently encountered of the giant creatures are the giant otters, beings much more likely to be hostile to humans than are giant fish or dinosaurs. They prefer to make their homes in rapids, river mouths, or the deeper parts of large lakes. The presence of giant otters, *nobiecho,* can be indirectly determined from their effects upon the surface environment. They can break apart the ice or raise the water level on small lakes, sometimes causing them to overflow and shatter timber along the shore. Nobiecho can make storms or large waves appear without warning.

A few of the lesser beings of inkoze may be vulnerable to the actions of human beings, but that is far from certain. The giant otters with which the Dene are familiar are far beyond the reach of Dene power/knowledge. I never heard any account of a giant otter being killed by another being of inkoze.

Dene have seen nobiecho. Paul and May told me of sitting for several hours on the shore of a lake in the Northwest Territories watching one play in the water. Their description of the giant otter as white and about the size of a seal led them to talk about other nobiecho. Some beings of inkoze appear to have individual origins and life histories, although these are not known to the Dene. Generally, beings of inkoze do not seem to be subject to the normal processes of aging and mortality that affect humans. The Dene react to some of these beings as if they have always been there and to others as if they are of more recent origin. They seemed to feel that some otters simply continue to grow past the normal size for an otter, presumably becoming more powerful as they grow, until they become nobiecho.

It is entirely reasonable there should be no hard division between ordinary animals and beings of inkoze. Paul's ambivalence in the fall of 1975 about whether or not he should try and trap a particularly large otter that had been leaving sign in the area demonstrated this lack of a hard division between the two. That he ultimately decided not to risk trying to trap the otter indicated the respect he held for possible beings of inkoze, but that he even considered the possibility of trapping it shows how Dene categories and explanations flow into each other.[4]

Nobiecho are about the size of the Steller's sea lion (*Otaria jubata* or *O. stelleri*), something I discovered when some Dene looked with fascination at a Pleistocene bestiary I had with me. The reported size of nobiecho loosely corresponds to now-extinct Pleistocene otter species, but neither the Dene nor I really knew what to make of that. There are stories of freshwater seal populations in Manitoba, and Dene have argued that if they are there, then why not in Saskatchewan or the Northwest Territories? The Dene are fully aware that their categories often do not correspond to those in English, and even in Chipewyan there is a good deal of ambiguity about the correct name for some rarely seen animals and birds.

Because giant otters might be found in any lake or river, water that a Dene has not ventured upon presents the potential for a chance encounter. If such an unwanted encounter should occur, it can usually be resolved through a small offering of the kind many men routinely give to larger lakes and rivers when they first venture upon them. These offerings may consist of tea, a coin, some tobacco, or whatever is handy simply being tossed into the water. Giant otters know what humans are thinking and feeling, so it is the "spirit" of the gift rather than the gift itself that is efficacious (Mauss 1967). Unfortunately, some giant otters are so hostile to a human presence that disaster will follow from even the most unintentional intrusion.

The role giant otters play in Dene life is generally not very significant as normal life proceeds on its merry way without reference to giant otters, giant fish, or other beings of inkoze. When contact with one of these giant beings does occur, it is rarely pleasant. The raw power/knowledge and the ill-tempered nature of some of these beings can lead them to violence, and they are capable of exacting retribution for decades.[5]

Chipewyan explanation tends to be symbolic rather than Cartesian (Sharp 1988a: 67–69). It brings together different, often entirely different, kinds of explanations that augment each other instead of comparing different explanations to eliminate some in favor of others. How individuals explain giant otters is both contextually and individually determined. The explanation given to another adult may differ from the one given to children, while Dene who have seen—have personal experience of—giant otters may give quite different explanations of them than will Dene who have never seen one and have no personal experience of them. Explanations may refer to natural processes or objects, personal experience, myth, stories, or other sources of knowledge. An individual may make several different explanations in a single conversation, and a group of Dene may well offer several completely different types of explanations without attempting to arrive at a consensus.

Whatever talking about things may accomplish for individuals, at a social level it is one of the means of creating order out of indeterminate data. Talking about things as an agent triggering social action is a fairly forthright aspect of creating a determinate reality within which humans can coexist. The process of creating a shared reality, with its orchestration of social action, thought, language, proxemics, myth, story, aesthetics, and everything else humans do and are, becomes more enigmatic when the abstractions of causality arise in complex events. Explaining these complexities still involves giving them meaning—that is, agreeing upon their meaning—and in the rare events and circumstances of Chipewyan experience considered here, it is inextricably tied to the nature of animals.

The causality of these events is determined by inkoze, the system of causality and being from which the Dene emerged as human beings. The essential core of Chipewyan awareness of inkoze comes from their understanding of the nature of animals as revealed to individual Dene in dreams, visions, and experiences of animals, although these beings do sometimes manifest themselves to groups of Dene. Animals, ordinary animals that The People hunt, trap, and eat, have a simultaneous dual reality—existence—as both natural and supernatural beings. As animals, they are the physical beings upon whose bodies the Dene depend for their own subsistence and survival. As supernatural beings, animals participate in inkoze, and it is in that realm that they have their "true" existence. This duality of being dominates traditional Dene thought, experience, and interaction with animals and is one of the root paradigms of Chipewyan culture.

This picture of the nature of animals and The People's relationship to them rests comfortably within the conventional conceptual categories of Western thought. A more trustworthy representation will not be so comfortable. Glimpsing a truer picture of the nature of what we conceive of as ordinary animals—of beings we often treat as almost mechanical automatons—is more difficult than understanding the nature of the giant beings of inkoze.

8

TIME

The giant beings of inkoze hinted at the indeterminate nature of social phenomena and some of the particularities of time in Dene reality. These aspects of Dene reality demand greater attention if we are to understand animals as persons. The Dene conceptualization of animals as persons is crucial, for their relationship to those animal/persons is one of the deepest and most profound paradigms of their culture.

The folk physics of Western culture, the expression of our cultural view of physical reality, views time as both a linear and a directional phenomenon, a presumption called the "arrow of time" in science (Hawking 1988: 145–53). In our ordinary usage, time is understood to be a flow from an already determined past toward an undetermined future. We believe these already-past-and-yet-to-come states do not exist. All that exists is the "now," a constantly moving point of contact that is everywhere in creation the same, that connects these nonexistent states. Instantaneous and universe-wide, now is the only reality.

We view the reality that time composes in two somewhat contradictory senses. One view regards reality as a series of events linked by time, like pearls on a necklace. Those events that are past are determined; they have happened and are forever fixed and immutable. We may not know enough about those events to understand or explain them, but they are unalterable. There is a partial parallelism between the way we think of the past and the way we think of the future. The future is also thought of as a series of events, but they remain undetermined until the flow of time—the now—sweeps over them. In effect, we view time much like a crystal dropped in a supersaturated solution. All the potentialities of the solution, all the possible ways in which its components might combine, are instantly and forever fixed into a single unalterable outcome by the arrival of that crystal. Likewise, the arrival of the now freezes the future into a single unalterable state that is lost, forever unmodifiable, to the past.

This view shares much the same theoretical underpinning as does calculus, but since we do not think about how long now is, now, in effect, is instantaneous. The interval between the last now and the current now is so short that the experience of time is of a flow within which the disjunction of events is perceptible only over longer intervals. This folk view of time is akin to a monothetic categorization process in which events are discrete and bounded entities linked into a seamless flow in spite of their discrete nature (Needham 1972, 1975).

Conversely, we also view time as a seamless flow of events. The past flows into the now without disjunction between them. Events are seen not as separate and time-fixed but as a series of transforming processes. In this view it is still only the now that is real, but its reality is that of a point along a continuous flow of events perpetually transforming themselves into something new. This folk view of time corresponds to a polythetic categorization process in which time consists of a series of overlapping mini–time lines (Needham 1972, 1975). The collective effect of all the mini–time lines is to create the perception of a seamless flow of time and events even though individuals can be aware of the disjunction between individual events and individual mini–time lines.

The difference between our two folk conceptions of time can be illustrated through the metaphor of a surface: one, made of separate nonoverlapping scales such as are found on some snakes; the other, a sheet of paper.

The monothetic conception of time is like the snake skin. Its constituent scales are separate and discrete. The smoothness of the surface they form is a function of the size of the scales. As the size of each scale decreases and the density of the scales increases, the apparent smoothness of the surface increases. When we think of time in this way, the intervals of time are so short that the effect is a seamless flow. The shorter the intervals, the greater the smoothness and the more time seems to be a continuous flow.

The polythetic conception of time is like a sheet of paper. The constituent elements of the sheet of paper—the fibers that compose it—are large and irregular. The distribution of the fibers within the paper is neither uniform or sequential. Individual fibers are of varying lengths and face in many different directions. Individual fibers overlap one or more other fibers. The apparent smoothness of the surface does not come from the smallness or uniformity of the fibers. Neither does it come from the uniformity of their distribution. The smoothness of the sheet of paper comes from the degree of overlap between the individual fibers, an overlap that gives the impression of smoothness because of the abundance of interconnections between the irregular fibers.

In our folk physics, both views of time, with their instantaneous now, are coupled to the three dimensions of physical space (length, width, and breadth) in such a way that the first three dimensions are seen as independently variable even though all three are seen as linked together by the fourth dimension (time). To reformulate the classic teaching example of a bouncing ball, a change in direction in one of these three physical dimensions does not necessitate a change in direction in either of the other two dimensions. A ball that is bouncing up can become a ball that is bouncing down without necessitating a change in whether it is going forward or backward, or left or right. The binary nature of this perception of space shows in the speech we use to represent direction: up versus down, left versus right, front versus back.

These conceptions of motion and direction in space contrast radically with the way we conceive of time. The metaphors we use for time are always at least implicitly triadic. The now always mediates between the past and present while any metaphor involving now and the past or now and the future will also imply the third component of time.

In our Western folk physics, and in the social world our folk physics constructs and reflects, time is not only directional but always unidirectional.[1] Even if time is thought of abstractly only as that which connects events, it is still unidirectional. The unidirectional nature of time is problematic in physics and the other sciences. According to physicist Stephen Hawking, "One must add up the waves for the particle histories that are not in the 'real' time that you and I experience but take place in what is called imaginary time. Imaginary time may sound like science fiction but it is in fact a well-defined mathematical concept. . . . That is to say, for the purposes of the calculation one must measure time using imaginary numbers, rather than real ones. This has an interesting effect on space-time: the distinction between time and space disappears completely" (Hawking 1988: 134). He concludes, "Which is real, 'real' or 'imaginary' time? It is simply a matter of which is the more useful description" (139). That time can flow in either direction is a mathematical feature of theories of relativity, but we ignore our physics and mathematics in the construction of ordinary life and experience.

Cyclical time—the alternation of day and night, the round of the seasons, the sequence of a ritual calendar—is often advanced in anthropological writing as a form of nonlinear time reckoning (see Gell 1992: 34–35, 84–85 for examples of this). There is merit in that argument. Cyclical time is not linear. Summer follows spring only to be later followed by spring; day follows night follows day; Christmas follows Thanksgiving. But if cyclical time is not linear, it is still unidirectional. Summer returns to summer returns to summer, but it does not reverse into spring; day does not reverse into day; Christmas does not reverse to Thanksgiving. The cycles return through the same points but they always flow between the points in the same direction. We begin to more closely approximate aspects of Dene thought when we cross-connect time by events rather than by connecting events by time. This is easier to see in cyclical time where a point on the cyclical calendar assumes a connection with other iterations of the same point on the cyclical calendar, as when we think on Christmas of other Christmases or of Christmas itself. Doing this creates a unity between events (Christmas) in which events are organizing time rather than time organizing events.

Science and ordinary life share one assumption about time: its linkage to the other three dimensions. The arguments about the arrow of time, whether from Hawking in physics (1988), Stephen Jay Gould in paleontology (1987), or in popular culture and popular scientific writing, all hold the ultimate proof of the directionality of time to be the absence of reversing events. If time reversed, not only would time flow backward but events would also flow backward. This is a common argument that matches our commonsense experience. Food does not fly from peoples' mouths and reassemble upon their plates; deceased humans are not lifted from their graves to live to birth and then ascend to the womb and oblivion; shattered pitchers do not reassemble on the floor while gathering their contents to then leap upon the table.

We conceive of time as linked to the other directions of space-time in such a way that a reversal in the direction of time produces a lock-step reversal in the direction of ordinary space. This assumption is the cornerstone of our cultural thought about time. Time cannot flow backward without every event in creation reversing its direction and repeating what has gone before. The idea that time might be independent of the other dimensions, that a reversal in the direction of time might have no more effect in a local space than a reversal in the direction of a bouncing ball along its vertical axis has on its direction of motion along its lateral or front-back axis, is unthinkable.

Dene time usage, though it uses linear, directional, and cyclical time, includes usages that do not correspond to any of these. Animal/persons are not limited by our perceived constraints of the physical universe. Their license to suspend the restrictions of what the West considers physical reality is embedded in their inkoze and is particularly conspicuous in their dispensation with the restrictions imposed by time. Dene culture is not dominated by the idea of a now, and time is not seen as a flow between a no-longer-existing past and a not-yet-existing future. There is a sense, and there are circumstances, in which the Dene conceive of reality as effectively being "simultaneous," that is, time is treated as a dimension that is independent of any flow or directional change within that dimension. The past and the future are as real as the present. Communication and connection between past, now, and future are all possible. The connections between time and the three ordinary dimensions of physical reality are uncoupled. Time sometimes becomes a thing independent of motion within it. All places in time become equally accessible. It is possible for some beings to move anywhere in time rather than having to move in only one direction in time. The effect of this is to make it seem as if the Dene sometimes use time the way Western culture uses place.

These differences in time usage are fundamental to some of the aspects of Dene reality explored here. A stranger is first likely to encounter these differences in time usage when the Dene encounter an animal or bird while they are hunting. A hunt is a ritual encounter between a Dene seeking the life of an animal/person whose power/knowledge is greater than his own. Any encounter with an animal/person is precarious. The potential risk in any encounter with an animal/person leads the Dene to concentrate wonderfully when they encounter animals. Beyond the peril of dealing with a being of greater power/knowledge is the never-absent chance that the animal/person may be a being of inkoze. If the animal/person is but an ordinary animal/person rather than a being of inkoze, the intensity of the experience of the hunt creates a situation in which experience orders time rather than time ordering experience. On those very rare occasions when the encountered animal/person is a being of inkoze, the entire encounter moves beyond directional time (see, e.g., D. M. Smith 1993, 1997, 1998).

The discussion of the nature of the giant beings of inkoze largely involved events that occurred before I came to Mission. As the discussion shifts from giant beings to ordinary animals, lesser beings of inkoze, and the reincarnating culture hero Lived-with-the-wolves, the nature of the evidence will change. The evidence for the following events is largely based upon that which I have experienced. It is one thing to hear about a being of inkoze or the supernatural aspect of ordinary animals. It is quite another to personally encounter one. Nothing I can write can quite express the shock of hearing a loon call your name from a few feet away on a stormy lake, of feeling the presence of caribou from twenty miles away, or of watching a being of inkoze in the form of a loon mock the efforts of skilled hunters.

9

ANIMALS *The Nature of the Beast*

Animals are living beings with bodies of flesh and blood. They are conceived through the sexual activities of their parents and are born or hatched through the ordinary processes of biological reproduction. They live their lives contesting the forces of an exacting environment. They must hide or insulate themselves from extreme cold and have physical adaptations to withstand it or knowledge of how to avoid it. Food is generally scarce except during the summer, but even in the face of scarcity animals understand how and where to find food. At times they need shelter for safety, reproduction, or to escape the elements. Shelter generally must be made rather than found, but when it is needed, animals know how to make it or where to find it. They must escape or evade predators intent on consuming them and, unless they are unlucky, have the strength, speed, and skill to do so while their bodies remain healthy. They must be able to move, often for the sake of their lives, as quickly as they can over terrain where footing is almost always treacherous. They have the coordination and skill to do this but are not immune to broken bones or other injuries. The land takes a toll of them. They can become ill, suffer skin disorders that destroy their hair or feathers, or develop cancer and must face fire, famine, and epidemic. All who live in this land, whether amphibian, bird, or mammal, must cope with parasites and the enormous populations of biting insects that come with warmer weather and longer days. Some animals choose to live their lives in the company of their kind while others spend their lives without such company. Virtually all attempt to reproduce themselves. They are beings that live and die and, as is the fate of most organic life on this planet, their commonplace destiny is to die while being eaten.

The Dene know all these things. They have interacted with the animals of this land since time immemorial, and their experience of that interaction has helped them develop an extensive practical knowledge of them. For all those thousands of years animals have been more than food; they have been a dominant passion of Dene life. The People have thought long and deeply about animals even as they have observed them with intensity, perception, and sensitivity. They have learned their habits and characteristics in often minute detail, but The People have watched and thought about animals not just to prey upon them but with a passion to understand them.

Much of what the Dene have learned of animals is known to whites, for the experience whites have of living with and upon the animals of this and other lands is not entirely dissimilar. Whites have also their science, their folklore, their natural history, their religion, their economics, and their emerging understanding of ecology to teach them about the behavior and habits of animals. Where Chipewyan knowledge transcends Western knowledge, where their knowledge most offends the values of whites and leads them to disavow Dene knowledge, is not their knowledge of animal behavior and ecology but their knowledge of their nature.

What differentiates animals from humans is the fact that humans do not KNOW; they do not have the power/knowledge to survive unaided.[1] Humans must be taught; they are not complete unto themselves. No one, no person, no being, no power needs to teach the animals; they KNOW. This news of the animals' power/knowledge is unambiguous and transparently obvious, for the animals do survive, and how could any being survive here without the power/knowledge to do so? Animals are, as they are, complete unto themselves. From time immemorial, the Dene have understood this, and it is the center of their knowledge.

As the giant beings of inkoze exist in dual form as an embodied animal and a supernatural being, so ordinary animals exist in a dual form. The basis of their duality rests in their power/knowledge. If this duality of existence seems cryptic, its ambiguity rests in the thought of Western culture and the grammar and categories of the English language.

Our culture and the English language distinguish between the natural and the supernatural as modes of being, experience, and causality. It is this distinction we see as the core of the difference between ourselves and the animism of the other that has fascinated our intellects since the halcyon days of Sir Edward Burnett Tylor (1958) and Lewis Henry Morgan (1964). This distinction is not present in Chipewyan thought or culture. What in our reality is the disjunction and incompleteness of unknown causality through the agencies of accident, coincidence, and chance, the Dene see as a far more complete and comprehensible reality within a unified field of causality. This difference in perspective, between animist and we who choose to imagine we are not animists, has driven scholars from Sigmund Freud (1983), Henri Levy-Bruhl (1967), and E. E. Evans-Pritchard (1952, 1956) to Claude Levi-Strauss (1963, 1966) throughout the twentieth century.

The essential task in trying to understand the nature of animals in Chipewyan thought is learning to unlearn the distinction between the natural and the supernatural. Animals are unified beings who exist within a unified field of causality. It is not a question of learning to integrate the natural and the supernatural for what is not separated cannot be integrated. Perhaps the most comprehensible facet of this unlearning can be found in the English language's use of articles when people talk about animals.

What is true for the caribou is true for the way the Dene use English to speak of all animals. The Chipewyan word for caribou is "EtⲐhen," a word they frequently prefer to the word caribou even when speaking English. The Chipewyan do not say "an EtⲐhen" or "a caribou," they do not say, "the EtⲐhen" or "the caribou" but EtⲐhen or caribou, regardless of number. EtⲐhen is simply EtⲐhen; caribou is simply caribou. There are words for kinds of caribou—for a cow, a calf, a large bull, and so forth—and the Chipewyan are perfectly capable of distinguishing between one individual caribou and another as well as between kinds of caribou. Nevertheless, caribou are, simultaneously, individual animals and "spiritual" beings.[2] As individual caribou they exist in the realm of inkoze even as their bodies walk the earth, but their spiritual status is also simultaneously individual and collective.

Each caribou has an ordinary life history and a fate for its earthly aspect to meet, but that individual history is of no concern to the Dene. Caribou and other wild animals exist in Dene society as but iterations of their kind. What concerns the Dene is not the individual identity of the caribou but the tie between the ordinary form of caribou and its spiritual aspect. What happens to the embodied animal reverberates in the spiritual realm, but killing an animal is not offensive to it. Animal abuse is not about predation but about why an animal is killed, the wastage of an animal that has been killed, the means by which the animal is killed, or the exposure of its remains to pollution. The manner, for example, in which a caribou is killed reflects the regard the hunter feels for it. Caribou are not offended by being shot, stabbed, snared, or speared but even if they have been wounded and are already dying, they are offended by being beaten to death. Beating an individual caribou to death offends all caribou. Once offended, all caribou may respond to the insult by abandoning the area where it occurred and refusing to return to it for perhaps several generations of human lives.

The spirit of the caribou acts as an entity and responds through the actions of the physical forms of all of the caribou. That the species responds to the treatment of the embodied individual indicates animal is collective as well as individual. This idea of the species as an entity is one I think is routinely misunderstood. Again, the problem is number. The species, caribou, is a collectivity as well as individuals, but the collectivity and the individuals are the same. Neither is it accurate to understand caribou, or any other animal kind, as a single entity controlled or represented by a single being.[3] Too often it is presumed that the First Nations' idea of a species is merely a personification of the species, a simple anthropomorphization of the idea of the species in a convenient symbolic form. In actuality, the individual and the collective are not separable even though they are distinct. Mystery is not bound by English grammar. The number of the beast is singular and plural without separation or disjunction.[4]

The problem of number with kinds of animals is pervasive. It particularly effects our understanding of Native American thought about animal renewal and reincarnation. The Chipewyan, in common with many First Nations' cultures, hold that, dogs excepted, the animals "become young again" or "become new again" every spring. With our understanding of the specificity of number, we customarily believe this to mean that Native Americans think that individual animals become young or new again each year.

Of necessity, people who butcher thousands of animals in the course of their lives become skilled observers of animal anatomy and physiology. They must learn to identify diseased tissue in order to discard it. They must be exceedingly attentive to the condition of the animals they kill and butcher, for their survival has often rested upon their ability to identify and pursue fat and healthy animals to the exclusion of those who are in ill health or who carry no body fat. They learn the articulation of skeletons from countless hours of cutting and processing animal carcasses. They learn the easiest means to deflesh them if for no other reason than to spare their own muscles, hands, and joints the excess strain that would come from not knowing what they were doing. They learn from their own bodies' demands for nutrients and vitamins the identity of the animals' internal organs and the signs of pathology within them.

Old animals are found at all seasons of the year. To presume the Chipewyan, with their tremendous pragmatic understanding of anatomy and physiology, do not know that individual animals do not become "young" each spring is an absurdity. Granted, individual Dene, rather like the rest of us, may take their symbols, myths, and metaphors too literally. I remember the confusion George felt as we butchered an old bear late one summer at Foxholm Lake. In George's eyes, that bear should have become young again the previous spring, yet here it was with its greying hair and broken and missing teeth. His inspection of the bear unquestionably indicated that it was so old as to have been unlikely to have survived the coming winter. George was anxious to hold to his belief. As he worked the carcass he searched for an explanation of the information his eyes and hands made part of his own experience. All through the skinning and butchering he talked, searching for a resolution to the conflict between his belief and his experience before finally finding a satisfactory explanation. Because bear possess particularly potent inkoze, that very inkoze must prevent them from becoming young again each spring. His pragmatism and experience of the details before him allowed no interpretation other than that the bear was old, and they forced him to modify a firmly held belief.

Although individual Dene may not always understand the meaning of their oral traditions and belief, their statements that animals "become young again" or "become new again" are not statements about the physiology of individual animals. They are statements of another kind, about the collective aspect of being an animal/person rooted in inkoze as well as being a biological entity that renews itself through sexual reproduction. Once this is understood, the statements can be seen to convey a complex set of meanings about continuity, renewal, and the processes of nature. These statements are not just metaphors, for they transcend metaphor. They are commentary upon the nature of inkoze, the nature of animal/persons, the nature of number, and the nature of the ongoing relationship between Dene and animal/persons within the folded time and perpetual processes of their shared non-Euclidean reality. They are intelligible because within their reality, animals are neither singular nor plural, biological nor spiritual, but unified beings participating with the Dene in the enduring relationships of inkoze.

The multiplicity of being that animals have in Dene reality is roundly at odds with Western folk thought equating the individual with the body. We have a long history of recognizing the spiritual aspect of being through the concept of the soul as well as a perhaps even longer tradition recognizing other aspects of the spiritual such as ghosts (Fustel de Coulanges 1956). Our conceptualization of the body as a vessel for the spiritual reflects the dualism of Western thought. The spiritual aspect of the living is seen as embodied, so the body becomes the marker of the individual while unembodied spirit is the marker of the supernatural.

The specificity of the individual is sometimes problematic in our own thought. The equation of the individual with the body is dependent upon the presumption of scale, the limitation of consideration to a certain size range. Marking the individual by the boundaries of the body is not operative when the focus is microscopic. Genetics in particular discards the primacy of the individual—the body—in its focus upon the gene. At that scale the continuing element of being is not a body but a patterned strand of chemicals. Although the gene itself is but a segment of a larger chemical strand (the chromosome), it is the gene that has continuity and upon which natural selection operates. The individual becomes little more than an incidental mechanism for the production and distribution of genes. Since identical genes appear in many bodies, both sequentially through time and simultaneously in time, an equation of the body with the individual is meaninglessness.

The problem also exists at larger scales. Many species of aphid regularly pass through periods of parthogenetic reproduction in which large numbers of genetically identical individuals appear over several generations (Moran 1992: 35–38). These clones "include two, three, sometimes as many as eight distinct types of individuals that look and behave very differently, even though they are genetically identical" (Moran 1992: 33). The equation of the body with the individual becomes problematic for these beings among whom genetic identity produces not only such divergent body forms but so many different bodies of each form. Is each aphid an individual? Are all the aphids sprung from a possibly still living fundatrix but a single individual?

Since the parthogenetic offspring may continue through several seasons, are all the genetically identical aphids—living and dead—but a single individual?

Identical twins are not so rare among ourselves that their genetic identity does not disturb our neat equation of the body with the individual. If we go neither so far as to declare identical twins an abomination and destroy them at birth nor so far, as with the Nuer, to declare them a single person (Evans-Pritchard 1956: 128–33), we remain discomfited by their presence and have developed a substantial folklore about them (not least of all in academic psychology's passion for twin studies). Among the strongest aspects of our folklore about identical twins is the presumption that a similarity of being, intensified communication, and understanding exists between them. This folklore verges toward that Nuer notion of shared personhood, but we are more likely to explain it in spiritual or quasi-spiritual terms.

If the observation of nature and consideration of scale confounds the equation of the body with the individual, it also confounds the presumption of number in Western thought and grammar. This disjunction is necessary to understand the issue of reincarnation (both human and animal) in Dene reality. When the Dene speak of animals becoming new again or becoming young again, they are primarily engaging in commentary upon the cyclic nature of natural processes, but there is a component of that commentary that is directed to animal reincarnation.

The Dene have not directed a great deal of attention to the specificity of individual identity among animal/persons. There are particular beings of inkoze or culture heroes, such as Lived-with-the-wolves, whose individual identities and some of whose reincarnations are known, but by and large they do not know of, or think about, the reincarnation of specific animal/persons. The Chipewyan do not think of themselves as hunting the same animals over and over again or that the spirit of a specific animal returns to a particular hunter to be killed again and again.[5]

The lack of identity between the individual and the body is apparent in the phenomenon of transformation. There is a level of power/knowledge beyond which beings have the ability to transform themselves into other kinds of beings. Beings of inkoze are able to appear in forms other than their own, and they so appear to Dene with some regularity. Any animal a Dene encounters may be an ordinary animal, in all the aspects previously considered, or it may be a being of inkoze that has assumed the form of the encountered animal. These beings, as beings of inkoze, are not ordinary animals and do not have the other aspects of ordinary animals of the form they have assumed. They are, as it were, wild cards that appear in the form of animals of a specific kind but are divorced from the relationships and being that exist for other animals sharing that form. A being of inkoze in the form of a loon need not be a loon, and its actions may have no bearing upon loons as individuals or as a spirit collectivity.

The Dene experience these kinds of transformations, but they have chosen not to systematize their knowledge of them. It is unclear if a being of inkoze assumes the body of an existing loon or simply takes the shape of a loon. Confounding this is the fact that a loon that displays the behavior of a being of inkoze may in fact be a loon that is a "loon-spirit" whose actions do effect the behavior of other loons. Such interactions between Dene and these beings may lead to the establishment of relationships between them and are a source of a great deal of Dene knowledge.

The separation of identity from embodied form is a characteristic of human transformations into animal form. The power/knowledge to transform is rare, the marker of a very substantial degree of inkoze. When ordinary humans exercise their ability, their human body becomes vulnerable. If it is but a soul journey out of the body into an animal form, then the human body is left behind in a sleeping or dreaming state. More powerful adepts seem to have the ability to have a temporarily dual existence in which their mundane body continues to function in ordinary life although, since the animal is subject to ordinary injury and death, it is vulnerable to death should the animal form die (D. M. Smith 1973).

If transformation is a disjunction of the individual into multiple forms at a single time, reincarnation is a conjunction of multiple forms through time. The majority or perhaps almost all Dene are reincarnated. The identity of the reincarnated is determined within the first few years, often within the first few days if not at the birth itself. Normally the reincarnated is a recently deceased relative. The disjunction of number and specificity operates in reincarnation, for what reincarnates is not the soul of Western understanding but something of an entirely different order. The reincarnated individual is the newborn child, but the newborn child is also a being independent of the reincarnated. It is as if each person is simultaneously themselves—a new creation, a new person—and the reincarnated person. The reincarnated aspect of the new person remains with them throughout their life, but its influence and relevance fade as the new person grows and assumes a social identity of its own. By adulthood a Dene is the reincarnated, but they are also completely themself. This gives a duality of being to each Dene, further pushing the disjunction between the body and the individual.

It is in light of this disjunction between the body and the individual that animals need to be considered. Animals KNOW, they are bodies, individuals, spiritual beings. An animal may be purely a being of inkoze who has taken the external form of that animal or it may be a human using its power/knowledge to transform into animal form. It is possible that any encountered animal might be a culture hero that has assumed that form, or the encountered animal might be something entirely unknown to the Dene. What the animal is can never be determined in the ordinary course of events by any means other than observing how it reacts to the encounter and the consequences of that encounter.

Animals are persons. As persons they individually, collectively, spiritually, and physically replicate the relationships with human persons that have existed within the realm of inkoze since before the beginning of time. It is not the individual that endures in Dene reality but those relationships between human and animal/persons. When the Chipewyan say animals become young again in the spring, they speak the truth, for it is not the individual that is renewed but those enduring relationships that are the covenant between human and animal within the reality of inkoze.

10

WOLF

The Chipewyan share their homeland with three species of dog: the wolf (*Canis lupus*), the domestic dog (*Canis familiaris*), and the coyote (*Canis latrans*).

WOLFING: THE COYOTE

Canis latrans is a remarkably adaptive species ranging from deep in Latin America to the interior of Alaska. Its range is now spreading rapidly throughout the eastern United States and Canada. Coyotes are colonizing areas where they have had no recent presence, including urban and suburban areas in the most densely populated parts of eastern North America. Short of chemical or biological warfare on a scale we cannot afford, the only thing that suppresses a coyote population is a healthy wolf population.

Most of the Mission Chipewyan homeland is beyond the margins of coyote range. There is still a healthy wolf population to the north of Mission and a significant wolf population near the village and some distance south of it. The wolf population, along with the terrain, climate, and scarcity of food resources, have long kept the coyote population to a minimum. Coyotes are seen near Mission, but their numbers are few and scattered, and they are seen mostly around dumps. In much of North America the coyote is a major symbolic figure, usually a trickster, but the Chipewyan call the coyote by a diminutive of the word for wolf and pay little attention to it.

Dogs and wolves are an entirely different matter. Both exist within a field of symbolic uncertainty and anomaly as dominant symbols with a consistent series of meanings in a variety of contexts and stories.[1] Dogs are most peculiar animals in Chipewyan thought while wolves are regarded as such competent moral beings that they are seen almost as good but somewhat boring neighbors about whom one is affectionately curious but not overtly concerned.

WOLF

Of all living land carnivores, the wild canids are the most complex and wolves are the most complex of the wild canids. If allowed to live undisturbed by human persecution, the species possesses a culture that varies considerably over its geographic range. As members of a species that is both social and cultural, individual wolves—in spite of lacking a human-like language—are sentient social beings in precisely the same way as are humans.

Neither the Chipewyan nor *Canis lupus* can be understood in isolation from their relationships with the caribou and each other. As social predators both prey upon the same large animals, although the Dene were more specialized in hunting the barren-ground caribou than were wolves. Nevertheless, caribou is the pivotal prey for both species, and they were inescapably entangled in a relationship of co-predation upon the caribou. Before the Dene entered into the trade relationships with European culture that allowed them to exploit European foods and material resources, Chipewyan and wolves existed in about equal numbers. The two species coexist rather than compete, but before the Dene acquired repeating rifles late in the nineteenth century, it would have been hard to argue that either species had a significant competitive advantage over the other. Even with all the advantages of modern technology, transport, and communication, the two species would still be quite evenly matched at the business of survival if humans had to live exclusively off the resources of the bush.

Dene and wolf have coexisted since even before the Dene became The People. As co-predators of caribou, the two species displayed a significant degree of parallelism in their annual movements until just after World War II, and there are still substantial parallels between them (Sharp 1978: 55–75). The People remember when their own movements were in accord with those of the caribou and, like wolves, they moved throughout their land in search of the caribou. The Chipewyan understand the ecological parallels between themselves and wolves just as they recognize their organizational similarities to them (Sharp 1976, 1978). The stories the living tell about their ancestors stress their constant movement in search of prey and explicitly liken the lives of their ancestors to the lives of wolves.

Although quite shy, wolves are conspicuous animals. The wolves of the Subarctic are large animals with huge front paws that leave massive tracks. They come in a wide variety of colors, but grey, black, and white predominate. Wolves are conspicuous as they move over open country, and in warmer weather they are often found out on flats and meadows seeking prey. They are large enough that Chipewyan watching from the elevated vantage points they favor for hunting can sometimes see them from miles away. As soon as the lakes freeze and snow begins to accumulate, caribou begin to spend a large part of their time out on the lakes. Both Dene and wolves use the lakes as routes of travel and seek caribou resting upon them. The two species often encounter each other upon the frozen lakes.

Most human contact with wolves is indirect. Their presence is announced by their tracks, their scat, and the remains of their kills. The Chipewyan and the wolf are constantly aware of each other through the remains of the caribou kills both leave upon the lakes. Wolves are considered clean animals (Sharp 1976). The People say they will take meat from a fresh wolf kill and will not abandon one of their own kills simply because wolves have eaten from it. Wolves regularly feed upon the remains of human kills, kills that are for them an often critical resource during the dying days that come with late winter and early spring. In a curious sense, the two species share food through the remains of their kills, and many human and wolf groups have survived times of scarcity by eating from the kills of the other.

Both humans and wolves are visual creatures. They use the same vantage points to search for prey and often start their hunts from the same locations. They often kill their prey in the same kinds of locations. Both leave behind the remains of those kills for the other to discover. As men move out through the land in the course of their own subsistence activities, wolf sign marks their land and declares the presence of their co-predator. Because decay is so slow in this cold place, caribou remains litter the treeline, and Dene often inspect even bone and antler remains to determine if the kill was made by human or wolf.

Wolves seek for their dens the same things—nearby water, suitability for surveying the surrounding country, wind for relief from insects—that Dene seek for their own camps, and they often alternate in their use of the same locations (Sharp 1988a: 39–59; 1996).

At all seasons of the year ravens cluster around wolves and humans where they rest or camp. Ravens that come upon wolves or humans often follow them as they move, circling around them and diving down close to them. Wolves and ravens have developed this interaction to a form of play. Perhaps it is not a game in the zero-sum sense of the word (Von Neumann and Morgenstern 1944), but when ravens and wolves encounter each other what passes between them is a noisy and visually conspicuous game both species seem to enjoy. At times it is possible to follow the movements of wolves or humans by watching the ravens circling around them and, with wolves, by watching the ravens rising into the air and dropping back to the ground as they tease the wolves and are chased by them. Both humans and wolves know this and sometimes mark the presence of the other by watching the ravens.

Wolves are vocal animals. They bark in warning if someone or something comes too close to their pups, but their usual sound is the howl. They howl singly and in concert, and the sound of their howls can be heard for miles. Many of The People are convinced they understand the messages wolves are howling. When the caribou are coming and The People are seeking information about their locations, some of them use the information gained from wolf howling to plan their own hunting.

Wolves often respond to human howls, and the two species sometimes engage in howled conversations that can last for hours.

All this interaction between humans and wolves through tracks, sign, visual sighting, and howls makes humans and wolves neighbors. The Dene usually know how many wolf packs live near where they are camped and may, unlike other wild animals, know the individual wolves themselves. Wolves, with their complex social systems whose size and distribution so closely parallel human social systems and distribution, become comfortable and familiar co-residents engaged in the same business of hunting the surrounding land.

With the collapse of the Roman Empire and the spread of Christianity throughout Europe, the symbolic nature of the wolf transformed from its various—relatively benign—pagan forms into a complex symbolic set expressing relationships between good and evil, culture and nature. This complex symbolic set contrasted the hierarchically ordered, working, property-owning life of Christianized Europeans to the unordered, free-ranging, property-less life of outlawed, feral, or non-Christian Europeans. In European culture, the nature of the wolf as animal was lost within its metaphorical and symbolic role as an anti-Christ expressing the Christian association between satanic forces and the natural world.

The Dene have long recognized the complexity of wolves and noted the similarities between their culture, diet, ecology, social organization, and family relationships and those of humans, but they have come to an almost diametrically opposed conclusion about the meaning of those similarities. Instead of perceiving wolf as an evil competitor beyond the twin realms of property and Christianity, the Chipewyan perceive wolf as the perfect natural hunter and the epitome of the wild animal as a moral being.

As animal/persons, wolves are thought of as clever, strong, and well tempered. Their bodies are valued for the high price their pelt brings. A few individuals hunt them, but wolves are thought to be especially hard to kill. Most Dene men will shoot a wolf if the opportunity presents itself, but only a few put any effort into hunting them and even fewer try to trap them. Most people say wolves are edible, but I have only met one person who admitted tasting one. Once they have reached a reasonable size the Chipewyan have no fear of wolves. Many people have encountered wolves at close proximity while they were small children, but they remember those encounters as being startling rather than frightening.

Besides their role as gender symbols and as symbols of the natural world of inkoze, wolves are complex symbols of competence, self-control, responsibility to kin and family, and the ability to hunt. The basic ecological, behavioral, and social similarities between humans and wolves are reflected in some of the unusual characteristics that eighteenth-century explorer Samuel Hearne reported the Chipewyan attributing to them. In the bestiary appended to his journal he recorded that "all the wolves in Hudson's Bay are very shy of the human race, yet when sharp set, they frequently follow the Indians for several days, but always keep at a distance. They are great enemies to the Indian dogs, and frequently kill and eat those that are heavily loaded, and cannot keep up with the main body. The Northern [Chipewyan] Indians have formed strange ideas of this animal, as they think it does not eat its victuals raw; but by a singular and wonderful sagacity, peculiar to itself, has a method of cooking them without fire" (Hearne 1971: 338).

The animosity between DOG and WOLF is still characteristic both of the lives of both animals and of their role as symbols in Dene thought (1976). As animals, wolves tend to be nonaggressive toward dogs or else to regard them as prey. Dogs are very aggressive toward wolves and clearly regard them as objects of fear. Contemporary Chipewyan still regard wolves as having a number of unusual characteristics, including being exceptionally intelligent and capable of understanding human intentions and thought. "They knows what you is thinking," one person told me.

As animal/persons, wolves are frequently referred to as the most powerful of the animals ("strongest").[2] They are significant figures of inkoze and enter into relationships as power sources and teachers to humans. Wolves are peculiar animal/persons, ones whose individual identity is sometimes known and whose family membership is often known. The indeterminate nature of animal/persons—as well as their power—can be seen through their involvement in Dene life.

In its common form, power/knowledge comes to men from animals they encounter in the bush or in dreams. These encounters can, if all goes well, turn into lifelong relationships between individual men and particular animal/persons. Some Dene men receive songs of power while others may have relationships with more than one animal/person or other beings of inkoze. Others may not be favored by any animal/person and establish no personal relationship with any of them. The Mission Chipewyan are unusual—if not unique—in their belief that women do not have inkoze.

The relationships that come to exist between men who possess inkoze and the animal/persons who reveal power/knowledge to them appear to be bound into relationships of asymmetric if not hierarchical reciprocity, and men become bound by their relationships with the animal/persons that have chosen to reveal power/knowledge to them. Those animal/persons often give them rules and food prohibitions they must respect in order to maintain their relationships with the animal/persons, but those relationships, like the comparative power of humans and animal/persons, is asymmetric. The animal/persons owe no one or no thing for their inkoze or for their gift of power/knowledge to a man. If a man fails to follow rules that have been imposed upon him by the creature(s) that gave him power, those being(s) are free to withdraw that power/knowledge at any time.

Men who have power/knowledge become bound into relationships with other humans by using their inkoze to help or harm them. The use of inkoze to help, particularly to heal—outside certain boundaries of kinship or residence—requires payment for the service inkoze performs. Just as a plant taken for *nydie* (medicine) must be given a return in the form of a gift slipped into the ground among its roots, so the human cured by a healer must make payment to preserve the relationships between nydie, healer, and the revealer of the knowledge of how to heal. A man who heals sets no price and asks no payment for his healing. It is incumbent upon patients to pay what they think is appropriate. If a patient makes no payment to the healer, makes a payment that is too small, or takes too long to make the payment, the cycle between patient, healer, nydie, and revealer of inkoze is not closed. If this happens, the inkoze may rebound upon the patient, causing the condition of which the patient was cured to reoccur in a more virulent and perhaps incurable form.

During the 1960s and 1970s, when I was most actively pursuing my study of inkoze, information on the specific attributes of individual practitioners was elusive and the subject was shrouded in secrecy, but of all the animals, wolf was identified most often as the one into which sorcerers transform themselves. It is also the being of inkoze most likely to transform itself into a human being. One particular being has a timeless history of interest in human affairs and appearance among the Dene as a living human being.

During the time before humans and animal/persons became distinct kinds of beings and both spoke the same language, Lived-with-the-wolves was young. He lived with his grandmother and her other children, whom he regarded as his own sisters and brothers. Each spring while he lived with his grandmother, she led Lived-with-the-wolves away from his siblings and their home to a place of jumbled rocks near a high rock spire. Each spring she made him climb to the top of the spire and told him to remain there while she was away. She would leave him there for a week or two before she returned. Each time she returned she was pregnant with a new litter of pups that became his brothers and sisters. In time, Lived-with-the-wolves became curious about what his grandmother was doing while she was gone, so one year he crept down and followed her tracks for several days. When he finally heard his grandmother behind a bush, he carefully peered over it only to see his grandmother copulating with a wolf. After he saw this, he came to the realization that he could no longer live among the wolves but would have to live instead among The People.

Since his first appearance in the time before humans and animal/persons were separate kinds of creatures, Lived-with-the-wolves has lived continuously as a wolf. On rare occasions, Lived-with-the-wolves reincarnates into ordinary human form by entering into the fetus of a pregnant woman. It is within the power of a pregnant woman, by consuming wolf flesh during her pregnancy, to call to Lived-with-the-wolves to be reborn as her child. Lived-with-the-wolves is not bound to respond to her call to be reborn. In body, Lived-with-the-wolves is mortal. Whatever body he occupies may be killed, and he remembers the circumstances of his death in other manifestations. As a being of inkoze, Lived-with-the-wolves's power/knowledge overrides the constraints of ordinary existence. Lived-with-the-wolves exists simultaneously in multiple forms, appearing here as a wolf, there as something else, and elsewhere as a human being.

Whenever Lived-with-the-wolves does choose to be reborn in human form, his birth is attended by miraculous events. The last reincarnation of Lived-with-the-wolves was born in the neighborhood of Cold Lake, Alberta, in the late 1940s or early 1950s. In 1969, when I first came to Mission, the "Magic Boy" was described as "a young boy" about eighteen to twenty-one years of age. The night before Lived-with-the-wolves was born wolves surrounded the village of his birth and remained outside howling all night long. His natal village is located in an area rich in the origin of previous Chipewyan prophets (Janes and Kelley 1977), but the land around the village is overhunted and wolves are scarce. That was the first time wolves had been heard near the village in many years, and never in living memory had so many wolves been heard nearby.

While his mother was still in labor, two very large white wolves entered the village. To the terror of the village dogs—and the discomfort of the human inhabitants—the two wolves wandered calmly and unhurriedly throughout the village before vanishing into the bush before dawn. At dawn, shortly after the birth of Lived-with-the-wolves into the body of the person who was to become the Magic Boy, two arrows flew into the village and struck, one above the other, the trunk of a tree beside the cabin where he had just been born. Little was ever later said of these arrows, for they were magical arrows giving their owner the power to ascend to the sky and the realm(s) above the clouds.

During his visit to Birchtown in the winter of 1969–70, the Magic Boy stayed at the home of an in-law of the chief, himself one of the village's more important political figures. During that stay, Lived-with-the-wolves on several occasions displayed his power to transform into a wolf. The best known of these transformations occurred early one morning when a fresh snowfall had blanketed the ground. The Magic Boy had retired for the night but rose well before dawn and left the house. Those in the house noted his departure but assumed he was making a trip to the outhouse. When he did not return until just before dawn, they became curious. When the Magic Boy did return, he went directly to bed and slept late. By dawn others in the house were up and about. As they left the house they saw his tracks heading toward the road to the abandoned airstrip behind the village. The Dene often stay up late during the Christmas season, but there were people out and about even in the early morning and a small party formed to follow the Magic Boy's tracks in the fresh snow.

The Dene are subsistence hunters, and many of them are skilled trackers whose livelihood often depends upon following faint and sometimes very old tracks and sign through the bush and over hard and rocky ground. A set of human footprints in fresh snow along a deserted path was not difficult for them to follow, but they were not prepared for what those tracks revealed.

Along the route to the airstrip but outside the village the Magic Boy's boot prints were replaced by a set of wolf tracks that continued on to the middle of the airstrip. In the middle of the airstrip, the wolf tracks of the Magic Boy were joined by the tracks of two different wolves coming in out of the bush from different directions. The three sets of wolf tracks then led off in many directions from where the three wolves had run all over the airstrip in a glorious romp. Ultimately, as people from the village walked along following the three sets of tracks, they found where the two sets of tracks that had come in from the bush led back, in separate directions, into the bush where the two wolves had gone their separate ways after their romp with the Magic Boy.

The third set of wolf tracks turned away from the bush, crossed the airstrip, and began to follow the trail back to the village. En route to the village, these tracks were replaced by the boot-shod tracks of a human whose trail led directly to the door of the cabin where the Magic Boy was sleeping.

11

DOG

If the indeterminate nature of animal/persons is now more intelligible, the depiction of the nature of animals is not yet complete. The covenant that exists in inkoze between Dene and animal is imperfect. Wild animals are persons, but not all animals are wild animals. The Dene have little firsthand experience of whites' domestic animals, but they do have enough knowledge of them to know that domestic animals are incapable of feeding and caring for themselves. This inability to care for themselves is crucial. Without it the Dene see domestic animals as beings that do not KNOW. Among the animals they know from personal experience, the dog alone is incapable of caring for itself. To the Chipewyan, Dog is the quintessential liminal being. Animals that are not animal/persons, beings that do not KNOW, entities that do not have a "soul."

When I first analyzed canid metaphors some decades ago (Sharp 1976), I was seeking clarity, order, and resolution in the way symbols related to each other but was uncomfortable with the structuralist assumption that symbolic oppositions led to mediation. I expressed that discomfort by stressing that symbols were also values, citing Meyer Fortes and E. E. Evans-Pritchard's *African Political Systems* to make the point "that symbols are often values and as such have a final meaning in and of themselves" (Fortes and Evans-Pritchard 1940: 17).

I do not know if it is just because I have continued to observe and think about the way Dene use canid metaphors or because I have aged and gained experience, but I have come to realize that life is not as simple as it once seemed. I continue to agree with Levi-Strauss that the symbolic material of cultural life is as amenable to symbolic analysis as is the symbolic material found in myth (Levi-Strauss 1969b: 3). However, I have now come to think that the ambiguity, paradox, and unresolvable conflict generated by symbols are often more to the point than are resolution and orderly systems of classification. That very conflict and ambiguity now seem to me to be a major factor in the generation of culture and its transmission through time. The irresolvability of the paradoxes festers within the body social, perpetually drawing attention to the values expressed by the conflicting symbols.

Values are the intersection between the social and the individual, the mechanism that links symbols—which are social—to emotion—which is individual. The relationships between symbols and the manipulation of these relationships is the primary way in which the social generates action from abstraction by forming a shared communication system that generates emotion within the individual and makes each individual responsive to that which is social.

The symbolic oppositions expressed in Dene canid metaphors lead not to resolution or mediation but to the creation and re-creation of a series of inescapable and unresolvable conflicts in Dene values. The conflicts between the symbols become, in effect, affect generators. The irresolvability of the conflicts—the structured and inescapable clash of values—continues generation after generation in individual after individual. Every Dene, no matter what their individual capabilities, talents, or the degree of their reflexivity, is caught by the paradoxes engendered by the metaphors. Internalized, these enigmas produce in each Dene a never-ending clash of values and emotions whose expression in speech, thought, and action helps in the continuous re-creation of Dene culture.

A number of the Northern Athapaskan peoples of the eastern and central Subarctic have traditions that trace the origins of humans to dogs. I have never been able to discern this tradition among the Mission Chipewyan, although a human origin in dogs is sometimes ventured as an explanation of conflict within particular kin groups (Sharp 1976: 30). Samuel Hearne published a myth of a dog origin recorded among eighteenth-century Chipewyan that would have included groups living in areas occupied by Dene ancestral to the Mission population (Hearne 1971: 324). I have read and told that story to a number of people from Mission, but it has never elicited any sense of recognition or called forth similar stories. The usual response to the story was a blank stare, although some people responded by offering counter origin stories. If the story Hearne recorded seems to be absent from the contemporary Chipewyan repertoire, there is little reason to doubt that it was current among the early historic Chipewyan among whom Hearne resided, and the symbols and the dynamics of the relationships expressed in that myth still resonate in contemporary Chipewyan culture.

Sled dogs are the most familiar of the Dene dogs. There may have been a traditional breed of eastern Northern Athapaskan sled dog distinct from the Eskimo husky, but if that was the case the breed has long faded from the memory of the Mission Chipewyan. When I began fieldwork, long-haired, narrow-chested dogs with erect ears predominated. These animals had extremely large front feet that, proportionately, were nearly comparable to those of wolves, but their chests were broader and their canine teeth were shorter. Their legs were not as long as those of wolves of comparable size. Their weight, at fifty to sixty pounds, was substantially less than that of the wolves of the forest or tundra (sometimes classified as different subspecies). The sled dog population contained a variety of types of dogs, and The People had experimented with a wide variety of breeds brought north by whites, including even standard poodles (of which they thought highly).

The extremes of the temperature, the work, epidemic disease, the scarcity of food, and the blood loss to insect bites are hard on dogs. Their need for food and care are substantial, and the Dene make little effort to keep them if they anticipate no further need for them. They are generally kept only so long as they can work before they are shot or abandoned. Modern times have not made the subarctic climate any less harsh, and food is still scarce. Chipewyan dogs are chronically underfed and always hungry. They will eat virtually anything of organic origin. The Dene have observed this willingness to eat almost anything, and that lack of selectivity in their diet is reflected in their thought about dogs.

Sled dogs are work animals. Their lives are short and harsh, and they are handled roughly. They are the only animate being the Dene treat akin to the manner whites treat machines or domestic stock. Unlike wild animals, it is within the right of Dene to beat their dogs.

The Dene are neither cruel nor fools. They knew how to care for their dogs and usually did so. Dogs had to be fed to work, so they were fed as well as they could be. Dogs had to have water, so they were given water. Dene sometimes take pride in their sled dogs' beauty or their performance, and a fast, reliable team may bring prestige to its owner (Savishinsky 1974). Although individual Dene may like individual sled dogs and keep them long after they are able to work, they are not pets. Not only do few Dene feel affection for sled dogs, they see white attitudes toward dogs as producing unreliable and lazy dog teams whose incompetence—and they have many stories about this—becomes a hazard to life and limb under the harsh conditions of the Dene homeland.

White Canada and the United States are paradoxical in their treatment of dogs. Our thought about ourselves is so dominated by our ideology of the dog as family pet that we are essentially oblivious to our own abuse of dogs. In practice our treatment of dogs is brutal. We abandon and destroy them by the millions each year. Abandoned animals gone feral roam our cities and countryside while people "put down" their dogs because they are going away on vacation, or the puppy messed on the rug, or the dog barked at night, or because they were too lazy or unwilling to make even minimal accommodations to the animal's need for exercise and affection. We keep them isolated in labs and use them for medical testing when other substitutes are readily available. All too often academic and commercial users are not even capable of giving a coherent explanation of why they are using dogs as lab animals or relating the purpose of their testing to any clear body of knowledge. Our culture supports an industry populated by vermin who steal family pets and sell them to labs that ask no questions about the origin of the dogs they buy. All too many animal shelters support themselves by selling pets to labs and, in the Lower Mainland of British Columbia, the Society for the Prevention of Cruelty to Animals wages an incessant war on any dog not confined or tied. Their tactics include "executions," calling dogs off their owners' property, and aggressive patrols that go so far as to stop children and threaten to seize and destroy the leashed dogs they are walking. We raise dogs to be vicious for the sake of displaying our own toughness and keep hunting dogs in packs and give them no better treatment—and show them no more affection or compassion—than we do domestic chickens. Every one of us, even those who are themselves abusive to dogs, has horror stories of about the mistreatment, abuse, neglect, and torture of dogs.

Ironically, within the paradigm of the dog as family pet, the dog—above all other measures and means for defining the family—provides the most coherent definition of family in American culture. Within the family the dog is granted personhood. It is treated, not as a human, but as a person who is a participating member of the family and whose needs, wishes, and demands are factored into the operation of the family as a unit. Within the context of a family, a dog's actions are related to the shared context of the family and given meaning they do not have outside the family. Communication is largely a product of shared context, and we know—and understand—our dogs far better than we understand those—even the human "those"—with whom we interact merely by speech rather than through shared context. Within the family, the dog is a person. Beyond the family the dog is but a pet. That distinction, between person and pet, is the clearest marker of family in American culture.

The Dene are as paradoxical in their treatment of dogs as we are, but their values and beliefs about dogs bear little resemblance to our own. Within the direct experience and the oral tradition of the oldest Dene I have talked to, the Dene have always kept two kinds of dogs: pets and sled or work dogs. Now that the Dene are concentrated in permanent settlements, their sled dogs receive better treatment than they did even twenty years ago. But the Dene still do not much like sled dogs. They may respect a dog's performance or take pride in a dog's skill as a leader, but they are not pets.

Sled dogs are basically things of male concern. Pet dogs are more things of family, women, or children. The dogs the Dene kept as pets were mixed-breed mutts: the classic thirty-five-pound, short-haired dog that can be found wherever feral or semiferal dogs survive at all. These dogs receive far different treatment than do the sled dogs. They are usually allowed to run free in the bush camps. In town, many sleep inside Dene homes at night, and when the Dene are in the bush they are usually allowed to sleep in the tents. Their food is far better than what the sled dogs receive and contains a much higher percentage of table scraps, which rarely reach the sled dogs. Pet dogs have become much more common with village life, and over the last few decades the number, size, and variety of pet dogs has increased. The small generic mutts have mostly been replaced by larger mixed-breed dogs descended from those brought in by whites or obtained by the Dene on their trips outside. In the mid-1970s, mixed-breed Labrador retrievers were in vogue. As the Dene gained greater access to the animals in the animal shelter in Parklund and brought them north to Mission, their tastes changed (Dyck 1980). By the early 1990s, bigger, longer-haired German shepherd crosses predominated although Lab crosses were still popular. Some Dene become quite fond of their pets, and a few keep rather improbable animals such as toy breed crosses that require a great deal of attention and protection to survive. However, most Dene retain an ambivalent attitude toward dogs of any kind, and the surplus of food at Mission is not so great as to have much changed the dog's dietary habits.

If Dog is not an animal/person and lacks power/knowledge, dogs do seem to have some aspect of the collective spirituality of the kind wild animals have even if they lack the individual spiritual aspect of wild animals. They lack a "soul" but have power at least in their ability to bring retribution upon humans who mistreat them. If a man abuses a dog(s) by killing without reason, by beating too harshly and without good reason, or by otherwise abusing it, misfortune may come upon him (Sharp 1976).[1] The harm that comes from dog abuse is of a peculiar variety. It strikes not directly at the man who committed the abuse but indirectly at him by bringing harm to women (and their children) with whom he has a sexual connection. It may strike his children or his lover if he is married or may fall upon his girlfriend if he is not married. The tie between dogs, women, sexuality, dependency, and reproduction is so strong that the usual consequences of dog abuse are a miscarriage or stillbirth, the birth of a deformed or monstrous child, or the death of the abuser's wife during her next childbirth. Dog abuse particularly brings miscarriage or monstrous birth to the wife of the abuser if she is newly pregnant when the abuse occurs or if she becomes pregnant soon afterward.

Dog is paradoxical. Its power, whatever its nature, is closely tied to Chipewyan conceptions and symbolization of gender. Its presence indicates dogs have some aspect of the collective identity characteristic of wild animals, but the individual and the collective aspects of dogs are devoid of inkoze. Dogs are not persons; they are dependent beings unable to produce their own food or to survive on their own.[2] This inability to survive independently and its concomitant dependence upon humans essentially demonstrates the absence of power/knowledge in dogs.

What dogs do have is a social identity as individual beings who participate in Dene social life and culture. The Dene deal with dogs as individuals. They have names and social identities as co-resident beings living within human culture. Dogs have a place in specific human kin and residence groupings through their membership in a dog team owned by an individual Dene or their residence within a Dene household. They are referred to by their own name, by reference to their owner—so-and-so's dog—or by membership within someone's dog team. Even when a dog or a dog team has been abandoned to fend for itself and runs feral within the village or in the bush, other Dene remember the tie of identity between dog and human owner and refer to it by that identity.

The Dene presume that dogs understand kinship rules and, after their fashion, though to a much lesser extent than wolves, respect those rules in spite of their indifference to committing incest. They presume dogs know and respect their siblings. Whereas wolves are concerned with the rules of kinship, dogs are more concerned with the rules of co-residence or team membership.

In their identity as individuals, dogs stand in stark contrast to wild animals, whose salient feature is their membership in a spiritual collectivity but whose individual identity is unknown. The power of this distinction is seen in the disparity between the treatment of the living and dead bodies of dogs and wild animals. The Dene do not much touch living dogs, even pet dogs, or treat them as objects of comfort or affection. Living dogs are rarely petted, hugged, or cuddled. Dead dogs are touched only of necessity and then only to remove or destroy them. By preference, dog carcasses are burned or abandoned where they die. If they have died where it is not practical to leave them, for example, when they are staked among other members of a dog team or alongside a dwelling, they are unceremoniously removed to the bush and dumped.

The body parts of a dog—including the teeth, fur, meat, hide, feet, and tail—are never used in an object made for human use, practical or religious. This stands in dramatic contrast to the individually unknown but "spiritually" potent wild animals from whose remains came food, clothing, shelter, and tools. Indeed, from whose remains came life itself.

The mistreatment of a dog shows this contrast, for it is always seen in a more focused manner than are the relations humans have with wild animals. The retribution from dog abuse usually is referred to a particular incident (e.g., "he shouldn't have beaten that dog so much") with a specificity that applies to both the person and the dog. Even a general statement like so-and-so "is bad for dogs" has a social and individual specificity to it that is lacking in a statement about wild animals, for example, of a good fox trapper "fox, he like him." The equivalent statement about dogs, "dog, he like him," would be nonsensical.

The harm that can come from mistreating a dog is of such a nature that it can only be regarded as having a nonmundane origin, but the agency of that retribution is nebulous. Individual dogs, living or dead, are not persons and have no "soul." They are therefore incapable of wreaking retribution for abuse committed upon them. The retribution seems to come purely from the collective aspect of Dog rather than from the individual dog. In this sense, the liminality of the dog is enhanced, for their power is not inkoze yet it brings retribution. The very individuality and social identity of the dog as a living being that separate it from wild animals are powerless to bring retribution for a dog that is abused, but the collectivity of dogs seems to be outside the covenant of relationships between Dene and animal/persons defined by inkoze.

12

LOON III

It is not abnormal or threatening for an animal/person to refuse to die for any given Dene or for all Dene at any particular place, time, or set of circumstances, but it was—or should have been—apparent to these two men after their first few shots that the loon on Foxholm Lake was not just a loon. This loon was not merely refusing to sacrifice itself to the hunters, it was exhibiting its power in an almost mocking manner by remaining in the area and causing the bullets to miss it. The refusal of an animal to sacrifice itself produces no sense of fear or anxiety on the part of the Chipewyan. In this environment they would not have long survived as a people if individuals reacted strongly every time they encountered an animal that was not willing to die for them. They are, however, chagrined when it happens. The refusal of that loon on Foxholm Lake to die for these two men at that particular time and its blatant exhibition of its power not to be killed by them was as natural and normal, albeit less frequent, a piece of behavior as would have been its death with one of the first shots. By the same token, just because these two hunters failed to kill it, it did not follow that the loon would not have been willing to die for one of the other hunters or for me.

What made this encounter noteworthy was the extent to which the loon displayed its power. If they had killed it, they would have eaten it and recognized its sacrifice. In the normal course of events, when an animal chooses not to die for one of the Dene, it simply escapes. That this loon not only chose not to escape but repeatedly exposed itself to the shots of the hunters and dramatically paraded its presence raised the prospect that the loon was a being of uncommon power/knowledge. If it had chosen to die for one of the hunters, its death would have made a powerful statement about the favor in which that loon/person held the human/person who killed it. As it was, Phil took this encounter as the initiation of a relationship between himself and the loon. Each time it displayed its power, its "value" as an indicator of the favor given its slayer by the person of power/knowledge increased, as would the value of the remnants of its body.[1]

At the most abstract—in our terms—this encounter was conducted at a spiritual level in which material forms are irrelevant except as a means to embody relationships between nonmaterial beings and the Dene. To kill a loon is an act that results from an aspect of inkoze as well as from mundane mechanical skills. The People have lived by their skill with weapons for a very long time. They are perfectly aware of the mechanics of shooting. They know that skill at shooting varies individually and from time to time for every person. They know that factors like the heating of a rifle barrel or wear on the rifling affect the performance of any rifle. They know that some rifles are more accurate than other rifles. But the mechanics of shooting a rifle, unlike the mechanics of splitting a log with an ax, are not an adequate explanation for the death of an animal. Above and beyond and far more basic than the mechanical level of causality and explanation—the "things" of the Dene myth—is the level of inkoze. The willingness—or not—of an animal/person to allow itself to die for a hunter is the relevant issue, and the embodiment of power/knowledge in this loon is a sufficient explanation for the encounter.

The Dene conception of the universe is not mechanical, and time is not always linear or even directional. There was no beginning. There are creation myths, but the myths and stories are not sequential, successional, or linear. The first stories do not come first and the later stories do not come later. There is no temporally ordered sequence to their telling or to the meaning they convey. How individual Dene experience time is beyond my knowledge, but they sometimes use time in their social relationships and their explanations of the world in ways that move beyond directional time. The events of myth are timeless, relativistic in a language and mode of thought that is Einsteinian rather than Newtonian. In this respect Mission Dene thought resembles that of the Australian "Dreaming" (Stanner 1965). The Murinbata "everywhen" well represents an aspect of Chipewyan inkoze, for mythical events can occur everywhen and anywhere.[2] One never quite knows. Not only might an encountered loon be not so ordinary but it is impossible to determine its nature until one has begun to interact with it.[3]

It is difficult to guess the emotional reactions of Phil or the other hunter. Perhaps it was the powerlessness of the situation that dominated. It felt to me to be a lot like I had walked unarmed around a turn in a path and found myself face to face with a very large predator. One that simply snorted at me and then walked off, unbothered and unthreatened. I had the strong impression (and later was so told by other Dene) that our fellow hunter from Birchtown had made a hurried decision to depart the following day, made possible by the chance arrival of an aircraft but brought on by his discomfort at this firsthand encounter with a being of inkoze in a place that was strange to him. Nevertheless, neither man felt that his failure to kill the loon resulted from a failure on his part. They missed the loon not because they shot poorly but because it did not wish them to kill it.[4] The reason that the loon escaped was external to them and lay in their relationship to that particular loon at that particular time and place. No action they could have taken would have resulted in the death of that loon. This position is not psychological defense or rationalization; it is a social judgment operative in the Dene field of meaning. The only judgmental comments I was able to uncover about this incident came from Phil's elder brother George, who felt that Phil should have realized the loon would not allow itself to be killed before he had shot at it twenty times.[5] Phil's judgment might be questioned for shooting so often, but it was never stated (or, I am certain, felt) that he shot badly or that he had failed.

If we return to those two men while they are at Foxholm Lake firing at the loon, we can see the essential duality—again, a duality only in our terms—of the events that occurred. The mechanical aspects of shooting can be and are learned. Ability and practice can make one a better shot, but these are not enough. Anyone can learn to shoot a rifle with some degree of competence, but something that anyone can do cannot explain why some people succeed and some people do not succeed. It cannot explain why a person fails at one time and succeeds at another time. Inkoze provides this explanation, for any incident of hunting involves not merely the hunter but the prey as well. The prey is an active participant in the system of relationships inkoze creates, and it is as much of an actor in those relationships as is the hunter. Since the hunter can be trusted to perform competently at the mechanical level, or to know when he did not, control of the situation passes to the prey. The hunter becomes passive, performing his actions flawlessly but depending upon the goodwill of the prey for his success. Each Chipewyan, even in non-inkoze contexts, is enveloped in a web of relationships with the realm of inkoze and the beings of inkoze, and it is that web of relationships that determines Dene behavior and that bears responsibility for the consequences of Dene actions. Causality is external rather than internal. Phil did not miss the loon; the loon did not wish to be killed.

These two Dene and I had encountered a being of inkoze. It displayed its power and its unwillingness to die, and it quietly left when we stopped trying to kill it. The interaction took place outside directional time at a locus of conjunction between these Dene, myself, a being of inkoze, and the universe/dimensions embodied in the being of inkoze's power/knowledge. The loon itself was indeterminate, its nature known only through its interactions with us. The Dene do not know if that loon was just a bird before they encountered it. They do not know if it became just a bird after they ceased trying to kill it. They do not know if the loon simply winked into existence before the encounter and winked out of existence after the encounter. They do not know if a being of inkoze simply took over the body of an ordinary loon that happened to be nearby only to abandon it afterward. The loon demonstrated that it was a being of inkoze and that it did not choose to die for them. Its being a being of inkoze is sufficient explanation in and of itself. None of the other questions is intelligible, reasonable, or rational.

13

TALKING ABOUT THINGS

Creating reality is an imperfect process. Within the field of meaning that each culture generates there are discontinuities of knowledge and experience that force individuals to constantly refashion themselves to match the context created by their fellow cultural beings. Talking about things is not reality itself but a mechanism through which an observer, Dene or alien, can begin to uncover the nature of Dene reality.[1] Even though talking about things is but an effect of Dene reality manifesting itself in Dene behavior, it is a primary means an observer has for gaining insight into the causal system within Dene reality.

Talking about things is a mechanism for the cultural construction of reality and for the individual's adjustment to that reality, but behavior is performance and performance that has an audience can feed into verbal gossip as effectively as words can.

The relations of men to inkoze illustrate this, for inkoze is secret knowledge that must be expressed by performance, allusion, and metaphor.[2] Inkoze is never directly claimed. To say one has inkoze offends the beings of inkoze who give power/knowledge. They respond to such claims by taking away that which they have given. As no man who had power/knowledge would risk losing it by talking about it, the closest one ever comes to hearing a man with power/knowledge assert that he has it is when he says "I'll try it" when facing a situation that calls for power/knowledge. Unfortunately, this statement is also a common response when the only issue is confidence in one's strength or skill.

Nydie itself is not inherently secret, but it must be guarded from pollution to protect its relationship to inkoze and preserve its effectiveness. Nydie's power to heal does not come from its physical properties or the properties of its constituent elements but through its existence within the relationship between the healer and the being of inkoze that revealed the power/knowledge to him. A man's reputation for power/knowledge is dependent upon his actions being noted and talked about by other Dene. Reputations may be built through the choices men make in recommending a particular man to deal with problems requiring a solution based on power/knowledge. Inkoze is always a dangerous topic for men to speak of, but they are freer to speak of the power/knowledge of others than they are of their own. Dene tend to tout the power/knowledge of their kin, and for a man's reputation to become established outside the circle of those who see his performance in everyday life, it must be talked about. Not only must it be talked about, the details of its source and the specific domains of its applicability must become widely known.[3]

Women, who cannot have power/knowledge themselves, are freer to speak of inkoze than are men.[4] Even for women, inkoze is a dangerous and sensitive topic, but their talking about the power/knowledge of individual men is among the most crucial factors in creating and maintaining a man's reputation for inkoze.

Men learn to use means other than speaking to bring their claim to power/knowledge to public attention. On my first stay at Mission a healer lived only a short distance from the cabin I was renting. A small but animated man no more than five feet, six inches in his prime, he was approaching seventy and becoming stooped with age. He had already outlived four wives and had married his fifth wife, an active woman in her thirties, when she was in her early teens. Even if he were not a healer, he would have been suspected of having inkoze because of his longevity and his continued success at hunting and trapping. We developed a curious relationship and liked each other from the time we met. Perhaps because I was interested in what he did, he took it upon himself to instruct me. We both tried very hard but never got very far with the process. He was nearly deaf and spoke only a few words of English while I had been at Mission only a few weeks and spoke but a few words of Chipewyan. Because the secrecy of inkoze limited what he could tell a translator, we were unable to use an interpreter very effectively (see Goulet 1998: 56). The most difficult problem we faced was that inkoze is revealed in dreams and can be taught only imperfectly or not at all. I did, however, learn a great deal about his movements and was able to see how the secrecy he imposed upon his inkoze became a vehicle for making his healing public.

The Dene approach the application of inkoze to specific tasks—healing, hunting, divination, gambling—in a decidedly empirical fashion. Men may dream how to accomplish the task they have in mind, but they carefully observe the results of their efforts and incorporate those results into their future efforts. Successful cures become experiential knowledge that can be used lifelong, and each healer builds up a body of knowledge about what he can cure and what he cannot cure.

Healing is a social act with a widespread social context that provides an audience for any man attempting to heal. Dene healers do not seek out patients and should not volunteer to heal. The choice of a healer is carefully discussed by patients and their kin before the appropriate healer is approached. The old man had built his reputation for inkoze through his record as a healer. He had a long lifetime's worth of experience and knowledge beyond that revealed in his dreams and visions, and he had developed a large pharmacopoeia that included animal parts and inorganic materials but was mostly plant material.

The old man's desire to protect his nydie from pollution had developed into a performance scripted upon secrecy. His performance of secrecy became a way to make the secret public, a nonverbal performance that regularly became a topic of gossip. In a community as dense in social relationships as Mission was then, few illness remained private. Illness or injury, whatever the cause, related directly to the ability of individuals to perform as competent participants in social life. Knowledge of who was under stress from illness or injury was significant knowledge and quickly became known to the community. I do not mean to imply that all of the people living at Mission knew—or cared—whenever a child had a cut or a cold, but when illness or injury threatened one of The People or reduced their effectiveness, it was information worth knowing. The significance of that information meant that people at Mission knew who was in need of healing, what kind of healing they needed, and what actions had been—or were being—taken to obtain healing. Above all, The People knew who had attempted to heal them.

The Dene know who among them are healers. When the old man took on a patient, it was in a context that would give a Western physician fits. The community knew the symptoms of the patient's problem, speculated as to its causes, and tried to guess the appropriate treatment. The performance of the healer was private, often secret, but the entire community was aware of any attempted healing. They talked about it and ruthlessly judged its results. If others had tried to heal a patient and had failed, the potential for success by other healers was gossiped about in conjunction with the gossip about failed attempts. No case the old man took could be anonymous; it was public even before he tried to heal, as would be his refusal to try.

When the old man did decide to tackle a patient he always followed the same routine. He only healed after dark, or, since it never really gets dark in summer, late at night. On the appointed night he would close and secure the door to his cabin. He would then draw the curtains and extinguish all the lights except for a single candle. He kept his nydie carefully wrapped in the thin translucent pastel scarves favored as headgear by the women. In his dimly lit cabin he would remove his nydie from the various places where he had secreted it. Each kind of nydie was separately wrapped and tied in a bundle bound by colored ribbons, the meaning of those color combinations known only to him. He would open and carefully inspect each bundle, selecting the appropriate ones and returning the remainder to storage. While his preparations were under way, he would periodically stop and look out the windows to ensure no one was watching.

Once the correct nydie had been selected, they were gathered—still separately wrapped—together in a single large scarf and concealed beneath his coat. Guarding against prying watchers, he left his home and moved carefully through the village to the house where his patient awaited. He did not move openly upon the paths in the ordinary manner but secretly in the shadows from house to house, building to building. Mission was an active place with folks out and about until the wee hours of the morning. In warmer weather, foot traffic was to be expected at any time of the day or night. There were usually people about even in the cold and darkness of winter. The Dene are customarily open about their activities, and it was passing strange for someone to be sneaking in the shadows from house to house.

The old man often brought a nydie bundle near the size of a basketball to a healing. Stooped with age and bending almost double to hide his nydie bundle beneath his coat, his efforts at secrecy were not terribly successful. Long before he reached his patient he was seen and his activities passed into gossip.

He tried to ensure the secrecy of his actions once he reached the home of his patient. He closed and secured the door of the patient's dwelling and put out all the lights, replacing them with a single candle. The curtains were drawn or coverings were rigged over the windows, each in turn inspected by pulling back a corner to search outside for prying eyes. Every time he drew back a window covering in the now darkened cabin a flash of candlelight beamed out from its darkness. The Mission Chipewyan announce their desire to be left alone by securing the door of their cabin and covering its windows. The main lights are darkened and only candles are used to give a dim light inside the home. A darkened house with its dim internal light is a signal to others not to intrude without good reason.

The old man's routine for ensuring privacy was conspicuous enough to ensure that every attempted healing would become widely known. Closing up the house where a person awaited healing and peering through the windows while sending out the dim flashes of candlelight were a claim to the patient and a declaration of his power/knowledge. It was never necessary for the old man to talk about a patient or a cure. The social context within which both healer and patient existed ensured that Mission would observe the process and talk about its results.

The form of Mission's political structure was determined by the laws of Canada and the conventions and practices of Indian Affairs. As far as the government of Canada was concerned, Mission was but another case where the regulations were applied to provide equity under the law. In practice, as is usually the case with a bureaucratic structure, Indian Affairs' primary concern was control of Native life in order to maintain the administering bureaucracy and prevent the Indians from interfering with its interests.

The separation of a political sphere of activity from a domestic sphere of activity is not justifiable for the Mission Dene. The two so interpenetrate each other as to make a division between them invalid. The formal political structure imposed upon the Dene bore no relationship to the way the Dene had conducted their political life, and, as always happens, the Dene adapted the imposed structure to their customs and needs (D. M. Smith 1992). The way talking about things operated in the arena we call politics can be illustrated by the career of the first elected chief (*denegothera*). The man they elected (Denegothera) dominated the political articulation of Mission with the outside world from 1949 to 1972. The priest who had founded Mission reluctantly supported his bid for office, regarding Denegothera as the lesser of the two evils represented by the leading candidates, a position he still defended twenty years later.

Elections were new to The People, and election by secret ballot was utterly alien to them. The priest had to wear many administrative hats, but his most crucial role was that of broker between the Dene and the English-dominated Canadian authorities. What he brokered was legitimacy and information. It was his responsibility to conduct the election: to assist the largely nonliterate Dene with marking their ballots, to tally the results of the balloting, to certify the results of the election to Indian Affairs. If it is little surprise the priest's chosen candidate won the election, the alliance between them did not last long. They quickly became political rivals who disagreed on almost every secular issue. The priest suspected that Denegothera was a magic man who "raised the spirits" to support his positions. Although the priest knew the Chipewyan far more thoroughly and intimately than did any other white, there were curious and substantial gaps in his understanding of them. He did not understand the kinship system, casually dismissing as inconsequential many of the relationships it structured. Myth remained beyond his very formidable linguistic talents. To his everlasting credit, he saw no contradiction between Roman Catholicism and what he felt were "remnants" of the old belief system.

Denegothera was born among, and grew up as a member of, the eastern Chipewyan who traded at Brochet, Manitoba. As a young unmarried man he affiliated with the Chipewyan who were later to settle Mission. In time, he married into the Mission Dene, choosing for his wife the only surviving female in a large set of siblings. As this sibling set reached adulthood and became heads of families, they came to constitute the largest single bloc of kinsmen among the Mission Dene. A bloc of siblings, particularly male siblings that are relatively close in age and able to remain on cooperative terms, has the potential to form the nucleus of an extended kin and affinal group capable of dominating the politics of a small local population. Denegothera's genuine bent for politics allowed him to develop his affinal connections to this kin bloc into a solid platform for his political activities. He retained this base of support into its third generation when its grandchildren began to reach maturity. At that point it became so large and so diverse that it had few common interests and splintered.

When Denegothera was elected, The People had opted for the Indian Affairs rules making the office of chief a lifetime incumbency. This choice gave Denegothera a solid hold on his office, and his time of political leadership spanned the transition of the Chipewyan from a residentially scattered hunting society to a largely sedentary village society. From the time of his election, Denegothera became a professional politician. He curtailed his hunting and trapping activities and settled at Discha, later at Mission, becoming one of the first people to take up village life. In spite of his origin among those who hunted and trapped in the Northwest Territories, he built his political base around the concerns of the Dene majority nucleating into the settlement.

If the priest's position in the early 1950s was that of a broker to the outside world, that position was based upon his racial acceptability to the white world and to the control of communication that came from his designation by the white world as the only person fluent in both languages. The chief and council were the formal liaison between the Mission People and the outside world, and all government resources were channeled through them. Denegothera maintained his position through his control over the allocation of government resources and the official flow of information from the Dene community to the white world.

Denegothera had total control of the Chipewyan side of the political process. The council, formally a counterweight to the influence of the chief, was completely controlled by him. Over the years he had managed to strip the council of its power by removing or adding members as he saw fit. The chief and council made up the list of individuals to receive the new houses and distributed the treaty goods (rifle shells, fishnets, and so forth) delivered to the Dene each year to honor the treaty obligations of the Canadian government. The white Indian agent would allow only the chief or a councillor to approach him to correct errors in Ration payments. Officially, the chief and council alone consulted on the list of persons to receive Ration payments each month, but in practice the Indian agent consulted with the manager of the Hudson's Bay Company store ("the Bay") to try and determine the previous month's income of individual Dene families before determining the amount of Rations assistance they were to receive. These unofficial consultations were the bane of local politics as a means by which both "the Bay" and the Church enforced their various agendas through the reward or punishment of Dene individuals and families.

How the despised Denegothera remained chief was a painful mystery to the local whites (Sharp 1991). At times it was a mystery to the Dene themselves. How a man could support a family without working or trapping on the chief's yearly stipend of fifteen dollars supplemented by Rations vouchers, his gambling winnings, and the expense account for his official visits to the outside world was a deep mystery to everyone. There were whispered allegations of misappropriated funds and mysterious sources of revenue, all most probably unfounded.

Denegothera, who did not speak English, adopted me as his letter writer as a way to escape the control of the priest. My first glimpse of the way he maintained his power came while reading to him a letter from a Toronto charity that wished to give used clothing to the residents of Mission in what promised to be a distribution of substantial proportions.[5] From the wording and tone of the letter it was obvious that the charity had been previously stung by charges of patronizing Indians and wished to use local political figures in order to avoid further embarrassment. Mission was poor in the early winter of 1970. Caribou were scarce, and fur prices were low. There were no jobs to be had, and The People were having a hard time obtaining enough to eat, let alone money or credit to buy clothing.

I read the letter to Denegothera and watched as the interpreter translated. Networks, redistribution points, scarce resources, Saints, and Bigmen—all the hot theoretical issues of my youth—danced through my mind as I awaited the chance to see Denegothera occasion the power that maintained his position through his shrewd appropriation and control of the scarce resources he would later allocate to the community.

Denegothera thought briefly about the offer from the Toronto charity, then replied that he "wanted a pair of size 34 pants."

I was stunned. Denegothera showed no awareness of the power and prestige that would flow to him from his role in distributing the badly needed clothing. In shocked disbelief I drew upon my student understanding of theory and explained the situation to him in terms he surely would understand: unlimited clothing for everyone, *he* would be the one to give it away, the one to receive credit for obtaining it and distributing it. Everyone at Mission who wanted clothing would receive it from his hand. Surely this astute practitioner of semi–Stone Age economics and politics could not fail to grasp the significance of this event that years of study of various powerful theoretical models had made obvious to me.

We watched each other carefully while the interpreter conveyed my words to him. Of such stuff do charitable intentions die and abstract models meet social reality. Denegothera quickly repeated his answer. He "still wanted a pair of size 34 pants."

Denegothera kept power not because of what he got for The People of Mission but because of what he could keep individual people at Mission from getting. Month after month the Ration list came from Indian Affairs and recalcitrant opponents found themselves short of Rations or without them entirely. Denegothera alone could go to Indian Affairs to set things right so that after a week or so of deprivation the error would be corrected. The Indian Agent stormed at the damn chief and his inefficiency, knocking people off the list only to put them back on later. The Dene knew where the power lay and whom not to cross. Each spring Indian Affairs provided the nets, traps, and rifle shells called for by treaty for distribution to the Mission Dene on Treaty Day. Each year the items went into the footlocker in Denegothera's house. He gave them freely or sold them cheaply to his allies and not so cheaply or not at all to his opponents. He gambled with the shells. Sometimes, he even gave them to his opponents if it was widely known that they were in real need.

The theoretical models were incomplete. Denegothera led not by providing but by blocking, by bringing deprivation or easing his support of the factors that had brought deprivation. White Canada had declared that the chief was the only point of formal contact between the Dene and the government, that Denegothera alone was empowered to act for The People or be heard by the white government. He and he alone was the legitimate Indian contact point with the outside world. When fundamentalist missionaries arrived by ski-plane one winter it was Denegothera who told The People to use their tracts for toilet paper and told the missionaries to leave because they were "going to hell" for not being Catholic. When the government tried to start commercial fishing, Denegothera stopped it through his obstreperous demands and his greed. When representatives from the Indian Co-Op at La Ronge came to Mission to offer The People a market for their beadwork at two and a half times the rate they were receiving from the Hudson's Bay Company, he ran them off. Denegothera had a standard speech: The People needed more Rations and should administer them themselves.[6] That speech was the official response of the Mission Chipewyan to every question Canada asked of them. He delivered this speech to tourists, geographers, game officials, and government employees. He once had it translated and transcribed and then mailed it to Queen Elizabeth in England. He wrote letters to the "big boss" in La Ronge, Prince Albert, Regina, Ottawa, and London. He wrote to the queen several times, once trying to sell her his old caribou-hide coat for a thousand dollars after he heard that she had been presented with a buffalo robe by another Indian group. His reputation spread all over the northern part of the province. Every letter he wrote was, in the jargon of the whites, "circular filed." The local whites detested him (Sharp 1991). The bureaucrats despised him. Every plea he made was met with contempt. Only the politicians listened; there were not many votes at Mission, but they were cheap.

Denegothera was effective in dealing with the white world because of the reputation he had established among the white bureaucrats for ignorance, greed, and incompetence. Of the substance of his reputation Denegothera was either unaware or unconcerned. The effect of his reputation was what concerned him. By law, all of the formal dealings of the Canadian government with the Mission Dene had to pass through him. He did not answer letters. He did not fill out forms. He did not respond to requests or queries for information. He was nearly immune to threats. Mostly, the representatives of the Crown did not even bother to try and deal with him. His determined insistence upon his wishes and his absolute refusal to respond to the bureaucratic forms demanded by the Canadian government resulted in a near paralysis in their dealings with the Mission Dene. The whites thought him a fool, but for twenty-three years this remarkable man blocked or slowed virtually all the programs of deliberate social change that whites tried to initiate at Mission. Often the very knowledge that he would have to be involved with a program was enough to kill any attempt to implement it there. For those twenty-three years of his term of office, The People of Mission lived behind a protective barrier they did not know existed, a barrier that let them control the pace and tone of their adjustment to the expanding influence of the imperialistic new Canada that existed beyond their homeland.

Denegothera was a small and slight man, but he could sometimes be a man of no small presence. One remarkable display of his power was relayed to me by a distinguished Canadian anthropologist accompanying a delegation of Cree and Sioux visiting Mission to extend the constituency and influence of a Saskatchewan Indian organization. By this time Denegothera was no longer the chief at Mission, and he had no basis for attending the meeting. He simply came, sat with his peculiar poker face, and said nothing. At the end of the meeting, when he joined the line to be paid for attending, his manner was too much for the Cree members of the delegation. They paid him rather than risk the power/knowledge of this strange man in this strange world so far from their home.

If Denegothera maintained power by frustrating the intentions of the white world and by selectively denying and then delivering the benefits of that white world to his own people, gossip was the means by which he translated his actions into political effectiveness. Inkoze played a curious role in Denegothera's maintenance of his position as chief. He had a reputation as a healer at Wollaston Lake and Brochet. Even before I went to the field I had heard from the late James G. E. Smith that a man with such a reputation lived at Mission. Jim was then working for the National Museum of Man and engaged in fieldwork at Brochet. He did not know to whom the reputation belonged, just that there was a healer at Mission who was held in high regard by the Brochet Dene but whose name they did not reveal. Denegothera's reputation there was so great that people from Brochet sometimes chartered aircraft to fly him from Mission to heal their sick.

His reputation for inkoze did not extend to his home settlement. When visitors with reputations for power/knowledge came to Mission they stayed at his house and performed there. He knew the Magic Boy and all the other men of notable power/knowledge in the region, but The People of Mission did not credit him with power/knowledge. Most Mission Dene laughed at the idea of his having real power/knowledge. They pointed out that he was afraid to break up fights, that he was afraid of bear and had never killed one, that he did not hunt, and that he did not trap. All he did was gamble and get along with the "Old Women." If he had inkoze it was no more than the mundane dose to which any man might aspire.[7]

Gossip is a fickle thing, especially when dealing with those close at hand, but it is also a primary mechanism of social control in Chipewyan society. The Dene had it right about Denegothera; he "got along with the Old Women." Individually, the "Old Women" of Mission occupy positions that are categorically low in status, but collectively they exercise substantial power (Sharp 1976, 1994a). Femaleness among the Dene is not a highly valued symbolic category. To be an old woman brings no public respect. Being an old woman can, and usually does, mean that that woman has access to a large number of her own children and grandchildren as well as to the children and grandchildren of her siblings, most all of whom have themselves married and developed networks of kin and affines. Each of those "Old Women" sits at the apex of a wide-reaching network of junior kin and affines, and along each of those networks she has free access for communication with the expectation that what she has to say will be heard. The old women are the mothers and grandmothers of all of Mission, and they are individually connected by ties of sentiment to the entire community. From those ties of sentiment and the access they provide—in a society where political enfranchisement is the power to speak and be heard—come power and influence. Denegothera assiduously courted the old women of Mission, and their ability to move information along the communication networks centered about each of them was a major factor in maintaining his political base within the community.

By 1972, Denegothera could no longer stem the tide of change at Mission. He lost his exclusive access to the Indian agent when a Dene from Discha was appointed to the position. That appointment was one of a series of changes in the bureaucratic structures that administered Mission, and it came at a time when there was a general increase in English-language proficiency among the Mission Dene. A series of younger rivals were receiving strong support from the local whites, and there was a cumulative frustration from the governmental bureaucracies demanding the removal of Denegothera. It was a period of uncertainty, turmoil, and promise. There was enormous pressure on the white world to get the Mission Dene under control. The energy crisis was on the horizon, and there were uranium deposits that needed to be developed. The new precedent of the Alaskan Natives' land claims settlement and the halting negotiations over James Bay carried the fear of much greater costs if settlement were delayed. The band was persuaded to switch to the rules of election making the chieftaincy subject to periodic election and, in the turmoil, an election was held and the son of one of Denegothera's original allies was elected chief (Sharp 1975, 1986, 1987).

Gossip is blind and uncaring. It is blind to truth and facts and uncaring of the havoc it can wreak in the lives of its subjects. Anyone who was a member of a birth cohort that passed through its period of sexual awakening in a North American secondary school is fully aware of the unfairness of gossip and its power to inflict pain. Talking about things orders and explains the experiences of Dene life. The very act of talking to others moves experience from the individual to the social, where the fact that experience is shared is far more significant than the nature of the experience itself. Shared experience, shared reality, need not be logical, coherent, or true. It need only be shared to form the context within which human lives and human actions are ascribed meaning.

If the mechanisms that had maintained Denegothera in office were fairly subtle, the role of talking about things in driving the newly elected chief from office displayed the worst features of a gossip system. The newly elected chief retained neither support nor his office for very long. He lost the support of the government when he refused to sign the papers to make Mission a reserve and instead insisted upon negotiating over land. His stated definition of a good chief as "one who breaks the government" cost him the support of the local whites. One of the most effective means the white world uses to control the Dene is the sudden enforcement of laws, practices, and regulations that have been previously unknown. The tactic is used most effectively by new RCMP officers under pressure to increase arrest rates and make their own records look better. What had been represented as a five-thousand-dollar expense account for the new chief to attend meetings on behalf of the band was suddenly determined to be a double signature account intended for the band's use. Rumors flew that the new chief was about to be charged with misappropriation of band funds.

What finally drove the new chief from office was not the threats of white bureaucrats but a gossip morality play about drunkenness and sexual misconduct. The Chipewyan tend toward the austere regarding the public display of affection, sexuality, and nudity, although their conceptions of what constitutes each of these is quite different from those of Western cultures in North America. Ribald behavior is not appropriate in the presence of certain categories of kin but quite acceptable in their absence. It is quite permissible to joke with sisters and sisters-in-law, but not in quite the manner or about quite the same topics as with non-kin. Private displays of sexuality among persons of appropriate kin and age status are normal, but public expression of sexuality is frowned upon. The Chipewyan are not a people who slavishly express affection in any case. A stylized handshake is the appropriate response to first seeing a spouse, sweetheart, or kinsman who has not been seen for months.

The new chief and his wife were visiting Birchtown and staying at the home of that village's chief. During the course of their visit the new chief had far too much to drink one night. He drunkenly grabbed his wife and began to undress her, publicly exposing her genitals before retiring with her to the privacy of a back room. This action was consonant with a form of male assertion of supremacy (as well as hostility, control, and in a curious sense, respect for her status if not for her personhood) in which men expose and comment possessively upon their wife's genitals before an audience of other males.

Word of the new chief's action spread quickly at Birchtown and soon reached Mission, where it was rapidly disseminated throughout the community. Three days later, when he and his wife returned to Mission on a chartered aircraft, they shamefacedly rushed home. The new chief did not appear in public for three days after his return, and his wife was not seen in public for another week. The gossip stemming from this incident was choice. Other, more political gossip related to his dealing with the whites, but the stories of this event removed his last vestiges of legitimacy. A special election was held that summer, and he was voted out of office.

To castigate the chief for sexual misconduct by making a joke is, as Marcel Mauss put it, "a total social phenomenon" (Mauss 1967). The joke is at once moral, religious, political, and humorous, a statement of position and alliance, and many other things besides. The separation of politics from reputation, inkoze, morality, and most other issues is both an analytical strategy and an artifact resulting from the demands of writing about them. The Dene live these experiences without any separation between them.

Dene life is much denser in social relationships than is typical of the world that lies to the south of them. For all the vast space and great distances in this land, the Chipewyan are rarely alone. Adult men can gain temporary solitude in their bush activities, but their life in camp or village is as open to the view of others as are the lives of women (Foucault 1979). Privacy, in the Western sense, does not exist. The Dene have strong cultural conventions about the kind of behavior that is seen and that which is not seen, what to comment on and what not to comment on, but the possibility of observation is always present. The very density of social relationships and the omnipresent potential to be observed—and for that which is observed to be commented upon—allow for a system of social coercion of staggering power.

14

LOON IV

Talking about things as part of the process by which humans observe/measure the indeterminate chaos of individual experience to create a shared reality shows in why the Chipewyan regarded "just Phil shooting at a loon" as a sufficient explanation for all the shooting that August day at Foxholm Lake. Like so many things that involve inkoze, that explanation involves Dene uses of time, which, if we hold to our own ideas of the relationship between time and events, make Dene ideas of causality seem a chaotic nightmare.

From our perspective, the Dene interpretation of the encounter makes effect not only precede cause but determine it. Through our use of English we understand that "just Phil shooting at a loon" was a sufficient explanation because the potential actualities of Phil's future experiences, reputation, and development that might come to be actualized in the course of his later life were immanent within the part of his experiences, reputation, and development that had already been actualized in his life. That, as a sentence and as a set of ideas, is a mouthful.

This encounter with the loon was a hunt, the ritual activity that enacts the inverted sacrifice paradigm that orders the relationship between the Dene and inkoze. A hunt shifts the ordinary experience of causality into the full non-Euclidean geometry of time and causality that mark inkoze. The meaning of the encounter within that warped geometry was not determinable when the encounter occurred.[1]

Within Chipewyan reality, what the "event" is, what the "event" means, cannot be known until related "events" have played themselves out through time and space to reveal the meaning of the original "event." The "event" was not one that was organized by time and bounded by the now but an "event" that organized time.[2] Within this framework of causality, the boundaries and meaning of this encounter have to be seen within the history—past and future—of Phil's life and his ties to loon in inkoze.[3] Full and immediate explanation is not determined by "events." It is as if the Dene put meaning and interpretation on hold until the rest of the "event" becomes visible as time passes. Only then can the original "event" be understood and its correct meaning determined.

Within our framework of reality there occurred, at a specifiable time and place, an event whose meaning could be interpreted, whose nature could be fully understood, and that could be fixed in time and forgotten. Within Dene reality there occurred at the same place not an event that could be interpreted and frozen in time but a contact with inkoze whose nature was known but whose meaning would remain undetermined for years to come.

Insanity and inkoze are both associated with the head. The distinction between the two is not a clear one. Inkoze can lead to insanity while insanity may be distinguishable from inkoze only by the fact that inkoze produces concrete results. These two things are not discrete states but aspects of causality that can only be inferred from behavior and the consequences of behavior. Throughout his life Phil has walked the borderline between insanity and inkoze. This relationship began when Phil was a toddler. While playing with friends he received a hammer blow to the back of his head. The force of the blow was severe enough to have fractured his skull and exposed his brain. The wound refused to heal, and for years he endured a suppurating wound exposing his skull and brain. Phil was treated by both Western and Native medicine, but the wound remained open until he reached adolescence.[4]

Before Phil was old enough to talk he began to have fierce and violent dreams that continued for years. In some of these dreams he acted out violent wrestling matches with the creatures of his dreams. Once, during a particularly violent dream he had at home while in his early teens, he grabbed a knife to fight off the being in his dream. His father took hold of him and attempted to wrestle him to the ground to protect other family members from injury, and he narrowly escaped having his hand severed.

In Mission Dene reality the beings of inkoze must take the initiative and come to the person to whom they seek to give inkoze. Individuals may not seek out beings of inkoze and ask for power. There is no vision quest in Mission Dene culture. In strong contrast to practice among the Athapaskan peoples of the American Southwest, the beings of inkoze that come to the Mission Dene are not bound or regulated by traditional rituals or songs (Basso 1976). The beings of inkoze remain in absolute control of their relationship with individual Chipewyan and may punish them or withdraw from the relationship at whim.

The term "pity" is sometimes heard. In the relationships between the peoples of the American Northern Great Plains and the supernatural beings that aid them, being in a pitiful state often elicits sympathy from supernatural beings or has a coercive aspect compelling them to assist an individual in that state (see, e.g., Radin 1990: 118, 214). Being pitiful has no coercive power over the beings of inkoze.[5] For an individual Dene to be reduced to a pitiful state might prompt a being of inkoze to aid them, and many stories of receiving power/knowledge involve those who are destitute, abandoned, orphaned, or being mistreated by their relatives. However, being in that state in no way coerces a being of inkoze to assist a person or to enter into a relationship with a person. Being pitiful is more likely to generate hostility or disgust from one of these beings than it is to garner sympathy or help.

One of the ways beings of inkoze can come to a man is by attacking him during his dreams. He must fight off the being of inkoze during the dreams, otherwise he will die. If he successfully overpowers the being of inkoze during the dreams, he then enters into a relationship with that being and is given power/knowledge. From the time that Phil could talk, his brothers questioned him about the nature of his dreams. After years of persistent efforts they finally prompted Phil to reveal that snake was coming to him in his dreams and attempting to kill him. If Phil had not been able to resist snake, he would have died. By successfully fighting him off, Phil should have gained power/knowledge in the relationship that his resistance should have led to.

I am unable to say if control over snake would have resulted from a victory but am inclined to think not. It seems not to be a case of mastery over the source of inkoze but of establishing a relationship by proving oneself deserving of inkoze. The relationship between a man and a being of inkoze that has chosen to aid him—"likes him" is the operative English phrase—is a secret one. By finally telling his brothers that it was snake, Phil offended that being of inkoze and it withdrew from him.[6] Revealing this power source provided only a temporary respite. In a short while Phil began to dream again, although less violently and less frequently. The new dreams also featured snake but one of a different appearance and manner.

Phil's behavior was often violent, with mercurial transitions between rage, violence, compassion, and tears. As a youth his parents took him to the priest, who was often used as a shaman, to remove the visitations of snake and help him gain control of himself, but the priest's actions had little effect upon him. As Phil grew into his teens and became stronger and more mobile in the social world, concern about his behavior spread beyond his family and immediate neighbors. Paul was a man with far more than the normal power/knowledge. He had placed his healing power in abeyance when I knew him, but neither he nor the local *segolia* were able to control Phil's behavior.[7] As he grew, the formal Canadian institutions at Mission began to take notice of him. He was expelled from school for fighting and, following this, ultimately sent to Saskatoon for psychiatric evaluation and treatment.

In Saskatoon, it was decided that he was mildly retarded. He was placed on medication and sent home. Phil was anything but retarded, but his inability to prevent sudden violent emotional reactions was unabated. A few years later Phil again came to the attention of the local authorities and was placed under the jurisdiction of the medical system and sent to the hospital at Uranium City for diagnosis. The hospital there forwarded him on to mental health authorities in Prince Albert for further diagnosis and treatment. When put on the plane to Prince Albert, Phil understood the authorities to tell him he was going home to Mission.[8] The flight from Uranium City to Prince Albert had to make a stop at Discha, and when it did, believing he was free to go home, Phil tried to get off the plane. His protests that he was to go home were ignored, and he was overpowered by the flight crew and taken on to Prince Albert in confinement. This provided a choice bit of gossip for Mission as well as considerable anguish for his parents, who only learned of the events through the ensuing gossip. Phil's frantic parents phoned me, and I was able to find out for them where Phil was and what was happening to him. At Prince Albert he was diagnosed as schizophrenic rather than retarded and placed on medication. He spent a few months in occupational therapy working on a farm, which he rather enjoyed, before becoming too lonely and being allowed to return home.

In the fall of 1975, Phil was still supposed to be on phenobarbital for his "schizophrenia." He had dozens of phenobarbital tablets. Neither he nor anyone else in his extended kin group knew quite what they were or just how dangerous they could be. They were simply Phil's medicine, which he sometimes took if he felt a burst of rage coming on. At one point, a five-year-old boy got into the medication and scattered dozens of tablets around the cabin. Fortunately, respect for nydie kept the youngster from taking any. Phil himself would sometimes throw down a few if he felt bad, but they had been, by and large, supplanted by more effective medicines provided by one of the first of the traveling Cree medicine men to come to Mission. His nydie for Phil was based upon reeds and water plants taken from a lake where there had been an appearance of the Madonna. These plants, steeped in hot water and taken as a drink, succeeded where all other treatments had failed.[9]

Inkoze ultimately is knowledge, and knowledge is the power to produce concrete results: animals killed, animals trapped, races won, targets hit, people healed, people punished by sorcery, card games won—all the competitive activities men engage in that have a clear outcome. Inkoze is a performance system, and without sustained performance there is no acceptance that an individual has power/knowledge. At the time of the loon encounter, Phil displayed all of the aspects of behavior that demonstrate strong inkoze except for self-control and the ability to consistently produce positive results from his actions. The factors that produced his erratic behavior could be construed as revealing inkoze, but they could also be construed as the results of insanity. There was ample evidence to interpret him either way.

In spite of his occasional brilliant performances, Phil had not yet demonstrated that he could consistently perform successfully the male activities that allude to power/knowledge. Though he clearly was associated with inkoze, the consensus outside his family seemed to be that he was crazy. These issues in Phil's history were known to all the Mission Dene to some degree in their details and to all Mission Dene as a judgment on him as a person. The history of each person is carried in the gossip that circulates about them, but this gossip is not just a history. It is a series of shared judgments about each person that are made within in the gossip system and serve as the basis for interpreting a person's future actions.

It is in this context of Phil as a failing or failed medicine man that we must interpret the loon hunt and the explanation given for it. Erratic behavior is a possible sign of inkoze, so it was not surprising that a magical loon should appear around Phil, but as the only differentiation between insanity and inkoze lies in the results that the person produces, his failure to display control over either himself or events indicated that he was not a person of power.

Explanations are effects. They are ad hoc responses to events intended to provide order, meaning, and intelligibility in human life. Explanations are also causes. Explanation creates events by giving meaning to them, and once it is collectively assigned, that meaning then determines the nature of the events. The Chipewyan at Foxholm Lake, all the Chipewyan at Foxholm Lake, knew Phil either from their own personal experience of him or through the gossip history that surrounded him. The interrelationship between that personal experience and gossip history that guides the collective assignment of meaning to the encounter with the loon shows in the nature of Phil's life after that day at Foxholm Lake.

Shortly after our early return from Foxholm Lake in late November, Phil became involved with a young woman and lived with her before she—wisely—left him for being abusive. They had one child. His behavior remained erratic with rapid lapses into tears or bursts of violence, but his general pattern of behavior was more controlled than it had been when he was younger. He married a few years later and became a father for the second time. During that marriage, he worked at the mine in Uranium City and earned a decent income for his family. His behavior was more controlled than in his first relationship, but alcohol became a problem. His marriage lasted for several years but broke up when the mine closed and he was unable to find work. He resumed trapping and bush life, but his wife had no truck with bush life and left him.

After the breakup of his marriage, Phil alternated between time in the bush and wage labor. Phil tries hard to keep himself actively working when he is not in the bush. He contributes erratically (he was only in the community erratically) to the upkeep of his last child—the mother of his first child has severed all relations with him. His work history has been checkered. For long periods he vanishes into the bush, traveling hundreds of miles by canoe out onto the barren grounds or making long winter trips by snowmobile. He would prefer to travel by dog team but recognizes that he cannot trust himself to keep a team without killing the dogs in a burst of rage. He has

made a number of long winter trips, including one snowmobile trip all the
way to Churchill on Hudson Bay. When he is not in the bush, Phil works
until some incident sets off an outburst of violence and he ends up in jail for
a short stretch. In the winter of 1992, after my last visit, Phil was mocked and
attacked by a knife-wielding ex-girlfriend in the band office at Mission.[10]
Phil responded to her attack by disarming her and beating her soundly.
There were no witnesses, and it was Phil who was taken before the court. He
was banished into the bush in the Northwest Territories for a year but was
unable to remain away that long and was sent to jail when he returned.

This pattern of alternating life in the bush with life at Mission mixed with
episodic travel or work away from Mission has continued to the present. In
1998, Phil was living in Saskatoon. He had been sent yet again to a mental
hospital for observation and diagnosis with again inconclusive results. A
rather charismatic individual at times, Phil exerted such an attraction on
one of the nurses that she began dating him during his stay in spite of it
being against the rules. When their liaison was discovered, the nurse was
fired and she and Phil continued their relationship for some months after
his release. Phil returned to Mission in 1999, shortly before the death of his
mother in early summer. Her death was a heavy blow to him and he had
difficulty coping with it, but by the summer of 2000 he seemed to have
recovered.

In the years following the breakup of his marriage, Phil actively explored
not only Dene culture but the culture of other First Nations groups with
which he has come in contact. He has become an accomplished singer and
drummer, and both activities are a regular part of his life. His fascination
with traditional Dene culture and that of other First Nations cultures has led
him not only to innovate in Dene culture but to also be an agent for the
introduction of elements from those cultures. It was Phil I first heard refer to
"mother earth" in the summer of 1992. In the early 1980s, he and a few
friends were exploring the use of the sweat lodge, a custom whose practice
had long vanished by the 1960s. The Mission Dene retained an interest in the
sweat lodge, often pointing out the scars near old camping sites that had
been made by sweat lodges and the smaller shaking tents, but the Dene no
longer made them. The form of sweat lodge Phil and his friends reinvented
was based on the practice of other cultures and were much larger than those
The People had used earlier.

Phil explored the idea of the vision quest as found farther south and actively sought visions. This defiance of Mission Dene practice was probably tolerated only because interest in inkoze was coming to be seen as less relevant to the new micro-urban environment at Mission. The results of his dreams and visions were expressed not only in religious constructions in the bush but in artistic work. He became an accomplished artist who took delight in creating works of composite materials completely lacking any of the technological products of the white world.[11]

Inkoze is knowledge, inkoze is power, and inkoze is the ability to use knowledge to produce results. Although Phil remains actively and openly interested in inkoze, he still has never been able to display the consistent control of himself and the world he lives in that is its hallmark. The phenomena of inkoze occur all around him. He is almost like a conduit for inkoze, and it is not possible to be long around him without encountering manifestations of it. Most men who heal with plants must dream of them. As Phil walks through the world the plants sing out to him even through the snows of winter, telling him their locations and their uses. He says, "I see medicine everywhere. . . . I know it." Power/knowledge surrounds Phil, but he does not control it.

When we encountered that loon, I was the first to see it. The man from Birchtown fired ten times at it. Yet, because of what Phil was and because of all that was known by these Chipewyan about what Phil was and might become, that contact with the loon was immediately associated with Phil. Because of what he was, because of what he has become, and because of what he is yet to become, "just Phil shooting at a loon" was a sufficient explanation in Chipewyan reality for why those two men fired thirty shots at that loon that lovely day in August of 1975.

15

MEANING

The process of allocating meaning gives physical phenomena their order and creates a determinate and intelligible reality. It is the daily life analog to the use of instruments and recorded observations for measurement in science. There are two analogies that express what I mean by a "field of meaning." Of the two, the first is the easier to understand, but the second is more accurate and has greater explanatory power. Both analogies allow for the possibility that meaning is something potentially subject to scientific measurement, but in their use here they are analogies—analytical metaphors for interpreting and explaining social behavior rather than science.

The first analogy is to a magnetic field. A field of meaning is a property of socialness. It is generated by social beings. Human culture generates a field of meaning that encompasses all of humanity. Individual cultures generate fields of meaning of lesser breadth and intensity. The fields of meaning generated by individual cultures vary slightly from each other, and there can be slightly varying local spaces within a cultural field of meaning. (The analogy would be neater if magnetic fields had frequencies that vary like radio waves.)

Not everything that comes into contact with a field of meaning will respond to it, just as some objects do not respond to magnetism. The fact that iron is magnetic does not mean that it does not have physical and chemical properties that are independent of its magnetic properties. By the same token, there are events and processes that do not respond to meaning. However, when dealing with an object that is responsive to magnetism, it is impossible to understand it adequately without taking into account the effects magnetic forces have upon it. In the same manner, the behavior of human beings (and other social species) can only be understood by taking into account the culturally generated fields of meaning within which they exist.

The second analogy is to the concept of a dimension in the physical universe. The universe consists of an unknown number of dimensions, with seven the most frequently cited minimum number I have encountered.[1] Within Western reality, the first four dimensions are subject to human perception. The remaining dimensions are not discernible. The ones that are perceptible are unfolded; the imperceptible remainder are folded.

In the terms of the analogy, meaning constitutes a dimension that lies beyond the four recognized in the Western understanding of reality; it is a dimension that is present—unfolded—in the presence of a social species. Any locus or event fixed by the four coordinates of space-time is different for beings that respond to the additional dimension—meaning—than it is for beings that are unable to respond to that—for them—folded dimension. What Western thought regards as physical reality is what it sees as events and processes occurring in the absence (folding) of meaning.

The variances in the fields of meaning generated by human cultures create slightly different physical and social universes as a function of those variations in meaning. The influence of meaning upon what a Western perspective sees as physical reality is limited. Although limited, it is nonetheless real. An observer from one field of meaning will often find the effects of meaning upon physical and social reality within another field of meaning virtually imperceptible. It is a little like trying to understand the music of a culture if you are not able to hear some of the frequencies it uses in its music.

Meaning is shared experience, but it is also emotion. Meaning is a social rather than an individual phenomenon even though it exists at both the individual and the social levels. Individuals seek meaning, create meaning, and are influenced by meaning, but it is only at the social level that meaning is a causal force in creating a shared reality. The linkage of meaning, shared experience, and emotion is essential to understanding fields of meaning as a causal force in the creation of reality. I take it as the import of the essays by Raymond Firth, Mark Hobart, and David J. Park in Joanna Overing's *Reason and Morality* (1985), supported by my comprehension of aspects of contemporary physiological understanding of the operation of the mind (see, e.g., Gazzaniga 1985), that emotion is the primary thought process within the human organism. Human beings think first with emotion and, as an aspect of explaining themselves to themselves (Gazzaniga 1985), translate that emotional reasoning into the forms we recognize as rational and symbolic.

Emotion is the link between the operation of the individual and the operation of the social within the individual human organism. It is the operating system that drives socialness within the individual.

The interaction of this use of meaning and the contrasting ideas of time already considered enable a model of reality quite different from that framed by either our science or our folk physics. If we return to the analogy of a surface and now presume a surface to represent reality, a suitable metaphor for the surface, for reality, becomes that of something akin to a pangolin's skin. Pangolins are covered by scales composed of matted hair. The scales are large, irregular, and overlapping. The surface, the reality they form, is not smooth and continuous but irregular and disjointed. The appearance of a pangolin's skin, the appearance of reality, must be socially constructed out of the irregularities of overlapping and disjunctive scales.

Humans use the disjointed and irregular experience of living to construct reality through shared experience and shared symbols. The nature of the reality that humans construct need not be seamless and uniform but may be disjointed, discontinuous, and irregular. Individual humans are sometimes able to perceive these disjunctions and discontinuities, but the social processes of cultural life—the sharing of meaning between individuals—tends to smooth disjunctions and discontinuities into what seems to be a seamless flow of experience.

The role given a field of meaning in generating reality is not a denial of what we already know about reality but the recognition of an added bit of complexity in it. As far as we know, the universe created by the first four dimensions exists whether or not a fifth dimension is unfolded.[2] Stars are born and die—so far as we know—without reference to the unfolding of a fifth dimension through the presence of social beings in the universe. Nevertheless, the unfolding of meaning, of a fifth dimension, is a real phenomenon whose effects are inescapable. Its unfolding is the difference between an archaeological (or paleontological) site and an indeterminate patch of ground.

The root of these propositions lies in the fact that humans are social animals. There is no social compact. There has never been a social compact. We and our ancestors have been social animals almost as far back in the fossil record as we can read. We, as individuals, are not the unique creators of and manipulators of our universe but iterations of shared sets of cultural symbols and values. Looking at humans in these terms bears thinking about precisely because our culture is so committed to the idea of individualism that our political, philosophical, and intellectual history is one of hundreds of years of denying the implications of our nature as social beings.

We humans are a species rather than a series of species. The uniformity of being human overrides the variations of belonging to an individual culture but does not eliminate them. For several generations of scholarship it has been customary in anthropology to neglect the examination of human culture as a whole for the examination of the specificity of individual cultures, to ignore the whole in favor of the part.

In spite of the power given here to cultural variation to generate genuinely different realities, the differences between these realities are slight. All the different cultures of humanity are but iterations of a common set of organizing principles. The common set of organizing principles that makes—and keeps—us human results from a single survival practice developed by our hominid ancestors that unalterably transformed our ancestors and the path of their subsequent evolution. The basic pattern of primate subsistence is for animals to live within a group but for each individual animal within the group to gather its own food and feed itself.

At some time and place unknown to us, our ancestors extended this pattern to include organized hunting.[3] For creatures living in a human body, hunting is a risky and unreliable means of subsisting. Hunting is so unreliable that even specialized carnivores often live on the edge of starvation. Gathering plant material is much more reliable and has provided the bulk of the human diet at almost all times and places prior to the invention of agriculture. It is so effective a way to make a living that virtually every species survives by having each individual collect its own food.

The effect of hunting upon human evolution is not its nutritional effects or its presumed selection for intelligence, upright posture, or any of the other things that have been attributed to it. Taking up hunting was, in and of itself, inconsequential to evolving fields of meaning just as adding meat to the diet was, in and of itself, inconsequential to evolving fields of meaning.[4] What was important is that, for whatever reasons, some of our ancestral populations began to share that which they had obtained.

Other primates share meat, and sharing meat does not seem to be the reason some populations of primates survive while other populations of primates do not survive. Sometime in our ancestral past, our ancestors also began to share plant food. It is likely that they first shared meat, but that is neither certain nor consequential. The consequences of sharing plant foods were enormous and might have altered the course of human evolution in and of themselves, but the point is moot.

If sharing meat is not in itself a sufficient explanation for the evolution of fields of meaning, it is a precondition for it. The consequence of hunting, shrouded in time and probably lost forever, that is critical to the evolution of fields of meaning is organizational.[5] Where, when, or for whatever reasons that organizational change occurred I have no answers. In fact, there may have been no cause and it may have happened for no particular reason. Neither can I postulate an order to the sequence of events leading to that organizational change for there is no necessary order in the sequence, but the critical step in the process came when both plant and animal foods were shared.

This single step, even more than language, made—and keeps—us human. For the first time in hominid history, and almost alone among mammals, the social group became the unit of production and subsistence.[6] This simple transformation from individuals gathering their own food into a social group that amassed and distributed food among its members spread among our ancestral populations. It displaced all other forms of social organization. With the sharing of food that came from two distinct sources, each requiring different techniques to obtain, came a dual form of the division of labor and the potential to increase exponentially the number and nature of the social ties within the group. For the first time a sexual division of labor could be complemented by an occupational division of labor.[7] As the number and nature of the social bonds within the group expanded and the mutual interdependency between the members of the social group increased, the primary locus of natural selection shifted from the nature of the individual hominid to the nature of the social organization of the group within which the individual hominid lived. Social organization became a "thing" in a sense even Durkheim never imagined (Durkheim 1951, 1964), and it was that thing that is social organization upon which natural selection operated.

The time of this transition was brief, for in very short order this single form of social organization replaced all other forms of social organization that might have been present in our hominid ancestors.

This single change in social organization is the common core to all our diverse forms of social organization and to all our diverse variations in culture. It is what keeps us a single species, and it is the source of the field of meaning that socialness generates in humans.

We have been social beings from so deep in our evolutionary past that it is inconceivable to be human and not be a social being. As social beings, it is our membership in a social group that creates us, that creates our mind, that creates the categories by which we think, that creates the language, proxemics, and posturing by which we communicate, that creates our aesthetics, that creates our spirit/soul, and that creates our sensations and our perceptions. I take this simple notion—that we are social beings constructed by the symbols and values of our cultures—so far as to assert that the ordinary physical world we daily experience is an illusion crafted from the shared experience of the symbols of our culture.

I suspect that the experience of trying to hold within a single mind the interplay between life at home and life in the field leads every anthropologist to develop an idiosyncratic view about the nature of culture. This may in fact be one of the reasons anthropologists have learned to spend little time talking among ourselves about the nature of culture. The analyses in this work, directed as they are toward those few circumstances I have been unable to explain through more conventional means, necessitate a bit of discussion of the topic here.[8]

The idea of culture as an illusion is one I take seriously. To begin with, we take as a given that every individual human being is unique. That uniqueness is caused not just by the slight differences in genetic makeup that exist between us but primarily by the uniqueness of the experience and history that come to each of us from living our lives as social beings. That uniqueness, which I accept as a given, has severe consequences for the task of attempting to explain human social life and how culture works.

If it were not for the issue of scale, there would be little difficulty. Viewed from a comfortable distance, human behavior merges so fully into cultural patterns that human uniqueness all but vanishes into insignificance. (I do not mean that differences between individual humans become insignificant but only that the uniqueness of each human becomes insignificant.) It is when we look at human behavior at a very fine scale, put it under the microscope as it were, that the issue surfaces.

The first consequence of the uniqueness of each individual's life history and experience is to make verbal communication impossible beyond a certain point of specificity of meaning. Symbols, by definition, have multiple meanings. As a result of the uniqueness of each human's experience, and the meaning of that experience within each individual human mind, no symbol can mean precisely the same thing to any two human beings. Individual uniqueness means that full and complete communication or understanding between any two human beings is impossible. No human can know the full range of meaning of any symbol processed through the mind of another human being's unique experience.

Communication depends not upon the understanding of meaning but upon the *illusion* of the understanding of meaning. We learn not to examine communications and meaning too closely. We do not seek to find if what our fellow cultural beings understand of experiences, words, categories, and meanings is truly the same as is our understanding of them. For the process of seeking the full and complete understanding of our fellow cultural beings we substitute a reliance upon the shared understanding that can exist between us. Human social life must be conducted at a scale, at a distance from individual uniqueness, that masks the existence of that individual uniqueness, otherwise it would degenerate into babble, confusion, and mutual incomprehension.

As James Gleick has noted, "Categories mislead. The ends of the continuum are of a piece with the middle" (Gleick 1987: 108). Mutual intelligibility is achieved at the cost of the uniqueness of individual human experience. What is substituted for it is the illusion of understanding at a scale where the uniqueness of human experience is subordinated to that far more powerful demand for the sharing of a comprehensible reality. Each human being exists within a shared reality of meaning that is at odds with their own unique individual understanding of that reality. The disjunction between the two, between shared context and individual experience, is perceptible to all humans. It is a necessity of life as a social animal. It is not clear why we are social animals. It is simply the case that we are. As social animals we subordinate the uniqueness of our individuality to the necessity of sharing the illusion of communication and intelligibility with our fellow social beings.

The search for mutual intelligibility is analogous to a fractal process (Gleick 1987: 83–118). I do not care to take this analogy too far for it is not possible to say that the same rules apply at all scales of the process, but the process itself, the search for the illusion of mutual intelligibility through the sharing of meaning, exists through all the scales of existence from individual perception and sensation to mass political phenomena in nation-states. The power of this process and its ability to effect the physical world are the topics of the next chapter.

16

DEATH ·BY MEANING

Inkoze integrates the previously discussed aspects of time, causality, and meaning into a unified causal field. That reality is particularly efficacious at altering biological processes. It is not without reason the Dene regard inkoze as dangerous. It can be lethal.

At the height of the power and influence of the late 1960s and early 1970s reincarnation of Lived-with-the-wolves, his legitimacy was challenged by a man from Mission. A challenge to an established prophet was a known factor in Dene experience. The outcomes of such a challenge were well scripted. The most probable outcome of such a challenge is the death of the weaker of the two figures.

The challenger to Lived-with-the-wolves was a self-acknowledged fraud, a man who publicly claimed inkoze that others did not think he possessed and that he himself knew he did not have. His challenge led to his death, the death of a self-serving skeptic who became caught within the reality of what to him was but a web of deception.

Throughout his adult life Gleacho (Big Squirrel) had wished to be regarded as a magic man, but the Mission Chipewyan had never thought of him as having that degree of power/knowledge. His obvious desire for a reputation as a magic man was one of the greatest barriers to his ever achieving it. His attempt to deceive his community into according him a status he had not achieved came at a time the community was particularly attentive to the nature of traditional meanings and values. In spite of—or perhaps because of—the changes the local space in the field of meaning was undergoing during its adjustment to the new circumstances facing the Dene, the field of meaning asserted itself with such a force that the existence of the challenger as a social being could only be tolerated if he were a dead man.

The man who challenged the Magic Boy was the son of one of the most powerful sorcerers of the previous generation. I never heard in English any Mission Chipewyan do other than flatly deny that any living Mission Chipewyan knew enough inkoze to kill. That ability was always presented as a thing of outsiders or of past generations. The only story of contemporary sorcery that people would acknowledge involved a man who became incensed by a local woman's affair with a man of ambiguously close kin status. I suspect the story was only acknowledged because of its humor, because his sorcery was so weak that all he could do was make her hair fall out. Gleacho's father not only had the reputation for having the inkoze to kill but for the inclination to use it.

A man in his mid-fifties, Gleacho had been caught breaking into a store at Discha in his youth. The Chipewyan are not fond of thieves, and he had never been able to overcome the loss of respect stemming from this incident. Most men who have a reputation for inkoze achieve it through quiet competence and consistent performance. The verbal and physical performances that lead to establishing a reputation for inkoze are often emphasized precisely by their understatement (D. M. Smith 1973: 16). Gleacho was a garrulous man who often played the clown. In many ways he was too simple a soul to project the necessary image of competence, but he was nonetheless a very sociable and popular man.

Gleacho was quite senior in the community, but he did not have a particularly large network of kin to support a claim to inkoze. The marriages of his children had failed to give him strategic affinal ties to compensate for his lack of kin ties. Gleacho's youngest son had been in trouble with the RCMP several times. The lad (actually a truculent and somewhat nasty fellow) was coping with his emerging awareness that he was gay, and he was not having an easy time of it. His son's homosexuality was not widely known at the time of Lived-with-the-wolves, but his son's troubles and emerging reputation as a troublemaker diminished Gleacho's prestige in the community.

Inkoze is not based upon socialness or personal popularity, and it is not attributed lightly. Over the four decades since he had reached his teens, his living peers and their now-deceased predecessors had failed to recognize in

Gleacho the signs of power/knowledge. However harsh it might seem, it was the judgment of those who had known Gleacho from his infancy to his mature adulthood. That judgment was collective and it was cumulative, outlasting the lives of many of the individuals who had judged the younger Gleacho and found him lacking. When Gleacho let it be known that he questioned the legitimacy of the Magic Boy and indicated he was going to destroy him with his own inkoze, those statements were an affront to the social body that had for so long denied that Gleacho had inkoze.

My awareness that Gleacho was challenging Lived-with-the-wolves came in the winter of 1970, almost at the same time I learned of the Magic Boy. I only heard of Gleacho's challenge because there were individuals at Mission who were so fearful of the possible consequences of Gleacho's actions, including even the destruction of Mission itself, that they were driven to speak of things they would otherwise never have spoken of. Because the Magic Boy was the Magic Boy, it was assumed that he was aware of Gleacho's statements and actions.[1] Most people hoped that, since Gleacho had no power/knowledge and was only making a fool of himself, the Magic Boy would be tolerant and would take no action against him. However, if Gleacho were to persist, the consequences would be severe.

Whatever his intention, Gleacho had entered into a debate with the entire Mission community about the nature of his social personality. The community of Mission formed an arena within which the knowledge individual social beings had of each other was of singular intensity. The adults over forty years of age constituted scarcely more than a moderately sized lecture class, but those adults had known each other throughout their entire lives in a degree of detail almost unimaginable in contemporary North American life. The fears The People expressed about Gleacho's challenge to the Magic Boy and their certainty that Gleacho had no power/knowledge were more than casual worries. They were an offer to Gleacho from the field of meaning that constituted the lives of all the Dene of Mission to acknowledge that he was being foolish and accept the humiliation that was the consequence of his foolishness.

The Magic Boy left Birchtown after the New Year's celebrations of 1970. In his absence, Gleacho's dispute with him seemed to fade, although Gleacho made occasional claims that the Magic Boy had left the region because he feared Gleacho would ultimately destroy him. I do not know how widely this claim was circulated. Those I talked to who did know of it found it both absurd and dangerous.

I left Mission in September of 1970, and, save for a few days at Christmas of 1970, did not return until August of 1972. When I returned, interest in the Magic Boy was again at a high. He had spent Christmas of 1971 at Mission and was rumored to then be en route to Birchtown. At the same time, the first rumors that he had renounced the power of Lived-with-the-wolves were beginning to circulate.

Throughout the time I had been gone, Gleacho had persisted in his comments about the legitimacy of the Magic Boy as a reincarnation of Lived-with-the-wolves. His persistence in making these statements had crossed the line between idle braggadocio and the precarious. Inkoze is secret. Gleacho's very willingness to speak of his challenge to Lived-with-the-wolves was a red flag to the entire community that he could not have had inkoze.

I am not sure that the person who was the Magic Boy knew that Gleacho existed. I have no evidence that he knew of Gleacho's claims or responded to them. The Magic Boy's actions, however, were essentially inconsequential. The issue was the perception of Gleacho's actions by the local field of meaning at Mission. I thought at the time, and still think, that until the Magic Boy visited Mission over Christmas 1971, Gleacho could have exercised the option of appearing foolish in the eyes of Mission and escaped the consequences that were to follow.

Gleacho was not someone I knew well. I did not talk with him on a regular basis, though for several months in the winter and spring of 1970 we lived less than a hundred feet apart and in direct sight of each other. Gleacho sent word to me that he wanted to talk with me before I left Mission in January 1973. I made a point of visiting him shortly before I left. During that January 1973 visit he was alert, confident, and cheerful. He showed no fear of the circumstances surrounding him and seemed to be free of any signs of anxiety or physical distress. I think I remember him having a slight cough, but I did not record it in my notes. I did not know him well enough to notice any minor changes in his appearance or condition, but I could find nothing amiss during my visit even though I was looking to find something. He was disconcertingly well aware of events in the community and alluded to some of the more sensitive of them as well as making a few comments that indicated he was aware of the circumstances of my own life in Mission. He talked to me in English, which he did not particularly like to do, and did not talk directly about the power fight but did make allusions to it. The tone of our conversation was that of one between two outsiders to the situation at Mission, a conversation between two individuals—both of whom knew what was going on—but to whom the normal rules of conduct did not quite apply.

Gleacho later sent with my then-wife a message to be relayed to me only when we were back in the United States. In it he said he was engaging the Magic Boy in a power fight. A serious claimant to inkoze would never talk about the fight—even to an outsider—or relay a message through an unrelated female. His message overtly stated that he was tricking the community into thinking that he was a magic man, confirming my opinion that he was a sane and healthy man attempting to run a con on the community.

Throughout the fall of 1972, Gleacho persisted in his claim to power/knowledge and increased his activity as fall turned into winter. During the early fall the arena formed by the social field of Mission, the social fabric that expressed the power of the field of meaning that was Dene culture, increasingly hardened against him. Gleacho's claims became more and more offensive to the field of meaning that defined Mission Chipewyan reality, and it began to respond to Gleacho not merely as a foolish man but as a man who was losing a power fight with a superior opponent.

Ironically, Gleacho finally had the community of Mission responding to him as it would to a man of acknowledged power/knowledge, but the nature of Mission's response was not what he had anticipated. The field of meaning interpreted his behavior as indicating that he was a victim of inkoze instead of a skilled practitioner of it. The People of Mission began to think of him as an increasingly crazy man who would go insane. They began to anticipate his death.

As the weather turned cold and snow came that fall, Gleacho began to behave erratically. He spent most of his time at home and withdrew somewhat from his normal involvement in social activities. Stories began to circulate, telling how he would be sitting home quietly attending to some task or other only to stop what he was doing and ask his youngest daughter to get him a cup of tea. When she would bring him the tea he would, instead of drinking it, rise from the bed where he usually sat and walk over to the wood stove in the middle of the cabin. To the shock and horror of everyone in the house, he would throw the tea onto the hot stove. In the midst of the steam and the smell of the burning dregs, he would return to his bed and sit down, only a moment later to berate his daughter for not bringing him the cup of tea he had asked for. He would again demand a cup of tea and the whole process would be repeated, sometimes several times in a row.

As word of these performances circulated, individuals were not content just to hear of them. The People wished to see and experience the situation for themselves and visited him to see how he would act while they were there. He repeated this routine frequently enough for it to be witnessed a number of times. Stories about it spread widely. What was to the visitors and the community at large a scene of humor tinged with uncertainty became for his co-resident family a scene of increasing horror.

Through these visits the field of meaning at Mission was expressing itself at all scales of reality. It was not just an abstract debate over the interpretation of Gleacho's actions but a detailed involvement in what he was doing as part of a search for the meaning of his actions.

As the fall progressed, Gleacho began to chatter constantly to family or visitors or, if he was home alone, to no one at all. His memory and situational awareness began to seem faulty. He appeared to forget the names of individuals who had come to visit him even though he had known them for decades. Worse—but even more ambiguously—he seemed to confuse the identity of his visitors with those who were not present and then deliver sometimes quite pointed commentary on current events and gossip about the very individuals who were visiting him but whom he seemed to have confused with someone else. It was not long before he began to forget the names of his children or call members of his immediate family by the wrong names.

Although visiting Gleacho's house was sometimes embarrassing for the visitors, the social field at Mission remained in constant touch with Gleacho through a steady stream of visitors. The curious came to see what he was up to, providing him with an ever-changing audience while spreading the news of his actions throughout the village. This process of visiting Gleacho, talking to him, and watching him was followed by the visitors going away and talking about what they had seen. Gleacho was the subject of gossip, and the full power of talking about things was applied to finding the meaning in what he was doing. The People talked about him, his health and his appearance, his actions, and about his family. They talked about what they had seen, what they had heard, and what they had been told about his actions. It was through this process that they rationally sought the meaning of what they were experiencing and formed judgments about him and his actions.

These visits included all kinds of persons. His peers came to visit. The wives and sisters of his peers came to visit his wife. Young adults came to visit. Young children came, watched, then left with the hurried energy of children. The communication with Gleacho came partly with words but most of the communication was nonverbal. Visitors commented on their assessment of Gleacho's behavior through their actions, as much by what they did not do as by what they did do. They communicated their assessment of him and his actions through their posture. By standing along the wall of the cabin instead of sitting down as would a stranger, a youth, or someone distant to Gleacho and his kin; a furtive glance or hurried look; rigidity in movement as if they were in a public forum rather than the home of a life-long acquaintance; an unexpected stiffness of the upper torso or the halting of a motion to freeze and attend to Gleacho's words or actions—all these actions by the visitors communicated to Gleacho the concern, fear, and uncertainty Mission felt about him.

As judgments in the community were formed about him and as meaning was attributed to him, his actions, and his circumstances, those judgments were fed back to him. There are, for every person who is the topic of a gossip system, those who will relay back to its subjects the judgments applied to them. Information came back to Gleacho, telling him how he and his actions were being interpreted by Mission and offering him alternative courses of action, choices he could make to confirm or deny the forming judgments of him.

As the community's judgment of Gleacho solidified and became harsher, the attitudes of his visitors changed. Different kinds of people, particularly individuals charged with governance or leadership within the community, began to number among his visitors.

Before Gleacho took up sewing, what seemed to disturb The People most was his incessant questioning of his wife as to whether or not she loved him. Gleacho and his wife were notorious for their decades of conflict. The idea of love in their relationship was one the community regarded as absurd.

Although passion and infatuation had always been a concern in affairs of the heart, romantic love was a recent introduction into the calculations involved in arranging marriages. At best it was a concern of generations junior to Gleacho. A man of his generation just did not publicly ask his wife if she loved him. A woman of his generation might ask that question during, or to start, an argument, but romantic love was really a concern of the younger and less traditional.

Gleacho's wife was nearly blind and unable to get around without someone to lead her. This task usually fell to a grandchild, but there were long periods when she was unable to leave home because there was no one to lead her about. When Gleacho would ask her if she loved him, she would sit quietly, never answering his question. She often had friends and relatives stop in to visit her. They, like most of the people at Mission, were curious about what Gleacho was up to and what she thought of how he was behaving. Always, Gleacho was watched. Always, the curious stares or furtive glances of these visitors kept him in the public eye and in constant communication with it. As Gleacho's wife and her friends talked about the events in her home, she expressed her fears about what was happening there. Voices were lowered, whispering was common, and conversations stopped if Gleacho seemed to be paying attention to them. If Gleacho happened to ask her if she loved him while her friends were there, she would quietly tell them that of course she did not love him. He must be crazy to ask such a question.

Her comments were carried out into the social field of Mission and met with widespread agreement. Her comments were accepted by the community and became part of the judgment upon Gleacho, part of the community's increasingly less tolerant view of him that narrowed the options available for the interpretation of his actions: "He must be crazy to ask."

During this time, two aspects of the paradigm of a lost medicine fight were establishing themselves within the community. The most obvious was that Gleacho was beginning to behave in ways that indicated the onset of insanity. The most common interpretation was that even if Gleacho did have some knowledge of inkoze, he was into it way over his head with his challenge to the Magic Boy and clearly was losing the medicine fight. Many people did not even bother to consider that Gleacho might have some knowledge of inkoze because the symptoms he was beginning to display were those that might be expected to appear in even a powerless victim of sorcery.

Less obvious—I certainly missed it at the time—was the fact that Gleacho was beginning to undergo a gender reversal.

To understand how the field of meaning was affecting Gleacho and those around him, it is necessary to look more closely at the arena within which his actions were being interpreted. The essential arena was Mission itself, although Discha played a secondary role in the interpretation of the events. Mission itself then had a population of only about five hundred souls. There was a white population of about a dozen, but Gleacho was Dene business and I doubt that any of the whites other than the priest had any clue that something was amiss. Had the priest been familiar with the village he might have been a major figure in the interpretation of Gleacho's behavior, but the priest was new to the village and recovering from a stroke. His influence was powerful but wanting.

The Mission population of 1969 to 1973 showed the effects of the reduction of deaths during childbirth and infant mortality brought about by improved medical care after World War II. The ready availability of antibiotics at Mission from the early 1950s onward had contributed to a lowering of death rates among both adults and children, although the rates for accidental death had remained high. The children saved through improved health care were now old enough to reproduce, and the population of Mission was growing rapidly. Of the treaty population, 57 percent were less than twenty while fully 70 percent were under thirty years of age. Only 20 percent of the population was over forty. The number of living individuals who were more or less Gleacho's peers numbered fifty to fifty-five individuals, barely 10 percent of the population.

These few individuals, male and female, had known each other since they were children. Their experience of each other was decades deep, and each had a lifetime's worth of stories and gossip about each and every other individual in their age group. They not only knew the most casual details about each other but had years of experience observing or hearing about even the most intimate personal details and preferences of domestic life. Shared experience is meaning, and the web of meaning woven about each of these senior adults was generations deep. These senior adults were at apical points in their individual life cycles. Almost all of them had adult children, most had grandchildren. Many of those grandchildren were themselves married and parents. Each of these senior adults occupied a position that made them sources of knowledge about the past. Their knowledge created the context by which past "events" were ordered and tied to the "events" and context of the present. They were, for their descendants, the interpreters of what things meant precisely because of the kin ties that bound the younger generations to them.

The Dene do not particularly like to speak of death, and it goes beyond even poor manners to casually name the dead. But the dead, if not much spoken about, are not absent from Dene social life. The senior adults at Mission remember those who are dead and remember their own interactions with those now deceased. The prejudices, passions, and conflicts of the past find expression in contemporary life through the memories and actions of the living. It is not just that senior adults remember; senior adults order and define the present through their own experience, and a large part of their experience is their memory of those who are now dead. Each senior adult is a conduit for the aspirations and judgments of the dead into the lives and actions of the living. As the only ones living who have personal experience of the dead while they were living, senior adults transmit their own experience of past social life to younger adults not just as stories or details but as judgments upon and interpretations of contemporary events and lives. The young do not learn the details or the experience of the past but receive in their place the judgments, commentary, and interpretations of the senior adults—judgments, commentary, and interpretations based upon experiences the younger adults will never have and that are given for reasons the younger adults will never know.

The field of meaning of Dene life was woven from the experience of the living and the dead into a web of meaning and emotion that surrounded the senior adults and their actions. This web of meaning is so tightly woven that even facial expressions, gestures, puns, or postures could express conflicts, likes, and dislikes generations removed from the experience of younger Dene. Within this intense field of experience, emotion, and meaning there could appear scripts of enormous coercive power unperceived by those expressing them but devastating to those at whom they were directed.

As with the children and the younger adults, the senior adults came to visit Gleacho. Everyone, Gleacho included, knew why they had come and what they had come to see. Before them, Gleacho's performance was subject to an intensity of observation and judgment that was an expression of the cumulative experience not of a lifetime but of a lifetime amplified by the collective memory of generations recently past. This was not a process of rationality but an exercise in emotional reasoning. Nothing was said of the magic fight. Nothing had to be said of the magic fight. Everyone knew and that issue embraced Gleacho's entire being and his place within the social fabric of Mission. The People watched while their emotions responded to Gleacho's words and actions. His actions and his claim to inkoze were under judgment by the audience that knew him best and that most truly mattered (Foucault 1979: 216–28).

To be human is to be created through interaction with our fellow social beings. Our being is the iteration of the symbols and values of the cultural context that created us. We in the West value free will and the ability of the individual to stand against the context of their life, but the simple truth is that we are creatures of context and we cannot escape the context that creates and defines us.

That context, those symbols, values, and emotions, were not just internalized within Gleacho, they *were* Gleacho.

Gleacho, the rational man who made a deliberate attempt to advance his status and position through a false claim to inkoze, was no different from the rest of us. He was, as we are, a complex construction whose parts and natures we scarcely fathom, but that part of him that deliberately tried to manipulate the cultural context in which he lived was the lesser part of him. That greater part of him was in contact with and understood the meaning of the judgments and values of his culture. They worked through him and upon his emotions and that greater part of him accepted and responded to those judgments and values. As The People, young and old, child and adult, came to experience Gleacho's behavior, they carried and communicated to him their judgments of him and the meaning of his behavior.

Of all of this Gleacho was the target, and as time passed, the judgment of the context in which he existed became progressively harsher toward him and his claim to inkoze.

By late fall of 1972, the Mission community had more or less accepted that Gleacho was somehow flirting with some form of power/knowledge. Some had accepted that Gleacho had attempted to perform inkoze beyond the level of his power/knowledge and the inkoze had begun to rebound upon him. A very few credited him with actually being in a magic fight with the Magic Boy, but many more felt he was the victim of the Magic Boy's inkoze.

Those most optimistic about the situation felt that Gleacho would merely go crazy. The common view was that he would die. Even though rumors that the Magic Boy had renounced his power as Lived-with-the-wolves continued to circulate, the Magic Boy was hundreds of miles away and his fate had little to do with Gleacho's own fate.

As Gleacho continued to act in an erratic manner, his behavior began to frighten his family. The Chipewyan are a people who can be magnificently self-controlled in expression, speech, and behavior, but that self-control is commonly a thing of public places, interactions with wild animals, strangers, or circumstances where power may be present. At home, emblanketed by the presence of kin and family, they are far more relaxed and are expressive in a different manner. Fear, uncertainty, and anxiety are difficult things to hide. They find expression in posture and bearing even if they are cloaked from verbal expression. In the less disciplined arena of their home, their expression by Gleacho's family was inevitable. Posture was more rigid. Facial expressions were held more tightly in check. There were subtle shifts from relaxed normality to guarded stiffness as shifts in Gleacho's behavior led the realm of inkoze to intrude, vanish, then intrude again into their home life. Ordinary domestic life was disrupted. The routines of daily life became unpredictable, generating their own anxiety. Gleacho was constantly the focus of attention and a source of uncertainty.

If Gleacho were to have had any chance for his claim to power/knowledge to succeed, it would have required the partisan support of his family talking along their lines of friends, kin, and affines. His network of kin and affines was not particularly strong to begin with. Without its support spreading along these existing lines of affiliation and connection to the rest of the Mission community, his case was hopeless. Instead of sending out messages of support, this most intimate and supportive group became instead part of the social field denying him the status he sought. As fear of the aura of inkoze or madness surrounding him grew, his own family sought succor from the new chief and the council. Their growing fear and its expression to the authorities helped confirm the social field in its interpretation of his actions as those of a crazy man.

Once the problem of Gleacho had been dumped in the lap of the new chief and council, they found themselves uncertain how to proceed and in many ways powerless to deal with it. The chief and the councillors were young men in their thirties. They were not quite sure just what was happening with Gleacho, and none of them had any reputation for power/knowledge. This was a situation that should have been placed in the hands of an accomplished sorcerer or healer who might have tried to help Gleacho, but Gleacho's own intransigence prevented this even if a local segolia had been willing to tackle the now ambiguous power of the Magic Boy. Unable to find a solution to what had become an extremely delicate situation within the community, they tried to dump the problem on the white authorities and institutions (Goulet 1998: 119–28). Inkoze was far too sensitive to explain to the white authorities, so the chief and council reported it to the RCMP and the local nurse as a case of probable insanity with threatening overtones of domestic abuse.

Both white institutions responded to the concerns expressed by the chief and the council on behalf of Gleacho's family. The nurse made arrangements for Gleacho to be flown to Uranium City for a physical and psychiatric examination at the hospital. She, having not been told of inkoze, the Magic Boy, or the power fight, could make no mention of them to the medical authorities. All she was able to convey to them was that Gleacho's family feared that he might be going crazy and become a danger to his family. Sending Gleacho out for examination was not a bad idea, but it proved to be no solution to the situation. Gleacho was examined at the hospital but was only kept in Uranium City overnight. The medical personnel at the hospital apparently found nothing wrong with either Gleacho's physical or mental health. He was not admitted to the hospital and returned to Mission the following day on the next scheduled flight. With Gleacho formally diagnosed as sane and healthy, the nurse washed her hands of the situation after his return and confined herself to monitoring his physical health.

During his stay in Uranium City Gleacho had acted sanely enough to satisfy the medical personnel who examined him. On his return to Mission, he stopped at Discha and visited kin and friends there. They found him perfectly normal and were confused as to why he had been sent to Uranium City in the first place.

When Gleacho returned to Mission from Discha and the hospital, he resumed the patterns of behavior he had displayed before he was taken out for examination.

Insanity was beyond the RCMP's purview, but the threat of domestic violence was of real concern to them. Upon yet again receiving expressions of concern from the chief and council on behalf of his family, the RCMP came to Mission and removed Gleacho from his home. They took him to Discha, where they had made arrangements for him to stay with kin. During his stay, Gleacho behaved in a perfectly normal manner and the reasons for his enforced visit became an even greater source of confusion to his kin. When Gleacho's behavior at Discha had satisfied the RCMP, they allowed Gleacho to return home.

As soon as he returned home, Gleacho began to display the behaviors that had led his family to seek protection from him.

Gleacho's odd behavior continued through the fall and on into the winter and became a continuing source of fear for his family. At least four times, before and after his trip to the hospital, the RCMP responded to requests from his family through the chief and council and took Gleacho to stay with kin in Discha. Four times Gleacho was removed from the social field at Mission. Each time his health was checked and his behavior carefully monitored. Four times he was found to be perfectly normal. At Discha he displayed none of the behaviors that disturbed Mission. His forced removals to Discha eventually began to anger his kin there. They could see no reason for him to be treated in this manner. The RCMP were increasingly frustrated by the removals. They could find no evidence that Gleacho posed a threat to anyone or that his behavior was anything but normal. Yet the fear expressed by his family was genuine.

Gleacho, while he was in Discha, was within the field of meaning of Chipewyan culture, but he was removed from the intensive focus of the local field of meaning at Mission that was defining him as a man fated to insanity and death. Free of this focus, Gleacho acted like the sane and healthy man he was. Within the local field of meaning that surrounded him at Mission, Gleacho always resumed the behavior that so thoroughly frightened his family.

Shortly after the last time the RCMP removed Gleacho to Discha, I drove the chief and a councillor to visit the RCMP at Discha to once more convey Gleacho's family's fear of him and ask the RCMP to remove him. As I drove them to Discha, I asked them about the situation. Even though I had been coming to Mission for several years, I was still white and an outsider. We were not close friends and they had no clear idea just how much I knew about the situation. They did not want to discuss it with me but felt the need to say something to me. The three of us discussed several possible explanations for Gleacho's behavior: Cree magic, a possibility but one that seemed unlikely; a sorcerer within the village, an impossibility because they insisted that no living local had that much inkoze; a power fight with the Magic Boy, an impossibility. The only acceptable solution we could find was that Gleacho had incorrectly performed magic to improve the performance of a dog team and was now showing signs of its rebounding upon him because he had attempted something greater than he knew how to do. Once we had talked about this in English, they began to talk to each other in Chipewyan and, from my halting understanding of their conversation, spent the rest of the trip discussing Gleacho's power fight with the Magic Boy and how they were to deal with it. Their concern was that Gleacho was a danger to his family and the community because of his rash intrusion into the power fight. They sought some way to get him away from the village before his actions brought harm to others.

Among them the script was drawn. They expected Gleacho to lose his power fight at great cost to himself and with possible danger to his family and the rest of the community.

By this point the RCMP were utterly frustrated by the situation. They had more than enough awareness of the local Dene to realize that something was going on that they did not know about. They knew and resented the way the local Chipewyan would get them to intervene in situations to bring order to them and then fail to follow up with testimony or charges that would allow the courts' entry into the problem. This Chipewyan practice made them look inefficient and was bad for their careers. The RCMP had now had enough of Gleacho. Since there was no violence involved, they chose to dismiss the situation as a "domestic problem."

A domestic problem was a very different matter from domestic violence, and they felt that no further intervention was warranted. With their refusal of further involvement went the last possibility of an external agency removing Gleacho from the arena before the consequences of his actions had played themselves out completely.

Gleacho had managed by dint of sheer will and self-delusion to force himself into a position beyond his proper place. He demanded to be attributed with something only a man with exceptional inkoze could claim: the ability to challenge the now ambiguous Magic Boy. Forced entry is not consensual attribution, and the script had finally emerged. He could not have power/ knowledge; he could only have symptoms.

Gleacho's behavior continued to become stranger and stranger as winter approached. He had begun to sew moccasins early in the fall but soon had used up all of the moosehide he was able to obtain. When he could no longer obtain moosehide, he began to make moccasins out of other materials. He began to make them out of cloth purchased at the store and then began to tear up clothing for material.[2] He ripped up bedding for material to make moccasins and once cut his wife's dress right off of her back to get cloth to sew. As the fall progressed, he began to make moccasins out of paper. This outgoing and sociable man soon refused to leave his house so he could stay home and sew.

Not only did he incessantly sew his useless creations but the running commentary he delivered to his visitors become a castigation of every women who visited his home for her failure to stay home and work as hard as he was working.[3]

Sewing was one of those activities that was a defining gender task (Sharp 1975: 76–78; 1979: 47). It was the primary skill men touted in unmarried women and one in which a maturing female had to demonstrate her competence before she was considered ready for marriage. Sewing was intricately involved with the patterns of rights and obligations that interlock kin and affines, but it was also a competitive skill that formed an integral part of a woman's reputation among her peers. Men sew as a survival skill, a thing of patching and repairs during periods of isolation. Most are capable of sewing, even of making themselves gloves and mittens, but they do so only under the duress of isolation and at the first opportunity replace any clothing they have sewed with clothing made by a woman.

I was absent from Mission from January 1973 until April 1975, so I had to piece together what had happened after I had returned home. The chain of events, the judgment of the field of meaning upon him, could not be broken. Gleacho's sewing spread to other aspects of women's work, but sewing remained his primary activity. His sewing was an intensification of a single aspect of the female gender role: a caricature of the female gender role. As he

sewed and sewed, creating bags and bags full of paper moccasins, he under-
went a gender role reversal as he became insane and died.

Gleacho was a man formally judged at least five times by Western medicine
or supervised observation during the fall of 1972 to be sane and healthy. His
health was monitored by the nurse until his death, and he had no illnesses or
injuries in the year before he died. Inkoze is dangerous and maleness is a
fragile condition that must be achieved (Sharp 1976, 1988a, 1988b). The
inkoze Gleacho unleashed, the inkoze he demanded of a community that
said he did not have it, followed the script crafted by the social field around
him. In spite of his deliberate attempt to manipulate the social context of
Mission and achieve a desired status within in it, in spite of the rational and
calculating manner in which he attempted to achieve that end, Gleacho was
an embodiment of the symbols and values of his culture and they were the
greater part of him. The power unleashed upon him by the field of meaning
reversed his gender, drove him insane, and killed him in spite of the fact that
he was, in Western terms, a sane and healthy man to the day he died.

The social forces that led to Gleacho's insanity and death illustrate why the
concept of meaning has been developed as it has in this work. The concept of
meaning has been used as a metonym for the unified field of causality that
generates cultural reality. The concept contains aspects of a variety of normally separated concepts ranging from emotion to collective representations.[4] I have gathered these aspects under a single term to stress the unified
action of meaning at all scales of analysis. Meaning acts at the level of individual sensation and perception, proxemics, and posture as well as on emotion,
reasoning, rationality, and speech within the individual human organism.[5] It
controls communication—verbal and nonverbal—between individual human beings. It also determines verbal performances and social interaction at
larger scales of analysis from the passing chance encounter between two
people to formal debate in community-wide discussion. The analogy of a
fractal process remains a fruitful one, for even if we cannot say that the processes are identical at each scale of analysis, they are integrated into a single
causal phenomenon that exerts its power to create and order human existence from the level of the thought of the individual through the mass interaction of society as a whole to the enduring level of myth, stories, values, and
the structured conflict between symbols (see the beginning of chapter 11).

17

EVENT AND MEMORY

Social phenomena, like Schrödinger's cat, are indeterminate (Gribbin 1984: 1–4, 154–63, 203–13, 233–75). The role of meaning in the unified field of causality chartered by inkoze is such that it determines the nature of events. Common sense must stand upon its head, for events are a function of their meaning rather than their meaning being a function of the event.

It is the purpose of this chapter to illustrate that our conventional view— the projection of our folk physics—of events as naturally determinate things, the "that" in the view of events as "that which is connected by time" (Achenbach 1994), does not provide an adequate basis for the interpretation of social phenomena. Showing that something does not exist, let alone a thing so basic to our thought as the concept of an event, is a methodological nightmare.[1] My intent here is simply to illustrate how an event disappears under the conflicting construction of reality. Indeed, that it vanishes so thoroughly that it is a sounder approach to assume that events are created than to presume that events exist and are simply the subject of different interpretations.

The mechanisms by which events are created among the whites of Mission, belonging as they do to another culture and a different field of meaning, are different than are those of the Dene of Mission, but the process is the same in both cultures. The indeterminate experience of social life is made determinate through cultural processes to create an intelligible shared reality.

Memory, which will be taken up again in the next chapter, is one of the major mechanisms through which social beings apprehend and determine meaning. It likewise influences the ordering of indeterminate data into determinate experience. I do not interpret memory as a passive recording of events but as an active social creation. The analogy to a fractal process holds here because memory is both a sociological and an individual process. As I am using it here, the process of constructing memory is a culture-bound process as applicable to creating determinacy in the events of the past as it is to creating determinacy for the events of the future. Both, creating past and future, are aspects of a single process.

The incident—what Western thought would hold to be the event—was a scuffle between a local Dene (Charley) and a teacher following an indoor floor-hockey game held in the school basement during the winter of 1969–70. The Teacher involved in the scuffle pressed charges with the RCMP, and Charley was later tried, convicted, and given a short jail sentence for his part in the event.

The winter of 1969–70 was harsh and very cold.[2] Social, political, and economic conditions were unsettled. The winter caribou migration had not brought the herds close enough to Mission to allow effective hunting on the scale needed to feed a nonmobile community in excess of five hundred souls. Hunger and malnutrition were commonplace and were probably an aggravating factor in the deaths of several people. Food from the store provided a buffer from starvation, but it was very expensive and often of poor quality. Access to store food depended upon a cash income or receiving Rations. The traditional source of winter income, the sale of fur, brought little income into the community. Not only were fur bearers scarce and trapping difficult but fur prices were exceptionally low.

The hardships of that winter were aggravated by the turmoil in Quebec. The federal government's assumption of emergency powers had created unease among the local whites. Some of them feared for Canada's survival as a nation or that it would become a totalitarian state. On top of the anxiety caused by events at the national level, a few of the local whites had fore-knowledge of a series of coming policy changes. One of these changes, knowledge of which was held close to the vest by the white community, was the impending replacement of the retiring Indian agent by a Chipewyan man who had grown up at Discha. They understood this change was the beginning of the transfer of the administration of Mission to its own people. That change would profoundly alter their own positions in the community.

For the Dene the harsh conditions and lack of food and money were aggravated by the uncertainty surrounding the Magic Boy and the first murmurings of Gleacho's challenge to him.

The local white population maintained political and economic control over Mission through its staffing of the institutions that provided police functions, income, or services to the Dene. Locally, the church and store were longstanding enemies vying for control of the Mission population. The economic and social hold of the Hudson's Bay Company manager and the missionaries, locally the traditional agents of white control, had degraded by 1970, but the Hudson's Bay Company and the Roman Catholic mission, along with the public school, had residential agents in the village.[3] Relations between these institutions determined the tenor of Mission's white community and the local implementation of the ideology and rhetoric of white Canada.

The school was then under provincial jurisdiction and did not answer directly to Indian Affairs. The school was the only institution at Mission with a residential staff overtly committed to transforming the social practice of the Native population. It was under the de facto supervision of the local priest and functioned as a parochial school that gave regular religious instruction.

Teaching in an Indian school in the North paid more than did teaching in a regular school farther south in the province. Teachers were often hired with fewer qualifications than were standard for the province (some had only a single year of college). Romantic views of the North and its peoples brought some teachers north, but money was the determining factor for most of them. It was possible to teach a year at Mission and save enough money for two years of college in the south. The Principal would only hire Catholic teachers, and renewal of teaching contracts was at his discretion. Those who lacked a genuine belief in what they were doing rarely lasted more than a year, for the life of a teacher at Mission was isolated—socially and geographically—and often very uncomfortable.

The context of Mission that generated the event that was not an event began with the Principal of the school. He and individuals employed by various other public agencies saw themselves as advocates for the Indian population. The heart of their belief was their presumption that they knew what was best for the Indian population and that what they did was "for their own good." The educators seemed to see their role to be that of arbiters and interpreters of Western culture. It was not enough just to improve the Indians; it was necessary to direct them toward an almost utopian version of Canadian culture that I never actually recall encountering during my life elsewhere in Canada.

The Principal, a brawny man in his mid-thirties, was a gruff and sarcastic practitioner of this liberalism. His view of the Dene was predicated upon his belief in the unquestionable superiority of Catholic-Canadian culture combined with uncertainty about whether any "true Chipewyan culture" remained. He seemed to see his role as that of a secular missionary charged with modernizing a demoralized and decadent Dene into a morally acceptable component of Canadian society. The hallmarks of his success were to be found in the Dene abandonment of their own cultural practices and the adoption of those Western values that led to success in the job market and independence from governmental assistance.

The Principal was a frustrated man. He was neither optimistic about the chances of long-term success at acculturating the Dene nor satisfied that significant short-term gains had been made. One focus of his frustration was Denegothera, whom he saw as a corrupt barrier to change and modernization. Once, while I was standing in the Principal's office, we saw Charley's youngest brother walking up the road to gather wood. This triggered a long discussion about the members of Charley's family, centering on the statement that he "was going to get them." His comments were not fanatical ravings but the frustration of an upright, dedicated, and moral man who had committed most of his adult life to a vision of bettering the lives of others. What is crucial is that the Principal focused his frustration upon particular individuals who became focal metonyms for his moral imagination. Denegothera remained impervious to him, but other Dene were not beyond his reach.

The other side of the forming encounter by proxy was Charley and his siblings. Charley's father was in his eighties, his mother in her sixties. The old man had moved to this area in his early adulthood, long before Mission was founded. He had left his home to escape the aura of disapproval that surrounded him because he had killed a man in a hunting accident in his early teens. He was generally thought of as a "nice old man." In midlife he had married a woman who had moved to Mission either upon her widowhood or to flee a broken marriage.[4] She was now blind but, unlike her husband, had an aggressive personality and a sharp tongue.

The children of their marriage fell into two distinct sets. An elder group of four, two males and two females, were married and established in the community. The younger set of three males and a female were yet unmarried. They ranged in age from their mid-twenties down to seventeen for the daughter. There was an intermediate brother, Jim, then in his late twenties. His younger siblings were not as close to him as they were to each other.

Domestic life for Charley and his siblings was not always peaceful. The perpetual turmoil of their household colored the Chipewyan judgment of them as a kin group. Although this judgment was not positive, neither was it overly negative. The idiosyncratic personalities of the siblings and their lack of cohesiveness in most contexts led the community to judge them as individuals rather than as an entity.

The second eldest male was the best liked and the most economically successful of the brothers. Following the common northern pattern of working away from home until he came to miss his kin and village life too much, he had just returned to Mission after quitting his job at a mine. The daughter held a marginal position at Mission. Economic opportunities for males who were articulate in English were limited, but for women they were virtually nonexistent. One of the few alternatives to a traditional life available to a female involved exploiting her sexuality, preferably with transient whites. Her lifestyle was not regarded favorably, and she was continually accused of theft and troublemaking.[5]

Charley was the eldest. Among the whites he was already burdened by a reputation as a troublemaker—a reputation that had begun when he beat up an RCMP constable in a fistfight. In the Chipewyan community his reputation, based largely upon his hunting and trapping skills, was that of a young but promising traditional man. Naturally quick, compact, and extremely strong, he was by far the best fighter at Mission. One on one, no one in the village was able to defeat him. The Chipewyan value strength and endurance more than they value fighting ability, and they demand that individuals who possess it exercise effective control over it. Charley's peerless fighting ability—an intensification of a traditional virtue—was a potential problem in an egalitarian society lacking formal means of social control. Charley was marked among the Chipewyan not because of his deficiencies but because of the potential excess of some of his traditional virtues.

Charley and his siblings were among the brightest individuals in the community and had absorbed all that the local educational system had to offer them. These brothers were competent in both cultures and were capable of obtaining work almost at will, either at Mission or away from it. In spite of their skills, Charley and his brothers remained Dene in their outlook on life, their work histories, and in their personal lives. Charley remained a traditional man, happiest when engaged in bush life. The middle brother refused to adopt the white approach to economic values and leave the village permanently. The youngest showed no sign of amounting to anything. From the standpoint of the educators, these men and their sister made a mockery of their intent to "better the Indian" and make them like whites.

These young men were largely indifferent to village politics, but they were seen by the Principal as supporters of Denegothera. In the eyes of the Principal this again marked them as an enemy of the educators' efforts and goals.

At the best of times Mission was lacking in recreational facilities, but in midwinter they were almost nonexistent. Once a week the school opened its basement gym for the teenagers and young adults to play an indoor version of hockey. Though the game used lightweight pucks and sticks so that the puck had to be pushed and was difficult to maneuver, it was popular.

February is intensely cold and hard, a time of poor hunting, poor fishing, and deep snow. In the absence of caribou a significant portion of the village's fresh food came from fishnets set toward the north end of Mission Lake some ten to fifteen miles away from the village. The nets had been yielding poorly, and some of the men of Mission suspected that someone had been pilfering them. These suspicions seemed to be confirmed when an emptied net was found pulled out onto the ice and left to become a frozen mess. Leaving the net out of the water was seen as motivated by laziness or maliciousness rather than by need.

Jim had attached himself to the household of a girlfriend's father. He had been regularly using this man's dog team to check his nets for him and had been returning with consistently good catches. The damaged net belonged to one of a loose alliance of cousins whose nets were near the same part of the lake. They suspected that Jim was the thief and were neither subtle nor secretive about their suspicion.

The trouble at the hockey game began when Joshua, a cousin of the man whose net had been left on the ice, got into a scuffle with Charley's youngest brother over some minor incident in the game. All the brothers quickly converged upon him and interposed themselves between him and Joshua. The signal was clear: they wanted no fight, but if there was to be one, it would involve all of them. He was hustled off the floor and left to stand beside his team's goal. The Principal, who had tried to stand between the two groups, was shouting, "There will be no fight. If there is a fight all floor hockey will end right here."

Charley came up to his youngest brother and took the hockey stick out of his hand. No words were exchanged. The middle brother, who had been very aggressive during the incident, returned to his spot on the sidelines, as did Jim. The game resumed and continued without incident. During the game, Joshua was replaced by Luther, the best fighter present from the other kin set. One of Joshua's distant relations, who professed not to be afraid of Charley, also joined the game.

The Principal was aware of the tension over the fishnets. He noted these substitutions, saw the opposition between the loosely bounded kin sets, and discussed the substitution of each man with me in terms of his ability to stand up to Charley in the brawl he thought was coming.

The next game, which was to be for the girls of the village, never got going. The residual tension kept so many of the girls from playing that younger boys had to fill in to make up the two teams. As the game progressed, older boys and young men replaced the girls and the younger boys until it resembled the previous game. Luther was a better player than Charley and outclassed him in the game. Their matchup became rather physical, and Luther did not back down from Charley. Eventually, after Charley had begun to play dirty, Luther took a roundhouse swing at his head with his hockey stick. The game stopped dead and the building emptied in anticipation of a fight. The Principal, after hollering that there would be no more hockey, remained inside with the priest and the Teacher to put away the equipment.

A short time later, after a female spectator entered the gym with word that there was a fight outside, the Teacher decided the crowd watching the scuffle between Charley and Luther might break the windows and went outside to disperse it.[6] He targeted Charley as the source of the trouble and ordered him off the grounds. Charley declared, "I'm not a dog that you can tell me what to do." There was a brief scuffle between him and the Teacher, after which the crowd dispersed.

The RCMP were later notified, and the Teacher filed a charge of assault against Charley. At his preliminary hearing Charley was sent to a provincial mental hospital for thirty days of psychiatric evaluation.

It is tempting to view this situation solely as a rational exercise of power by two self-interested men exploiting a chance opportunity. The data are compatible with such an interpretation, but more subtle factors cast doubt on the adequacy of this perspective. At the most rational level, the Principal and the Teacher perceived Charley as an impediment to their mission as educators and as a threat to their positions as advocates for the Dene, but these two men were cultural beings, and within the context and values of their culture they were honorable men. As cultural beings they believed in truth, facts, honor, and rationality. They were fully aware that one consequence of their decision to bring charges against Charley would be a trial and that at a trial their testimony—sworn under oath in a public ritual—would be subject to cross-examination. The Teacher and the Principal shared a common folk belief that the court was concerned with facts (events) rather than with interpretation (meaning) and that it would exercise its particular methods of truth gathering to uncover the facts. Their adherence to this folk belief buttressed their belief in the sanctity of facts in their own lives. In the culture they had invented for themselves (Wagner 1981: 10), manipulation of the facts was intolerable.

Any deeper probing of their actions from a realist self-interest perspective must be able to explain the mechanisms that determined their actions. At the very least, it must explain the way in which the two men responded to Charley as a symbol, the role that emotion played in their actions, and the extent to which their commitment to their moral visions led them to take actions that the "facts" seem not to warrant (Sharp 1987; 1988a: 101–18). Viewing them simply as rational beings exploiting an opportunity provides no way to negotiate the paradox in their cultural values that would lead honest men to lie and risk perjury charges. The only possible avenue of explanation such an approach leaves open is to drop from a social level of explanation to the individual level of explanation and seek within each of them, after the fact, a weakness or flaw in their character or personality that would allow one culturally determined set of factors to overpower others held with equal conviction (e.g., emotion over reason). This is not explanation; it is begging the question.

Between the fight and the decision to press charges, the Principal and the Teacher discussed the incident. In those discussions several different facts emerged: the only contact between Charley and the Teacher came when Charley kicked at the Teacher and hit him on the coat. The Teacher told this with humor and presented it as a marker of Charley's ineptness. The Teacher linked this ineptness of Charley's to an earlier incident when, upon squaring off with the Teacher to shout at him, he began to pull off his winter coat.

Doing this immobilized his arms and made him a sitting duck. The Teacher noted that had he wished to fight Charley; that would have been the point at which he would have attacked as Charley's own ineptness had made him temporarily helpless. Basically, the Teacher saw the event as somewhat humorous because it was all noise and ineffectiveness.

Neither of these men knew much about Canadian law, but like most of us, they carried within themselves strong ideas about what the law was supposed to be and how it was supposed to work. The Principal's reactions to the event were quite different from the Teacher's reaction to it. Having heard that Charley had called him a son-of-a-bitch as he was leaving, the Principal declared that under the "laws of Canada" being called a son-of-a-bitch was the only phrase in the English language that constituted assault and that striking someone who called you a son-of-a-bitch was self-defense and not subject to charges. The Principal also took the position that under Canadian law the clothing a person was wearing was a part of that person so that striking a person's clothing was the same as striking the body.

Had the Teacher and Principal known that the court would not question their version of the event, things might have unfolded differently, but as it was, the concern that the court would inquire into the specificity of the event—their testimony—shaped their decision to press charges, shaped their testimony, and, ultimately, shaped the nature of the event itself.

The Principal declared that if the Teacher would not press charges, he would do so himself. The coercive forces acting on the Teacher are fairly obvious. The Principal controlled his job evaluation, the remainder of his term at the school, and the renewal of his position, but what he exerted over the Teacher was influence rather than power. The Principal relied upon the Teacher as his second and needed his support in order to be effective in controlling the school and maintaining his own position. He was not able to direct the Teacher to see things as he did, and neither of them was inclined to lie. They were friends and close confidants, however, and what they did do was talk extensively about the situation and the event.

The Teacher shared the Principal's basic moral vision regarding education and the improvement of Dene lives, but his own interests and ambitions ran toward politics. Maintaining his personal reputation and avoiding scandal were important to him.

All through that weekend the two men talked about the fight and the interpretation of the event. The Principal held out for charging Charley with assault. He supported this position in terms of the purpose of the school and its role in changing Mission Dene culture to more closely conform to that of the white culture the educators represented. He worried about the role of the school and the safety and authority of the educators within the community if the fight went unchallenged. He worried about Denegothera's role in blocking change at Mission. He worried about their own status if they allowed the fight to go unchallenged.

The Teacher thought the whole issue risked becoming overblown and wanted to just forget the whole thing. After all, he had not hit anyone and had not been hit by anyone. No real damage had occurred and no one was hurt.

If we conduct the examination of their behavior on the basis of a rational self-interest model of behavior, the conflict in their cultural values will force upon us a paradox that is sociologically unresolvable. The concept of rationality has received substantial scholarly criticism (Overing 1985), with rationality itself being recognized as a cultural form rather than a fundamental characteristic of human thought. In this light, the behavior of the Teacher and the Principal is more explicable if it is seen as an exercise in the "aesthetics of emotion" (Parkin 1985: 140). Shifting the analytical focus from the rational to the emotional is, however, insufficient.

The crux of the issue is the point at which a transition in explanation is made from the social level to the individual level (Sharp 1986: 268–69; 1987: 226–27, 233). One of the reasons that the concept of meaning has been developed the way it has in this work is to seek a way to bridge this problem by recognizing that meaning is socially created but that it works at both the individual and the social levels. These two men were seeking the meaning of an event—which one of them had not witnessed—in order to bring it into their shared reality as a determined phenomenon.

The idea of truth is a cultural construct whose nature is determined by the methods and evidence that are chosen to establish it. Social phenomena truly are indeterminate, but the customary assumption behind their analysis is that their indeterminacy results from inadequate data or a lack of observational rigor. Social beings exist not in a world of events but in a world of meaning. Within the realm of meaning, what we call events under our mechanical model of reality are available, instantly and without regard to temporal sequence, for modification of their property of meaning. The

Teacher and the Principal were not coldly calculating embodiments of rational self-interest in deciding to press charges against Charley. They did not plan a future course of action but interpreted the meaning of the events. In so doing, they modified those events by negotiating a memory of them that was in conformity with their meaning.

All weekend the two men talked, and as they talked the passion and certainty of the Principal's belief—as well as his authoritarian assertion of the nature of Canadian law—began to tell upon both of them. Neither man lied and neither man changed his basic beliefs about the incident, but their understanding of the meaning of the details of the event began to shift. The Principal and the Teacher discussed the fight again and again, arguing out its meaning. Details—events—were not changed to create a congruence between them and emotion and moral vision; instead the meaning of those events was changed. Once their meaning had been negotiated, the Principal's and Teacher's perception and representation of the "events" unknowingly shifted to strengthen and preserve the congruence of the created memory.

To them, the critical issue was the nature of Charley's contact with the Teacher. The Teacher initially said that Charley's blow had only struck his coat, and he dismissed it as a measure of Charley's ineptness. As long as Charley had merely kicked the Teacher's coat there was no fight. The Principal had not seen it that way, pointing out that his clothing was part of his person and that therefore the blow was an assault on his person. As the Teacher came to believe the Principal's assertion that his clothing was part of his person, the event—the fight—came into existence. With that change in the meaning of his clothing, from something external to his person to an integral part of his person, came a change in the nature of the contact. In the vernacular, the kick in the coat became a "kick in the balls" (later modified into a "kick in the crotch" to assuage the delicacy of the court).

I spoke to these men before the fight, after the fight, over the weekend, before the court testimony, after the testimony, and two years after the testimony when I happened to pass the Teacher at the airport. As time passed each man became more firm in his memory of what had happened at the time of the event. The memory had become reality.

Their argument over detail and meaning was intended not to sort out a sequence of events but to create a conformity between the rational mode of verbal or analytical life and the emotional state consequent upon their moral vision embodied in their shared status as cultural beings who were liberal and advocates for the Chipewyan. Their moral vision in this situation is essentially devoid of a fixed agenda or content. It has meaning and is therefore an emotional state with which the events of experience must be brought into harmony. Reality is not a perception. It is a creation in which rational thought and action are but one means of creation. In Marshall Sahlins's terms, the "cultural concepts engage the real world" of contingency in conformity with the logic of emotion through the construction of a memory (Sahlins 1985: 45, 145). The cultural now, the cultural past, and their consequent future were created by the allocation of meaning through the construction of a shared memory.

By the following Monday, when the RCMP were notified and a charge was filed against Charley, the memories of the event held by the Principal and the Teacher had aligned with the meaning of the event. Each thoroughly believed in, and the Teacher clearly remembered, the impact of Charley's kick in the balls.

One result of recognizing the indeterminacy of social phenomena is the loss of separation between events and meaning presupposed by the cultural assertion of a now. As my fieldnotes cannot be privileged as objective data (compared to verbal recollections) as they could under a deterministic metaphor of science, neither can my memory be so privileged. I saw and vividly remember the blow Luther aimed at Charley's head during the fight. I remember as vividly the blow Charley directed toward the Teacher, even though I stayed inside the school and never saw it. As writing (and reading) this is but a part of the cultural process of allocating meaning, so that process of allocating meaning continued through the trial and the production of the trial transcript.

That document is no more an objective repository of reality than are the other sources. Like them, it is but an aspect of meaning intelligible largely through its distributional position (Foucault 1974: 3–65). The concern of the Teacher and the Principal that their account of the events would be subject to cross-examination and verification in a truth-gathering ritual proved unfounded. The court accepted without examination the meaning of the events given by the Principal and the Teacher, thereby accepting their account of the event itself. The court's concern was with motivation and the identity of the accused as well as the enforcement of its own procedures.[7]

THE COURT: This is the trial ex parte in the absence of the accused, who is charged that on the 8th of February 1970 at [Mission] in the Province of [name], he did unlawfully assault [Teacher] by striking him in the crotch with his foot contrary to Section 3231 (1) of the Code. The Crown is proceeding by summary conviction. A plea of "not guilty" was entered by the accused on the 16th of March and the matter was adjourned to this date for trial. The accused released on Recognizance to appear; he is not present and the Court orders that the trial be held in his absence ex parte . . .

Charley was unconcernedly waiting at Mission for the RCMP to pick him up and bring him to the trial.[8] I was arranging the transport of another man facing trial at the same court session and had asked him earlier that day if he needed a ride. He assured me that he did not. The RCMP had told him that they would come and get him in time for his trial.

[Teacher] Sworn, states:
[RCMP Officer]—examining:
RCMP:
Q. I call your attention to the 8th of February 1970 and would ask that you tell the Court in your own words anything pertaining to the matter that is just before the Court.
A. Yes, it was a Sunday, Sunday evening and there was the custom that we have a hockey night for the adults, floor hockey, indoor floor hockey for the adults at [Mission], held in the recreation area of the school and during the game Mr. [Charley] was quite—he was provoking one of the other players quite often and finally . . .
Q. Can you be more elaborate, in what way was he provoking the other player?
A. Elbowing and just using a stick, interference and so on like that.
Q. Just continue then.
A. And finally, Mr. [Luther] I believe his name was, lost his temper and he swung this stick, it was a wooden stick and he swung it at Mr. [Charley's] head and he missed, it was above his head, and immediately after that a scuffle erupted which the Principal broke up by saying that if there was any fighting the hockey would be called off and there would be no more hockey in the school—or pardon me—before

that scuffle had erupted in the corridor the Principal had given warning that if there was any more scuffles hockey would be called off; at the time when the stick was swung he did call the hockey off and sent everyone outside. Immediate, as soon as the hockey was called off I noticed that the—that everyone left very quickly and it was obvious to me that there was going to be some excitement outside, nevertheless I stayed down in the basement and the Principal [name] and Father [name] remained in the basement as well as a couple of local people. Finally one lady was standing looking out the window and I asked Father [name] to ask her what was going on and so Father asked . . .

At this point the court, through the arresting RCMP corporal, who was acting as prosecutor, intervened to assert the primacy of its procedure for truth determining. Once this had been impressed upon the witness, the court was satisfied and made no attempt to consider the validity of the witness's statements.

Q. Mr. [Teacher,] just confine your evidence to what you yourself did, not what someone else said.
A. And then a girl came in and said . . .
Q. Not what she said; a girl came in—what did you do as a result?
A. She came in and told me that there was fighting on the steps outside and they might break the window, if we come out and stop the fight.
Q. The point is . . .
THE COURT: You went outside?
A. Yes, I went outside.
Q. The woman comes in and it is irrelevant what she says to you. What did you do as a result of what she said to you, you went outside, right?
A. I went outside.
Q. This is what I mean by confining yourself to what you did?
A. I went outside, they were fighting on the step and tried to stop it.
Q. Who was fighting?

In this brief statement emerged the legal description of the event as well as the acceptance of the event by the court.

A. [Charley] and Mr. [Luther] and I tried to stop it, and just kept on, more of a scuffle, they moved over to a different corner of the building, and I put my hand on Mr. [Charley] to tell him to stop fighting and while I did this he, one of his feet, he reached around and I don't know which foot the right or the left, brought it up and a back sort of kick and kicked me in the crotch, and after that the Principal came out and the crowd was sent home and that was the end, a few words exchanging between Mr. [Charley] and myself and the Principal.

Q. Mr. [Teacher,] returning back to the point where you left the building as a result of this lady coming in; can you tell the Court why you concerned yourself to go out?

A. Well they were fighting on the school property and as I said there was a danger of some destruction to the property, to the windows, and generally creating a disturbance on the school property.

The representation of events that became the legal version of the events reflects the created memory negotiated between the Teacher and the Principal. The court accepted without question that Charley should be seen as the source of the disturbance. The issue of the extenuating circumstance of the blow aimed at Charley's head is not considered.[9]

According to the Teacher's testimony, he grabbed Charley from behind in the middle of a fight. The fight itself becomes not a face-to-face confrontation but a kick backward by a man grabbed from behind. Perhaps a reasonable man should not be fighting, but it is hard to see how one can be faulted for lashing out to protect himself when he is seized from behind during a fight.

I interpret the Teacher's testimony as an honest but uncertain attempt to hold to the memory created by himself and the Principal. Caught between the ritual formality of the law, the Principal, and his own thoughts of a political future, the Teacher found himself in an ambiguous position. His own moral vision must have differed somewhat from that of the Principal. His commitment was different, the aesthetics of his emotion led in a different direction, and he must have had to work harder to generate conformity between memory and a rational ordering of the created reality. Two years later, when I saw the Teacher in passing at the airport and asked him about his statement that his coat was hit rather than his person, he angrily said that I was accusing him of perjury. Wherever the blow landed, if there was a blow, his memory of the event and his assurance as to its nature increased as it receded further into memory.

If the memory the Teacher and the Principal had constructed led the Teacher into ambiguity, the Principal had no such problem. His testimony is firm, heavy in motivation and judgment. In his certainty, in contrast to the difficulty the Teacher encountered with repeating the statements of others, he was given considerable latitude for interpretation.

[Principal], Sworn, states:
[RCMP Officer]—examining:
Q. Mr. [Principal] you have heard the evidence of the previous witness. I think in the interests of brevity if you could contain your evidence at the point where Mr. [Teacher] states you first took action and continue from there, against Mr. [Charley]. Your [sic] are acquainted with Mr. [Charley] are you not?
A. Yes I am.
Q. Mr. [Charley]?
A. I'd like to preclude my testimony with some remarks . . .

The "precluded" (a Freudian slip?) testimony was to have been an assertion of meaning, a rehearsed diatribe against Charley and his disruptive effects upon the community and the mission of the school.[10] The court responded with a strong assertion of its procedure regarding evidence and then promptly accepted the Principal's interpretation without comment or question.

THE COURT: You will contain yourself to the evidence; the remarks are not evidence.
A. During the course of the game it was evident to all the players and spectators that Mr. [Charley] was conducting himself in a very aggressive fashion and at one juncture he provoked a fight and this was stopped by Mr. [Teacher] and myself who told him and the other people involved that if the fight didn't stop immediately the game would be stopped. He continued in a very surly and aggressive manner [and] antagonized all the players, until he was delivered a warning blow which didn't come close to hitting him by Mr. [Luther]. At this juncture he told (Luther) to come outside and the two of them left. I

saw that there was going to be a fight so I said if there was a fight there would never be any more hockey and Mr. [Charley] replied that he didn't care. Mr. [Teacher] and I busied ourselves in gathering up the hockey equipment and a few minutes later Mr. [Teacher] went outside and a few minutes after that I also went outside and when I went outside I saw Mr. [Charley] had Mr. [Teacher] by the jacket and this was after Mr. [Teacher] was ostensibly struck by Mr. [Charley], and Mr. [Charley] made a number of threatening remarks to Mr. [Teacher] and myself and both of us asked him to leave the property and he refused to do this and we asked him repeatedly and told him that this would be a matter for the police to look into and he replied that he didn't care and he then threatened me, said that he had never struck me before but that he would, but at that juncture he decided to leave . . .

The rest of the trial was rapid and, like the testimony not presented, centered on the identification of Charley as the person in question.

[RCMP Officer]: Is Mr. [Luther] in the Court room?
THE COURT: I don't need him. I will call you as a witness.
[RCMP Officer]: Your Honour I would like to enter in evidence—if you recall on the 16th February you made an Order to have Mr. [Charley] mentally examined, I would like to enter as an exhibit the results of that examination.
THE COURT: Thank you. I find the accused guilty as charged.

After some jocular negotiation, in which the RCMP officer tried to have Charley incarcerated for more than ninety days, which would mean sending him outside to prison, Charley was sentenced to thirty days in the local common jail.[11]

This situation is reminiscent of what Carlo Ginzburg has described as "this discrepancy, this gap between the image underlying the interrogations of the judges and the actual testimony" (Ginzburg 1985: xviii). This "gap" existed between the court and the white laymen as well as between the court and the Chipewyan. The court was as little interested in the events themselves as it was in determining the truth of those events.

This process of trial closed the issue of the nature of the event in the white field of meaning. The created memory of the Teacher and the Principal had become the reality of the event. There are other aspects to the event (particularly Charley's role as a symbol) yet to be considered, but that the event—the fight resulting in a kick in the crotch—never happened was no longer relevant.

While the white community wrestled with the meaning of the scuffle, the Dene community had its own concerns and attempted to determine its meaning. Because the Dene were Dene rather than white, their search for meaning took up different issues. The cultural ordering of reality generated by the Dene was such that the events in their world were not the same as those in the white world.

The most conspicuous difference between the white and Dene views was that the Dene did not give a damn about the "fight." I heard a few comments from schoolchildren, young boys at the age where they were most worried about their own future size and strength and had the adolescent Chipewyan fascination with fighting. A few "Charley hit a teacher" or "Charley fight teacher" and even a "Teacher and Charley fight," but I heard nothing from the adults of the community. The trial and Charley's jail sentence were of more concern, the former for scandal, the latter as deprivation for the family during Charley's jail term. In Western terms, there were different events in the two cultures.

For the Principal and his educators, Charley and his kin symbolized a failure to transform and acculturate the Chipewyan. The comparable feeling among the Dene would have been that they stood for the questionable value of formal education. The Chipewyan of Mission believe in formal education, and many of their hopes are pinned to the delivery of an effective education to their children. The failure of Charley and his siblings to conform to white hopes and expectations was paralleled by their failure to conform to Chipewyan hopes and expectations. Their success in absorbing what education had to offer but without fitting in and becoming competent adult members of the community concerned the Chipewyan, although they did not discuss it as such or make it an issue of public notice.

The Chipewyan, from the publication of Samuel Hearne's eighteenth-century journal, have had, in the vernacular, "a bad press" (Koolage 1975). The one constant endearing virtue attributed to them by whites has been their honesty.[12] The repetitive accusations of dishonesty directed at Jim and his sister were significant markers of the discomfort the Dene community felt about all of them. If the court and the Principal were able to disregard the context of the theft from the fishnets, the Dene community was not prepared to do so. The allegation that fish had been stolen and the willingness to support that allegation through violence, no matter how moderate that violence, was the community's judgment upon them as social beings.

The Dene, like the court, were also interested in questions of identity. The nature of the Chipewyan construction of identity is unexamined in the literature, but it differs radically from that utilized by the court. Where the court was interested in specificity and the differentiation of persons, the Chipewyan were interested in the construction of a history and the placement of the individual within a social and moral context. The key issue in the Dene community was Charley's fighting ability and his ability to control himself. Neither the scuffle nor Charley's court conviction had a great impact upon his reputation among the Dene, but the psychiatric examination did. His being sent for psychiatric examination resolved the issue of control generated by his extraordinary fighting ability and strength. Instead of being a repository of traditional virtues to excess, there was now the hidden implication that he might be out of control and possibly crazy.

The intracultural situation is instructive. Charley's role as a symbol in the rest of the white community was best expressed by the words of a young Hudson's Bay Company clerk who said, "They have got to learn that there is a law here now." White folklore about Charley's aggressiveness and strength increased to the point that the RCMP appropriated it as a symbol. Incoming RCMP constables found their manhood questioned by their peers and others in the white community until they had fought him, with Charley always being charged with something whatever the circumstances of the encounter. It reached the point that once, after Charley had drunk too much and returned home to sleep it off, the RCMP initiated a new constable by entering Charley's house without warning and having the new man pull Charley from a sound sleep in his own bed. When Charley, still in a stupor, knocked him down, he was arrested, tried, and convicted for resisting arrest.

Charley's conviction for assault on the Teacher was his third one in less than three years and a benchmark in labeling him a habitual offender. Subsequent offenses (more were to occur, as he was marked by the white community) carried longer and longer sentences. By 1990, nearly half of his adult life had been spent in prison.[13]

At the time of Charley's conviction, jail time was stigmatized by the Chipewyan (Goffman 1963). Charley's conviction was one of many even less justified that changed the nature of the stigma the Chipewyan attached to jail time. While it has not ceased to be stigmatized, the routineness and the capriciousness with which incarceration occurs has forced the Dene to shift their concern from incarceration per se to the grounds for incarceration.

As the stigma upon Charley increased through the early 1980s and the sanctions of Canadian law became greater, he was seen more and more by the local whites both as a symbol of Chipewyan inability to cope for themselves and as a justification for the whites' continued presence and control. The assertion of control manifested through the growing RCMP presence in Mission produced many more arrests, convictions, fines, and incarcerations. It was local white folklore that RCMP assigned to this area were either promising young men sent for seasoning or older men being given one last chance before incurring a permanent denial of promotion. Either way, the only avenue to success in the RCMP was an increased arrest and conviction rate. Watching the process on the ground, field trip after field trip, left me with the impression that each Mountie sought more and more obscure laws to enforce in order to increase the arrest record during his tenure. From the conviction of 1970 on, arresting Charley was always a safe bet for a conviction.

The event, the fight that never was, was lost within the complex of concerns and meaning in the white field of meaning. It was replaced by an event constructed through a negotiated memory of its meaning. This process is a general human process brought on by the nature of being a verbal social being. The meaning of an event determines the memory of the event, which determines the nature of the event itself. An event exists only as a function of the means by which it is measured, which means that, in the conventional usage of the word, there is no such thing as an event.

EPILOGUE

By the time I returned to the field in 1972, the events of 1970 had lost most of their import. The white community had undergone an almost complete turnover in personnel. All the teachers had gone. The Teacher had found his entry into the political arena, and the Principal had moved on to a larger school. All of the RCMP and Hudson's Bay Company people were gone. Even the priest had moved upward in the church hierarchy and been reassigned. From the memory the Principal and the Teacher had labored so hard to create, all that remained was an erratic symbol who was a certain conviction, a man fated to pay for that memory and the moral vision that created it. Ironically, it was Charley who was fated to die a hero's death. On one of his rare periods out of jail in the early 1990s, Charley came to visit his family at Mission. While he was down by the store, two children fell into Mission Lake from the boat in which they were playing. Charley ran out on the dock and dove into the cold water of the lake to try to rescue them. The children, who could not swim, panicked. When Charley reached them, they attempted to climb on top of him. All were drowned.

18

FUTURE MEMORY

"Loon IV" (chapter 14) showed that the meaning of what happens in the present is sometimes left undetermined until the future has come to be. Meaning creates events while time, in a reality engendered by inkoze, is often better likened to place than to a flow. This aspect of time being like place also occurs in ordinary social life. Here I wish to extend these arguments by showing how, through the agencies of emotion and memory, the future can determine the present.

In April 1975 I accompanied Paul and May to South Lake for the spring caribou hunt. Our coming to South Lake was prompted by the presence of a fly-in fish camp that had promised the brothers summer work as fishing guides. In his youth Wellington had adopted the lake as a trapping area. He had camped there for the past few winters. Paul and May had spent the previous fall with him there instead of at their more usual haunts on Foxholm Lake or Adeker Lake. George had joined them late in the fall but had continued to set his traps to the north around Foxholm Lake. Both George and Wellington had their families with them, and all of us planned to stay until Christmas.

Relations between Wellington and George had become increasingly strained since George had married a few years before. Things were now approaching a crisis point. The problem between them was created by conflict between the role of birth order among siblings and Chipewyan egalitarianism (Sharp 1979: 10–19; 1988a: 35–37).[1] Among the determinedly egalitarian Mission Dene, social independence depends upon establishing a household capable of functioning independently as a subsistence unit

(Sharp 1977). Both men now headed families, but Wellington had been married long enough to have established his independence.[2] George was still striving to establish his.

The milieu of our lives there was one in which George and Wellington were each hoping that others might choose to stay with them. If Wellington had succeeded, he might have found himself exercising the influence and leadership over the extended family that his father was slowly losing because the early stages of emphysema and a recent heart attack had lessened his strength and endurance. Early in our stay George's perception of the social situation was disturbed by several weeks of bad luck in hunting during which he was unable to lay in a supply of caribou meat. Coming just at the time he was determined to demonstrate his ability to support his family without outside help, he worried that he had become offensive to animal/persons other than caribou and had lost his ability to hunt or trap.

George's continued association with his parents did not pose a threat to his attempt to establish an independent social identity because of his father's failing health. Staying with them might even have been seen as a virtuous act as it would allow his parents to continue to maintain a separate bush household. Coming to South Lake did threaten his fragile independence, however. Not only was his brother there, but Wellington's brothers-in-law were to join him there later in the year. George's problem stemmed from the mantle of leadership over the whole group falling upon Wellington if enough people came to aggregate around him. Younger brothers are supposed to respect and listen to their elder brothers (Sharp 1975, 1977, 1979), so too great an association with Wellington would lead the Mission community to see him as subordinate to his brother.

One of the consequences of conflict between symbols and values, as was the case with canid gender symbols, is that they sometimes create situations for which there is no satisfying outcome. The most desired outcome was for all of the extended family to live together in harmony. Chipewyan decision making is a lengthy process in which there is almost interminable discussion and consideration of all points of view. When an issue this significant to the lives of an extended family is under consideration, achieving an outcome can take seasons if not years. The People consider options and alternatives but do not spell out possible consequences or make predictions. They instead advance possible courses of action and leave the consequences of those actions to be thought about and decided upon by those engaged in the discussions. During these times of discussion and consideration of alternatives the issue at the heart of the matter is rarely foregrounded and may never surface directly. This creates an ambience in which the issues under discussion are a constant backdrop against which other relevant actions and ideas can be compared. The process through which The People search for and identify the best solution is low-key, subtle, and persuasive.

Wellington was making no overt attempt to gain control over the camp or to subordinate his younger brother. The situation was analogous to that when Gleacho's peers came to visit him during his moccasin-sewing phase in 1972. The issue hung inescapably over the camp and dominated relationships within it. The topic itself was never discussed. Nevertheless, every adult understood the situation.

Decisions had to be made about where to spend the fall hunting season, and those decisions would permanently redefine relationships among people in camp. As Chipewyan, it was in their nature to pursue their own vision of how things should be through the conduct of their own lives. They did not seek to control each other or determine how others were to behave, but that shared vision of all of them living together in harmony carried a very different cost for each of them. It was in conflict with other values and the need of each constituent household for autonomy. In effect, each adult in the camp had a shared vision of how life should be lived and of how they should relate to each other as kin. This vision of how things should be was in conflict with their visions of their individual positions within their family and the community at large.

Any time of structured liminality has built into it the risk of an adverse outcome. This time in their lives was a time of stress and uncertainty when nothing was quite what it seemed to be. This showed in how they related to each other even before the first caribou came. They were not visiting among themselves as freely as was normal and there was less cooperation than I had seen in previous years. They were not as readily doing for each other the small things that make bush life less taxing. Food for individual meals normally circulates among families (along with condiments, baking ingredients, utensils, sugar, tea, and all the small things that can be in short supply or temporarily unavailable) through the daily visits the women make to each other. Before meat began to flow into camp from the first successful hunts, there was a conspicuous restriction in the flow of food from household to household. The visits between the women, and the food exchanges that went with them, were so constrained that at times some households would be out of meat while others had a surplus. The restriction of this flow of food through the reduction in ordinary socialization meant people sometimes had to ask for meat—a significant indicator of tension within a camp—or do without.

The tension also showed in how George and Wellington acted toward each other. Relations between them were far more competitive than in past years. In early May we began to prepare to move from the winter cabins (off the east side of South Lake) to tents on its west side. We had taken my snowmobile and a toboggan out to inspect the site where we planned to put the tents. Several miles west of where we were crossing, we saw caribou standing on the ice just off shore. We immediately turned and headed toward them as fast as the heavily laden snowmobile would go.

The caribou stood and watched a while before they turned and ran a short ways into the forest. Wellington drove the snowmobile headlong into the willow brush that lined the shore. Both he and George leapt from the vehicle and tore into the bush at a dead run. Wellington, taller and stronger than George, ran more quickly. As soon as he saw the caribou he shot four of them. George saw them but did not shoot even though he could have killed some of them (Sharp 1988a: 55–56).

If all had been well between them, they would have cooperated by entering the bush line abreast and moving toward the caribou at a fast walk. The idea is for the hunters to come up on the caribou in such a way that they could shoot those leading the escape, which would turn the rest back in the other direction. The hunters then should have shot at those leading the escape in the new direction, thus turning them back to their original direction. Doing this would keep the caribou running back and forth in front of them, creating the opportunity to kill as many as possible.

Instead of cooperation, their pursuit became a footrace, which Wellington ended by shooting at the caribou as soon as he saw them. George responded to his brother's actions by refusing to cooperate and not shooting at all.

This hunt, such an apparently simple incident expressing pique between the brothers, illustrates how, even in ordinary life, time can act as place.

In the course of daily life, men are drawn into the bush to accomplish the various tasks necessary to feed a camp. They often enter the bush in pairs or in groups, but in this vast land each man has to go off alone for extended periods of time. In Dene bush life, people—particularly men—are routinely separated from each other for hours or days at a time. Their daily activities can scatter them over hundreds of square miles. Unlike in the village, where nearly every action is observed, much of their time, again especially so for men, is spent out of the sight or hearing of other Dene. What happens to them during this part of their lives is beyond the direct experience of anyone but themselves.

A number of years ago Basil Sansom developed the concept of the "happening" in his superb book, *The Camp at Wallaby Cross* (1980). One of his concerns in that book was the manner in which the Australian Aborigines he was working among created a public verbal narrative voiced as a running commentary in accompaniment to social events while they were in the process of occurring. This pattern of public narration could accompany any event that broke the calm of the camp, even ones as pedestrian as a scuffle or a domestic argument. Sansom defined the concept of a happening as standing "for the form that people bring to the flow of social action to shape it whenever they either present or represent events. Each happening has a typical, almost a classic form, and action that is worth noting or worth gracing with one's own participation is action that is shaped to accord with sets of culturally provided rules that govern proper performance" (Sansom 1980: 3).

The problem that Sansom addressed in his analysis of events among the Aborigines was an extremely difficult and complex one, for he realized that these verbal performances did not just reflect the events but actually shaped and determined them. Those verbal accounts are a form of knowledge that ordered events and integrated them into the cultural context of Aborigine life. Each event was narrated by an individual whose right of narration was determined by a series of statuses and kin relationships with the individuals involved in the event. The knowledge generated by those narrations is public and was generated in a public performance before the audience of the community or a segment of the community, an audience whose assent to the narration was a determining part of its power to bring order to the confusion of the raw events. Once the narrative had been generated, it was—as knowledge—a possession whose telling could be performed only by individuals vested with the right of its narration.

What is at issue in Sansom's analysis are two things applicable to all the Mission Dene and the behavior of Wellington and George during this phase of their conflict, specifically, to their hunt for the caribou. Sansom's insight was that events themselves are ordered by the verbal narrative created simultaneously with the events. The events are a social process whose nature—indeed, whose occurrence—is determined through the process of ascribing meaning to them by the narrator and the consent to that ascribed meaning by the social body acting as audience to the narration. Once a narration has been created, once it has become knowledge that is possessed by particular individuals, it is the narration itself—with its prescription of causality and meaning—that becomes reality. The reality of the "actual" events is superseded by the reality of the narration of the events.

Most of the Mission Dene are at least partly bilingual. Many of them are partly trilingual. Most of the Mission Dene are at least partly literate in English and many are competent in written English. The Chipewyan language has at times been written in syllabic characters whose use the missionaries taught and promoted, but those efforts have faded and only the elderly now write in their own language.[3] In daily life, the Mission Dene use their language as if they were a culture that had no written language. In the absence of written language, the Dene rely more on memory and the spoken word to convey complex issues of causality and meaning than is customary in ordinary American or Canadian life or, for that matter, in the academic world. Since the daily activity patterns of Dene life often carry them far from the sight and hearing of others, they bridge this separation from each other by talking about what has happened in the course of their daily lives—sharing their experiences with those who have not experienced them directly. This talking about the events of the day is not bound into a rigid rhetorical form or delivered before structured gatherings, but obviously there are conventions of cultural patterning involved in determining to whom they talk and in how they organize their talk.

As each man returned to camp at the completion of his activities in the bush, he would talk about what he had experienced during his time away from camp. Each man spoke first to those at his home while he ate and relaxed after the day's exertions. After he had relaxed a bit, he would generally visit his parents or move around outside caring for his dogs, talking with others, or engaging in small tasks and chores. It was not just the two men who talked about their day's events. Their wives and children also moved throughout the camp on their normal round of activities, visiting and chatting as they went about their business. The more interesting and significant aspects of George's and Wellington's accounts were talked about during these movements. The stories of the men became the experience—albeit not personal experience— of the others in the camp. The wives and children interpreted what they had been told in light of their individual concerns and experiences, often offering their own insights or adding to what they had been told.

In the process of carrying this information about the camp there was an enormous potential for the creative aspects of gossip to intrude into the process. Misunderstandings became new events. Misheard phrases created nuances of meaning that had not existed before. Children trying to repeat the words of adults could create mountains where not even molehills had existed by passing on their misunderstanding of what they had heard.

This was a typical Dene bush camp in which each person was connected to every other person in the camp by bonds of kinship or marriage. If our small camp offered large possibilities for confusion and distortion, it was nevertheless a very limited arena within which to gain support. Neither man could expect to gain the support of the dependents of his rival. My support for one or the other might be of temporary value, but everyone knew that I would not be there to play a role over the long haul. Wellington knew that other affines of his, over whom he already exercised a degree of leadership by virtue of his sheer competence at making a living in the bush, would join us later that spring. He knew he would be able to rely upon their support.

The persons whose support was crucial were Paul and May. Bush life is physically much more demanding than is village life, but Paul and May were devoted to life in the bush. The threat of losing their independence, emanating from Paul's declining health, was terribly distressing to them. They hoped to be able to spend the fall and winter in the bush surrounded by their sons and their sons' families. Where they chose to spend the fall season would determine the immediate success of George's bid to assert his independence. George was more than capable of caring for his family and buttressing the needs of his parents, but he was not yet confident enough of himself and his wife to spend an entire cold weather season miles away from other Dene. If Paul and May joined George in a move north to Foxholm Lake, then his bid for autonomy would succeed. If his parents stayed at South Lake, George and his family would have to stay there as well and the mantle of leadership over the entire group would pass to Wellington.

A few weeks after the end of the spring caribou hunt, Wellington would begin a telling attack on George's position and reputation through a series of brilliantly scandalous stories about the behavior of George's wife (Sharp 1988a: 86–89). The means by which the two men would express their positions would shift to other issues and to other kinds of stories, but at this time the effects of their stories about the events in their daily activities were the main venue through which each man had to seek the support he sought.

Each of these men had adopted a mode of presentation of self in their accounts of the events of their daily lives. Their relations with each other drew upon—and strongly reflected—their individual natures and personalities, but each man's mode of self-presentation contrasted starkly with that taken by his brother.

George was slighter and less aggressive than his brother. Not as ambitious or as insightful, he was more polite and far more openly concerned with the nuances of inkoze and how humans were supposed to relate to animal/persons. His manner of self-presentation was that of a strongly moral man concerned with the proper rules of conduct both among humans and with the nonhuman world. He made a consistent effort to follow all of the rules and conventions for conducting a hunt and for sharing both material goods and the yield of subsistence activities.

Wellington, whose status and reputation among his kin were being compromised by his abusive treatment of an infant daughter whose paternity he suspected, was a more complex, assertive, and aggressive man. He paid much less attention to the nuances of correct behavior toward animal/persons and hunting and was perfectly willing to bruise George's feelings in what became competitive hunting. He was less sensitive to the conventional nuances of sharing access to animal/persons, but in practice he was far more generous than was George.

The stance each man took toward the other, and presented to the camp through his account of the events of the day, was exactly that: a stance. It was created through emotional reasoning, the reaction of self to the actions of the other rather than a consciously chosen position. The men's patterns of behavior toward each other did not fully expose the range or complexity of their personalities. Their behavior toward others in the camp expressed a much fuller range of their personalities. Rather, each man's stance drew upon and emphasized particular aspects of his personality in his dealings with his brother. The determining factor in the stance each took toward the other was their striving to live surrounded by their kin. The stories each man told were presented in this context, and often the individual household members' retellings of those stories reflected this.

The accounts of the events that George and Wellington gave as they returned to their camp were not simultaneous with the events as was the case described in Sansom's work. However, their knowledge of the nature and the context of their lives meant that each man knew he would talk to others about the events of his day. Each man knew those—the audience—he would speak to. Each knew the verbal forms he would use to deliver his account. This knowledge of the conventional form of their lives and their speech, especially in this context of concern for the future of the family, gave their accounts similar power to determine the reality of events removed in time and space from the view of an audience that Sansom reported for Aboriginal audiences present at a happening.

These accounts were talked about by the audience. That process—George and Wellington telling of the events and the audience of the camp talking about the events—became the means by which the events themselves were aligned with their meaning. In effect, the meaning that was conveyed through the events became the interpretive framework for the events. As the interpretive framework, the telling of the events and the audience's talking about them came to determine the shape and character of the events themselves. As the accounts became the reality of the events, and the "objective" characteristics of the events were adjusted to conform to that reality, Wellington and George adjusted their subsequent behavior to conform to that reality. As was the case with the Teacher and the Principal, creating the meaning of the events altered the nature of the events.

This was not purely a rhetorical practice. The two men actually regulated their behavior toward each other to conform to the stance they had adopted toward each other and to the social reality that the stance had created. In effect, each man came to act the way he did as the result of his memory of the reality created by the future commentary upon the way the events of the day were to be recounted before the camp—a commentary that would embody the view that each held of his own relationship with his brother and of their individual visions of the moral case each was constructing to support his position.

Recognizing the nature of this transformation of order, from event determining the nature of the account to the account determining the nature of the event, is crucial to understanding why Wellington and George were acting in the manner they were. Each man had assumed a strategy for his own behavior in situations where they interacted with each other (Sharp 1988a: 53–57).[4] The audience was not physically present at the events, but it was present in the knowledge each man carried of his future representation of the events before that audience. This knowledge of future representations of the events affected the stance each man took in his behavior toward his brother. Knowledge of his stance and of his future presentation of the events in compliance with his stance became a determining factor in how each man perceived the actual events.

It was not just that future stories about events determined how the audience would—after the fact—perceive the events. Knowing that, in this context, their future stories would be told about the events became a determining factor in the how the two men perceived themselves and the events as they were happening. This perception became a determining factor in how each man behaved and thus a determining factor in how the events themselves unfolded.

In this context of stress, uncertainty, change, and competition, the future memory these men had of their accounting of the events of their days and of their interactions with each other became a determining factor in what each man saw, heard, felt, and in how he acted. The future was determining the present.

There are several factors that may help make the idea of the future determining the present through the medium of memory seem a bit less alien.

Some Dene religious convictions have their origin in the dogma and practice of Christianity and have been so thoroughly absorbed and integrated that they form part of inkoze itself, but inkoze remains the core logic of Dene culture. At times it seems as if the Dene recognize that the physical universe we experience is only part of a greater connected universe(s) we are unable to perceive. I cannot adequately map the nature of these realms or describe their geometry. The Dene either cannot do so or choose not to do so. Neither of us can explain these multidimensional realms in intelligible terms. Perhaps the idea of mapping such a multidimensional reality is nonsensical. We are like color-blind individuals in a world of color. The reality of the universe in which we live is created only by the limitations of our culturally determined perception.

If the geometry of these realms is not known, some of the ways in which the realms are connected can be known and observed.[5] The Dene know that animal/persons are beings existing in more than one realm. The Dene know that the homes of the giant beings beneath the lakes and rivers of Dene country are pathways between the realms maintained by the power/knowledge of those beings of inkoze. The Dene know that some beings, like the loon Phil tried to kill, can move between these realms of being.

Within a world chartered by inkoze, where time has the character of place and connection within what is always true rather than being the means of separation between events that once were or may once be true, time can fold upon itself and bring together events Western thought insists must be separated. History is not past, history is. Future is not may be, future is. Both are equally real.

Memory of the future is no more a different order of beast from memory of the past than the revealed truth of a dream is a different order of beast from the knowledge that comes from other kinds of personal experience. A happening, the verbal construction of meaning that orders events, takes on the temporal characteristics of inkoze. Happenings acquire the same reality as other kinds of knowledge not gained through personal experience. Their reality is less valid than knowledge gained through personal experience, but the locus of that knowledge is not bound by time and space. Future memory is not so dramatic a concept.

I am not particularly interested in psychological explanation. I have little faith in the validity of Western psychological models when dealing with cultural experience as alien to Western history and experience as is that of the Dene. Nevertheless, we approach Dene cultural thought and experience from the perspective of our own cultural ideas about the nature of the mind just as we approach the physical world of the Dene from the perspective of our own cultural ideas about the nature of the physical world. We bring with us, as it were, not only a folk physics but a folk psychology. As with our physics, our cultural thought about the nature of the mind is not uniform, and some of that specialized thought is rather at odds with our conventional understanding of the mind.

Our folk psychology, varying as it may be, hangs on certain assumptions about the how the mind works. We presume the mind is an integrated phenomenon organized in a hierarchical manner, even if not all of it is subject to rational control. We regard consciousness as the ultimate and only true aspect of the mind and rational thought as the highest aspect of consciousness. Other aspects of the mind, such as dreams, emotion, or trance, are secondary aspects of it that are inherently suspect as things that threaten the operation of rational thought.

It is no accident that we speak of being drugged, being in trance, or being hypnotized as altered states of consciousness. Whatever they are, they are not reality and we discount their validity. We are perfectly willing to allow the mind—or at least the brain—latitude to run our biochemistry, regulate our heartbeat, and to keep us breathing without the participation of consciousness, but we see these as incidental mechanical functions.

By the same token, we think of the mind's role in memory as that of a slightly inept librarian in a large library. Memory itself is thought of as passively recording everything it experiences. Consciousness, the librarian, has but an imperfect access to what the mind has stored. If we cannot remember something, it is not because the events have not occurred or the information about them is not stored within the mind but because our consciousness cannot locate it.

This hierarchical model of the mind is somewhat at odds with some of our contemporary psychological and physiological thought about the mind and the brain. It is being challenged particularly hard by analytical metaphors developing from the study of brain physiology (Gazzaniga 1985). The analytical metaphors emerging from these areas replace metaphors of hierarchy with metaphors that liken the mind to a committee or to forms of political organization. The key assumption, derived largely from the analysis of the effects of surgical or pathological breaks in neural pathways between brain hemispheres, is that the mind is organized laterally with only a limited degree of interaction and communication between the lateral components (or "modules," as Gazzaniga calls them).

An analogy with the computer might make the distinction clearer.[6] In our folk psychology, consciousness is like the screen and keyboard hooked into a mainframe computer. Reality is what appears on the screen (or printer). The operations of the computer itself are simply mechanical processes, functions that are necessary but incidental reactions to the keystrokes of the person using the keyboard. In our folk psychology, everything that occurs in the computer is designed to serve the interests and the commands coming from the interaction of the operator and the keyboard.

The newer metaphors in effect argue that the computer consists of a series of separate programs, each of which is of equal reality and validity. Each of these programs (modules) is running simultaneously with the programs generated by the interaction between operator and keyboard (consciousness and rationality). Those separate programs have only a limited communication with each other, although at times any of them may temporarily seize control of the computer, that is, take control of the body and its actions. In this view, consciousness is only one of the aspects of the mind and it is not a controlling aspect. It is simply the aspect of the mind that communicates with itself and with others, an aspect that Western culture has chosen to emphasize as the reality of ourselves.

There is a limit to how far an analogy should be carried (and this one is now close to its limits), but it should be mentioned that from this perspective it is not a case of altered states of consciousness but of different aspects of the mind that are always in operation but only sometimes in control of the screen and keyboard (that is, the body). The implication is not that the mind goes into an alternate state when it goes into trance but that some aspect of the mind is always in trance, an ever-present aspect of the mind that is only sometimes expressed in the body's actions so that it can be discerned by others. The same logic could be applied to visions, dreams, and a host of other alternate states whose validity is routinely discounted in the West.

The interactions between Wellington and George can be profitably viewed in the light of this analogy. The interaction between the two men was determined by the strategy of self-presentation each had adopted in his conflict with the other, but their interaction was contextually bound to that conflict. There was no transformation of their nature because of the conflict. They continued to act toward others in the camp as they had before the conflict opened. It was as if in their interactions with each other, a separate "module" (or program) had been opened that determined their behavior in that context but that did not operate in any discernible manner outside of the context of that conflict.

What connects happenings with the way the Mission Dene use time, what makes future memory reasonable, is the fact that memory is a social process over which culture exercises its sway. It is a social process rather than an individual process even though it occurs in individuals, just as speech is always socially determined even though only individuals speak.[7] Not only is memory always constructed with reference to the judgment and input of other Dene, it is the social context within which individual memory occurs that exercises the supremacy of determination. Memory is the process by which experience is created through an alignment with meaning. The nature of that alignment is determined by the nature of the meaning rather than by the nature of the experience. Experience does not exist in any objective reality but only as an expression of the means by which it is measured, and meaning is the means by which humans measure all events. As the process by which experience is brought into accord with meaning, memory operates in both temporal directions. Memory of the future is the same process as is memory of the past or the construction of the shared reality of the present.

Both are the same process of knowing that the Dene apply to dreams, visions, and other forms of perceiving what are alternate realities to Western culture. The events that Wellington saw during that caribou hunt were not the same events that George saw. In accord with the nature of Dene explanation, resolution of their differences in memory into a single authoritative version was not in the offing. Their separate future memories constructed the events each participated in. Sharing those memories at the camp fixed the events in the reality of Dene life.

Culture constructs our self and our individual minds. What we can see from Western culture's variation in its thought about the mind, as with its variation in its thought about the nature of physical reality, is that it allows us to consider that the self and the individual mind of each Dene might be as different from our own as the physical universe each Dene experiences within Chipewyan reality is different from that which we experience within our own cultural reality. Without denying the biological aspects of the shared genetic basis of humanity, the potential still remains that the way Dene culture organizes the Dene is sufficiently different from the way Western culture organizes us that it produces genuine differences between us. We accept that languages are genuinely different and that some of those differences cannot be bridged by translation even though all of the speakers of all of the languages share a common humanity and the languages themselves probably result from a common—and causal—genetic base. There are genuine differences between Dene and Westerners derived from their different cultures, and not all of these differences can be translated into terms readily intelligible to Westerners. All we can do is try to grapple with the differences.

19

LOON V

I always worry that writing about the Chipewyan relationship with animals and their conceptualization of them as persons simultaneously natural and supernatural may lend some toward going off the deep end toward the mystical and the romantic. Culture is coercive and obligatory. People think and act in the terms presented by their culture because their culture provides the only way individuals have to think, speak, and act in a way that is intelligible to their peers. These conceptualizations are deeply embedded in Dene thought and practice and pervade all that they do. The causal nature of these ideas is usually not terribly obvious. It is much like trying to relate modern ideas about jobs and work to the post-Roman history of the West, the triadic reordering of feudalism (Duby 1980), and Western traditions of philosophical and economic thought. The manifestations are apparent in daily life, but that does not mean that, even if they are aware of them, those who live that life expend much time or effort thinking about them.

The Dene are an eminently practical and empirical people who do not run around in a romantic fog seeing spirits, auras, or mystic forces in every action they take or in every thing they observe. The relationships between Dene thought about inkoze and about animals are much more subtle and complex than that. Those ideas have to work through Dene who disbelieve in inkoze or who are ignorant of inkoze as effectively as those ideas must work through those individuals who are the most knowledgeable about them just as, in a Christian culture, Christian belief must manifest itself not only in theologians and the clergy but in the thoughts and actions of individuals who are ignorant, atheists, or just plain thick.

In the last week of July 1992 we arrived at George's camp on Foxholm Lake. Our expectation was, as it always was there, that the caribou would arrive no later than the first week of August and that the mosquitoes and black flies would vanish with the arrival of the caribou.[1] Our expectation was wrong. The mosquitoes and black flies remained until the middle of August, and the caribou did not arrive until well into the second week of August.

Lake trout and the other fish of the Northern lakes are wonderful, but after several weeks of an essentially all-fish diet supplemented mostly by macaroni-and-cheese dinners, bannock, and Kool-Aid, our camp was edgy. The women were there to make dry meat and were anxious to get under way. The lack of caribou made them feel they were wasting their time. They were bored and restless.

We all had been seeing signs indicating that caribou were nearby. The feel of the place had become denser and more animate. Its quality was increasingly charged as if there were an extra presence in the area. Seagulls and ravens nest around Foxholm Lake so there are always a few resident birds nearby, but as caribou approach the edge of the forest, ravens and seagulls move with and ahead of the herds. One of the first signs of caribou to be seen from the ground is an increase in the number of ravens and gulls near treeline.

The local raven population had increased significantly, and as they do when caribou are in the area, they had begun to alter their flight patterns and their manner of play. The seagull population increased even more noticeably than did the raven population. By the end of the second week there was a small flock that spent a large part of its days floating several hundred yards offshore from our camp. Their presence was mildly annoying, almost a symbol of the lack of caribou and our uncertainty about why they had not come.

One afternoon, out of frustration and boredom, Phil and I were contemplating shooting at the seagulls when a loon flew in and landed near them. Remembering how good they taste as well as the encounter at the narrows, I urged Phil to shoot at it. It was far too far away to hit, but Phil, reluctantly, took a shot at it. His shell struck quite close to a seagull but very far away from the loon. Since it was obvious he had deliberately tried to miss the loon, I talked to him about it. He indicated that he no longer shot loons, indirectly confirming that he had acquired a relationship to the loon. That it stemmed from our shared encounter with the loon at the narrows was confirmed by his perplexity that I had urged him to shoot at it.

The local wolves were keeping themselves out of sight, but their presence was indisputable. Scat was everywhere, as were the remains of their old kills. They spent enough time within a half mile of our camp for us to cross fresh tracks from where they had moved out of our way while we were out walking about. We heard no sound from them until one evening when, after we had all gone to bed, a single wolf began to howl from the south shore of Foxholm Lake just across from our camp.

It would howl, wait a few minutes, and then howl again, as if it was awaiting a reply. After it had howled a few times, I howled back at it. It responded immediately, so I answered it. On my second howl, Phil joined in from his tent. The wolf answered us. All of us continued howling back and forth to each other for near to an hour and a half. We were joined, part way through the conversation, by two or more wolves who were on hills above the west bank of the northern bay of Foxholm Lake, a mile or so past the narrows where we had encountered the loon. I never figured out how many were over there. There were a number of different voices, but only a single wolf would howl at a time.

When Phil and I talked about it the next day, he was convinced the wolves were telling each other where the caribou were.

The high point of the day, if not the entire two weeks, came later in the day when the conversation again drifted back to caribou and wolves. May began, with obvious delight, to tell us about how many wolves had been howling the night before and how close they had been to the tents. I doubt I shall ever forget the grin Phil and I shared as we simultaneously realized she had not recognized the two of us as two of the wolves from the night before.

The issue of the missing caribou remained. George and his sons, now in their teens, had made a series of reconnaissances along the lake—once out about ten miles—looking for caribou, but George quickly decided to preserve his gasoline supply and wait for caribou to come. Phil was irritated by George's decision to wait and began a series of hunts on foot or by canoe to seek out the caribou he felt were nearby. Not finding sign along the northern shore of the lake within five or so miles of camp, he turned his attention to the south of the lake. When that failed to produce sign of caribou, Phil prepared for a long overnight trip. He planned to walk north to the next lake system, a distance of about six miles, and then go east for ten or fifteen miles. He traveled light, taking only a cup for water, a little packaged food, and a light blanket. His trip was difficult and the insects were a sustained torment. After hours of fast walking, he spent the night huddled beneath a tree, wrapped in his blanket and suffering from the cold and the insects. He saw no caribou. The only bright spot on his trip was watching a pair of wolverines unsuccessfully pursuing a red fox along the esker on which he was resting. He returned to camp late the second day and, after a quick meal, fell into an exhausted sleep in his tent.

Camps attract visitors. Wolves pass by the edges while going about their business. Fox and other small predators explore at night. The most common visitors are birds. We were joined most mornings by a small flock of ravens. Most of the birds, which might show up anytime during daylight hours, stayed in the trees a hundred or so feet away from camp, but one raven had the habit of landing in the small trees beside our tents and chattering loudly at us. Ravens have a complex vocal repertoire. Less eerie than loons, their vocal range seems even greater, and they are much more likely to approach humans and exchange vocalizations with them. The morning after Phil had returned from his long walk, this bird came into camp and began to raise bloody hell. Phil, still tired and somewhat cranky from being awakened by the raven, came out of his tent and told it to shut up. The raven was irritated by Phil's behavior and squawked at him. Their exchange took a nasty turn. Phil began yelling at the raven to go away and shut up. The raven, all the more irritated by Phil's comments, not only continued squawking at Phil but began to swear at him. Phil swore back and for a short time the two cursed back and forth at each other until a now intensely irritated Phil retreated into his tent for his rifle, came out, shot the raven, and went back to sleep.

Throughout the day, May—who had witnessed the shooting—was telling the story to others who had not seen it (virtually all of the camp was still asleep when it happened) and laughing both at the raven's display of bad manners and at Phil's response to it.

In Dene thought this incident was devoid of any "supernatural" component. That animals are persons is a given, as natural an aspect of their being animals as it is natural that there is air on the earth. As persons, animals—

like humans—can and will behave in a wide variety of ways, including those that are stupid and rude as well those that are clever or helpful. Because all Dene and all wild animals are embedded in the web of being and causality that is inkoze, the presence of an animal/person need not indicate anything other than the ordinary state of affairs. The presence of an unusual concentration of the power/knowledge that is inkoze, whether in human, animal, or other form, is noted, is sometimes disconcerting, and is always a factor for reflection, but it is as natural as breathing. If there is a problem with this view, it comes not from the Dene but from our own understanding of animals and causality. It is we whose scientists, psychologists, and theologians can insist that animals are souless unself-aware machines who do not suffer or feel pain and who lack volition and purpose. It is we who conceive of raven only as a mindless object rather than as a sentient being who might argue with a human and be shot for doing so. It is we who create a reality lacking a soul, not the Dene.

NOTES

INTRODUCTION

1. This work is not, in the presumptuous term of current rhetoric, about "giving voice" to the Chipewyan. The Chipewyan are perfectly capable of speaking for themselves and will write their own interpretations of their culture as it suits them. There are Chipewyan scholars, and at least one of the Mission Chipewyan is an anthropologist. If the Dene are not engaging us in a written discourse in our journals, it is not because a Western cultural or anthropological hegemony has denied them a voice but because our discourse has been of no more interest to the lay public among them than it has been to the lay public among ourselves.

2. Within this time usage, local spaces within time retain the linear flow of time from past to present—that is, events flow within time—but the local spaces cannot be placed before or after each other.

1. LOON

1. I did not shoot at the loon. I thought about it, but by now I was more worried about the consequences of hitting it than I was about those of missing it or not shooting at it.

2. MISSION

1. The uranium mine was several miles down the lake on the other side of the river flowing out of Mission Lake. The country was too rough to construct a road and the cost of a bridge over the river too great, so the ore was barged from the mine to the loading dock. From there it was trucked to Discha, where it could be loaded on barges and shipped out for processing. The mine did not stay in business for very long, but the contaminants from it are a problem to this day.

2. In the early stages of my fieldwork I saw versions of the plan posted in offices in

Mission and Discha but always found the idea of it too bizarre to inquire into the source of the planning. By the time I realized that it was other than an exercise in bureaucratic fantasy, its origin was moot.

3. Local politics were not factored into the federal regulations but were, of course, the determining factor in the allocation of the houses.

4. The offices and homes of the whites at Mission had long had electricity (and indoor plumbing) running off a separate generator system.

5. The mission church also had a radio, but its use was denied to Native residents of the village.

6. Early in the history of the modern snowmobile Pertti Pelto published an interesting work describing its role as an agent of change in the North (Pelto 1973). In that work, technology—the snowmobile—was seen as the driving force that initiated dramatic changes in how Northern peoples related to their lands and resources. My experience of the Chipewyan at Mission was the reverse of what Pelto argued in that work. At Mission, change came for social reasons, and those changes were implemented through technology. This was also true with changes in communication technology. The point is that where Pelto saw technology as driving social change, I saw social change driving the adoption of technology.

7. As early as the spring of 1975, it was possible to distinguish caribou who had not been exposed to snowmobile-borne hunters from those who had (Sharp 1988a: 55–56). Experienced caribou ran for thick brush as soon as they saw or heard one. Inexperienced caribou ran, eventually, but they were almost as curious about snowmobiles as they were afraid of them.

8. This idea died when the owner of the building dismantled it and burned it for firewood.

9. The Dene had taken to the use of charter aircraft for their trips between store and bush almost as soon as aircraft were available in the North. So many Dene lived and trapped so far from Mission—often well over a hundred air miles out—that land and water travel to the traplines was time consuming. It was also hazardous, particularly for families with children. The logical entry time, late summer or early fall, was the time of strong winds and storms. These winds and storms are deadly for canoeists during travel. People often had to put up for weeks on their journeys back north and often had to consume the bulk of their supplies before they ever reached their hunting areas.

10. Often called "baby bonus" checks, the Family Allowance was a payment intended to ensure that every Canadian child would receive a certain minimum income to assist in its health and well-being.

3. INDETERMINACY

1. To illustrate the point, look carefully at how the eminent military historian John Keegan grapples with the issue of the relationship between war (something we believe to be a rule-bound natural phenomenon) and culture in *A History of Warfare* (Keegan 1994: xiv–12).

2. This issue is explored at length in Jean-Guy Goulet's *Ways of Knowing*. An examination of chapter 2, "True Knowledge and True Responsibility," would be useful here for readers interested in exploring this issue (Goulet 1998: 27–59).

3. The third issue, the more general use of indeterminacy as an analytical tool in anthropological analysis, is beyond the scope of this work.

4. FOXHOLM LAKE

1. I am inclined to think the name Adeker Lake is a corruption of Arctic Hare Lake, but both Phil and George dispute this. The word is not Chipewyan, and I have yet to find someone who knows its meaning other than as one of the names for part of the northern end of a larger lake.

2. Individuals who have read certain works on the Dene Tha and the Dunne-za by Hugh Brody, Jean-Guy Goulet, and Robin Ridington will be familiar with the role maps to heaven play in those cultures. I wish to make expressly clear that this reference to a hand-drawn map refers to a terrain map. The concept of maps to heaven does not exist in Mission Chipewyan culture. As far as I have been able to determine, the entire notion of the soul having to follow a trail to heaven after death is also missing. I have never encountered any reference or allusion to such a journey among the Chipewyan.

6. LOON II

1. *Inkoze* is the term that David M. Smith and I have used to represent the entire complex of causality based upon dream-revealed power. Among the Mission Chipewyan the term actually refers to killing a person through sorcery, but they themselves often use it as a shorthand reference to what we think of as the supernatural and the magical. The word's pronunciation varies in different Chipewyan dialects. I spell it *inkoze* to reflect what I hear at Mission. David M. Smith spells it *inkonze* or $ı^n\text{KO}^n\text{ZE}$ to reflect what he hears at Fort Resolution (D. M. Smith 1990: 157; 1973). June Helm spells the cognate word *inkon,* as used by the Slavey (speaking a different language rather than a different dialect) (Helm 1994).

2. Richard K. Nelson's evidence about the nature of animals and power among the Koyukon is confusing and sometimes contradictory, but on this point it clearly seems

that Koyukon conceive of this relationship in exactly the opposite manner from the Chipewyan by presuming that animals once spoke a human language (Nelson 1983: 10, 20).

3. I have discussed this issue at some length in "Inverted Sacrifice" (Sharp 1994b). The issue is interesting because the form of the sacrificial paradigm is inverted from the normal and takes on characteristics of the sacrifice of the god (see Robertson-Smith 1901; Hubert and Mauss 1964: 77–94).

7. WILD THINGS

1. This phrase indicates that the events are not to be placed within the framework of myth but within the framework of recent experience.

2. The association of eagle with the Thunderbird is less certain. The Thunderbird concept is not well developed in Dene culture and probably should not be taken to imply any of the values and meanings associated with the Thunderbird figure elsewhere in North America.

3. To try and link the topology of inkoze into a unified form is a Western rather than a Dene conceit. I doubt if such a topology could be created under any circumstances, and the Dene certainly would not be interested in it even if it could be done.

4. This point about the nature of Dene categories is a recurring theme in this work. My thought on this is greatly influenced by Rodney Needham's work on polythetic categories (Needham 1972, 1975).

5. "Giant Fish, Giant Otters, and Dinosaurs" (Sharp 1987) gives an extensive case history of the decades-long vengeance one of Mission Lake's giant otters took upon a local man who had mocked it.

8. TIME

1. I do not wish to get into a which-causes-which argument here. Both construct each other, and neither has an independent reality apart from their social context. By the same token, it does not follow that folk physics is logically consistent or rational if subjected to the precision of analytical examination. What counts is that it is the reality we have created and the way we experience reality.

9. ANIMALS

1. Domestic animals are excluded from this discussion. Horses and cats are the only domestic animals other than dogs of which the Mission Dene have any real experience. Keeping cats, which must be indoor animals to survive the local predators for more than a few hours, is a new experience (mid-1980s) and confined to the

town. The Dene have not yet sorted out what they think of cats. They have a longer, intermittent, and not recent exposure to horses, but these animals also do not fare well here. All domestic animals must be intensely cared for by humans, and the crucial factor is that they are as unable to care for themselves as wild animals are self-sufficient.

2. I use the words "spirit" and "spiritual" out of a sense of frustration rather than because the words fit with Dene thought. I simply do not know of any alternative English word that is not an even worse match.

3. I mean this to be an explicit denial of the validity of the concept of the "master of the animals" so widely used in the interpretation of Native American—and other Northern peoples'—thought about animals.

4. I find myself uncomfortable with Richard Nelson's treatment of this issue (esp. Nelson 1983: 17). It is the tragedy of Northern Athapaskan ethnography that, even at the beginning of the third millennium, it is difficult to tell if the difference between the Chipewyan and the Koyukon on this issue is a difference between how Nelson and I interpret the evidence from our fieldwork experiences or a genuine ethnographic difference between the peoples among whom we have worked.

5. Again, these issues need to be contrasted with the treatment the same issues receive in Nelson as they contrast strongly with what he reports for the Koyukon (Nelson 1983: 107, 157–58).

10. WOLF

1. See "Man:Wolf::Woman:Dog" (Sharp 1976) for a structural analysis of canids as gender symbols with particular reference to the role of dogs as symbols of women and culture and wolves as symbols of males and nature.

2. These characterizations of the power of the wolf or other animals are not to be taken too strictly. The Chipewyan have no typology of the strengths of the various animals and certainly no hierarchical typology of them. The power of inkoze any Dene receives depends far more upon how much power and what kind of power an animal/person chooses to give him rather than upon some abstract ranking of the power of the giving animal/person.

11. DOG

1. I have absolutely no data about women abusing dogs, itself perhaps one of the strongest indicators of the symbolic links between WOMAN and DOG (Sharp 1976).

2. The ability to support oneself—to gather one's own food from the bush—is the core of the identity between Wolf and Man. The lack of this ability is symbolically

devastating in Chipewyan culture. It can be seen in Chipewyan ideas about domestic animals but also shows in the conceptualization of Raven as filthy because it scavenges and the ambiguity about Bear, also known to scavenge. Eating feces is the most extreme indicator of the inability to support oneself, so any animal thought of as eating feces is at least suspect if not outright filthy. WOMAN, as a category, is linked to DOG at least in part because of WOMAN's—within the symbolic system—status as dependent upon MAN to provide her with food (Sharp 1976, 1988a, 1988b; Carter 1974).

12. LOON III

1. I have highlighted the word "value" with quotation marks because I wish to make certain it is understood that I am not using the word in any sense that makes reference to the use of the term "value" in economic thought. There is no economic value to this loon, or to its feathers, feet, and so on. If the men had killed the bird it would have been eaten, and some parts of the bird might have been retained by the slayer as references or tokens of its power and favor, but even then they would not assume value in an economic sense. Economic thought is just not applicable to these events and circumstances, and trying to place them in that context would pervert their meaning.

2. There are substantial differences between the concepts of time embedded in the "everywhen" of the Dreaming and of time in inkoze that relate especially to the role of ritual in enacting the principles of the Dreaming (Sharp 1994b: 256–59; 1997: 95–97).

3. This is the nature of indeterminacy and a good example of it.

4. Let me reiterate that being able to kill an animal/person is not a measure of the power of an individual's inkoze. Humans may have the power to kill animal/persons with inkoze, but they will not survive the encounter. The animal/persons will spring back to life and destroy the presumptuous human. Killing an animal/person is more an issue of standing in good grace with the being, more an issue of morality—in the most general possible sense of the word—than of power, knowledge, or skill (Sharp 1996).

5. George had had a similar experience a few years before when he encountered five swans on a tiny lake a few miles northeast of Foxholm Lake. He was able to approach within twenty or thirty feet of them and fired at them several times without hitting any of them. The swans simply swam around on the small pond and displayed at him until he recognized the futility of further shooting and left them alone.

13. TALKING ABOUT THINGS

1. I should perhaps repeat that this chapter, like the entire book, is about explaining my experience of the Chipewyan rather than about the ways and means by which I have arrived at my understanding of that experience. Analysis of the processes by which the Dene constitute themselves and their interactions with each other, particularly through language (e.g., Goulet 1998: xli–xliv, 33–36, 147–55), is quite a different set of issues and not one I intend to take up. My intent in this chapter is not to analyze Dene speech but to illustrate how verbal accounts (as well as performance) create a field of social interaction and meaning, that is, context, sufficiently dense to have the effects upon living beings that I find necessary to explain the encounter with the loon.

2. This secrecy of inkoze contrasts strongly with what is reported for the Beaver and Slavey peoples. In those cultures, the performance of what would be inkoze among the Mission Chipewyan seems to be a far more public phenomenon than it was at Mission. Power is always a sensitive issue among Northern Athapaskans, but the situation at Mission may be no more than the case of a general practice carried to an extreme. David M. Smith seems not to have found the extreme secrecy surrounding inkonze at Fort Resolution that I found at Mission. Unfortunately, J. G. E. Smith died before we had the chance to explore the issue among the more easterly Chipewyan. I suspect that the minimal role public ritual played in the life of the Mission Chipewyan during my fieldwork was a major factor—whether cause or effect I cannot say—in the secrecy, although there are other factors for the absence of public ritual (Sharp 1988b). I respect that secrecy and need to make clear that it limits what I can say about the nature and the details of inkoze, dreams, and visions.

3. Power/knowledge can be quite limited and specific: the ability to trap red fox but not fox in general, the ability to heal only certain kinds of illnesses, the ability to win at cards. The greater the inkoze a man has, the more domains in which his performance will demonstrate its presence.

4. This statement should not be taken either as sexist or denigrating to women. Women lack power/knowledge (inkoze), but that does not mean that they lack power. The nature of female power is complex and confusing. At it simplest, it seems to be the negation of inkoze through pollution (Sharp 1988a: 81). I have written briefly on the nature of women's power (Sharp 1981a, 1981b, 1994a, 1997), but the topic is sufficiently complex and murky that I do not feel I have a sufficient understanding of it to say much more than I already have.

5. The Mission Chipewyan are not nearly as sensitive about their personal clothing as Goulet reports for the Dene Tha (Goulet 1998: 94–101).

6. Ironically, that speech reflected the true concerns of the Mission Dene in a way that white authorities still had not figured out by 1992. Rations were perceived as a right rather than as welfare, a distinction very significant to a poor and proud people. The Dene talked of Rations and demanded more Rations at every opportunity. Talk of Rations was a metaphor for the state of relations between the Mission Dene and white Canada and the Mission Dene attempt to gain more control over their lives and their economy. I never met a white administrator who understood the meaning of the speech. The Dene would speak of Rations even to whites who had nothing to do with the allocation of Rations and who became convinced that not only were the Dene obsessed with the topic but that they failed to understand the issues that had brought the whites to Mission in the first place.

7. In the mid-1990s, when Denegothera had become a man in his early nineties yet was still active and capable, his very longevity and vigor might finally have been the proof of the inkoze The People of Mission had so long denied his having.

14. LOON IV

1. The process of interpreting and assigning meaning to that encounter, even excluding this analysis from being considered a part of that process, remained active among these Dene at least through 1992.

2. The closest kinds of experiences to this that I can think of in ordinary life are those like getting into a dentist's chair or waiting for a car to be repaired. Once the experience has begun, it is ordered not by the clock but by the memory of past visits and the anticipation of future visits. It seems that all life is a seamless flow through the dentist's chair and all other experience is somehow beyond relevance to these replicating experiences.

3. I am excluding consideration of the consequences of the encounter—for quite different reasons—for myself and for the man from Birchtown.

4. This information comes from his parents and siblings and is a representation of a magical wound. I have no information on the medical description of the injury or its treatment. Surviving the wound as described seems rather improbable, which is, of course, the point.

5. Contrast this with what Goulet reports for the Dene Tha several hundred miles to the west of Mission (Goulet 1998: 64–79).

6. This is one reason Mission Dene are circumspect about talking about their dreams. Dreams come in many varieties. They may be true dreams or false dreams. They may be no more than the simple expression of indigestion, sore muscles, or an uncomfortable sleeping position. Among this swarm of kinds of dreams are those

that foretell the future, tell how and where to hunt, or are outright visions. One cannot go and ask about a vision or power dream (the latter at least seem unmistakable) without damaging or destroying the relationship with the being who sent it, yet dreams that foretell the future or warn of danger do no good unless their contents are made known. Confounding this paradox is the fact that women dream even though they cannot have inkoze. Women have the full range of dreams that men do (I have found no certain evidence for women having visions or power dreams, so I am uncertain about these). The conundrum about knowing what to do about a dream makes their interpretation very much an individual effort.

7. I use the term "segolia" much as Dave Smith uses the term "adept" or the term "Inkonze Helin" to refer to those Dene who have substantially greater than normal inkoze (see Sharp 1986: 258; D. M. Smith 1973, 1982, personal communication).

8. None of these periods of hospitalization were voluntary or had parental consent. The system simply did not take account of issues of informed consent at this time.

9. The Mission Dene think that plants generally have less potency the farther north they grow. The stronger southern plants were able to overcome the forces working on Phil.

10. One of the mixed blessings of modern times is the increasing readiness of younger Mission women to use weapons and initiate violence toward men or other women.

11. One of Phil's artistic creations, shipped to me by Phil and his brothers from Mission, was added to the collection of the Field Museum in Chicago. It would have remained there had not the U.S. Fish and Wildlife Service in a burst of bureaucratic excess entered James VanStone's office at the museum and seized the artwork because it had eagle feathers on it.

15. MEANING

1. None of the dimensions beyond the first four correspond to anything that can be put into terms relating to human experience.

2. There seems to be some argument about the truth of this proposition among cosmologists.

3. Yes, this is the "hunting hypothesis" that has been such a bane to our understanding of human evolution but in the form that I thought, thirty years ago, it should have been propounded. I should also make clear that I am using "social" in a particular and more restrictive sense than is customary. For example, as social is used here, wolves are social because they are organized to collectively obtain and distribute

food among themselves while monkeys are not social because they do not collectively obtain their food and distribute it among themselves.

4. Hunting includes scavenging. The difference between the two is inconsequential. By the same token, there is no necessary relationship between gender and hunting or between gender and scavenging.

5. Since all the evolutionary transitions in our history were necessary for us to evolve precisely as we did, no one aspect of that continuous chain of ancestry is more important than any other. Asserting the importance of one factor is not so much a statement of its importance in the history of our evolutionary biology as it is an after-the-fact emphasis upon aspects of our history that reflect issues that concern us at the moment.

6. The term "group" is deliberately not defined here. Such a definition would open a can of worms that is not relevant to this work.

7. Although the phrase "sexual division of labor" is the traditional one, it might be more accurate here to substitute the phrase "reproductive division of labor."

8. I am not adverse to using other models of culture or employing different aspects of various models of culture when I am writing about issues whose explanation I do not find so problematic as the ones examined here. Models need to be modified, changed, or flipped between to fit circumstances. After all, the point of models is that they be an aid in thinking and understanding rather than a substitute for them.

16. DEATH BY MEANING

1. For a fuller account of the Magic Boy's power and the social context of this time at Mission see "Shared Experience and Magical Death" (Sharp 1986).

2. Moccasins are made from home-tanned, smoked moosehide. Moosehide makes a wonderfully light and tough leather that both breathes and insulates. Its only point of weakness, other than being cut, is its susceptibility to water, which destroys its insulating properties and allows it to freeze. The People wear rubbers over moccasins when they fear exposure to water as when in the village or when the snow in the bush is wet. Moosehide moccasins were the most effective general purpose cold weather footgear available to the Chipewyan. (Moccasins made of double layers of caribou hide, not tanned but dried and worked with the fur on, sewn with fur facing out and in, are warmer than moosehide moccasins but are much more fragile.) Worn over two to four pairs of heavy wool socks, they are among the most effective cold weather footgear ever devised by the human species. Moccasins made of cloth are utterly useless and, in effect, a parody of the real thing.

3. The issue of women being out and about instead of staying at home to work was

a long-running thread in the Mission Dene debate about the nature of the social changes that were occurring with the micro-urbanization of Mission. Within the village, as within the large temporary bush settlements of the past, women had enormously greater freedom of movement through the social fabric than they had in the small isolated camps of the past. In traditional bush life, women stayed in camp unless they left as part of a group of women, usually escorted by an armed male. Gleacho's comments, and the presumed example he provided, aligned him with the largely older or politically ambitious and more conservative part of the community that wished to see no alteration in the existing patterns of social and gender relationships. His comments were, in effect, a call for the reconstruction of an earlier state of existence within which the moral order chartered by inkoze played a greater role in structuring Chipewyan daily life.

4. I am not interested in trying to map a precise definition. Doing so strikes me as a pointless exercise in definition that would accomplish nothing as, I think, the sense of the concept is intelligible.

5. In case it has not been clear from the context of their previous usage, I group the two terms "sensation" and "perception" together to deny the distinction between them customarily made in psychophysics and physiological psychology.

17. EVENT AND MEMORY

1. If nothing else, it means this chapter has to be organized around something that did not happen in order to show that it did not happen!

2. For a fuller account of the tensions at Mission and the social context leading up to the scuffle, see "Meaning, Memory, and Imaginary Time" (Sharp 1991).

3. All the other whites in the region, following the self-segregation between Dene and white originating in the placement of their dwellings during the years Discha developed as a settlement, lived in Discha.

4. Several versions of the story of Charley's parents were current in the village. The issue never seemed worth resolving until I began this analysis, and I am now unable to resolve it.

5. These accusations were not entirely without foundation. Her adoption of this role provided her with both the opportunity and the motive to make trouble.

6. The Principal had instructed the Teacher to remain inside even though he had wanted to go outside and watch, so this provided an excuse for him to go outside and see what was going on.

7. All quotations are from a certified copy of the trial transcript, modified only to disguise venue and the names of the participants.

8. Because of the emergency powers in effect, Charley could be tried in absentia.

9. In my notes I recorded that the hockey stick was one of the lightweight aluminum ones rather than a heavy wooden one, but I remember it as a heavy wooden one. My memory is no longer reliable on whether or not the Teacher and the Principal discussed the nature of the hockey stick among themselves, although they did discuss the possible consequences of a hit by the stick as well as how close the stick came to striking Charley.

10. The Principal was quite proud of the speech he intended to give but did not favor me with a recitation, only with a summary of its content.

11. Not only would the longer jail sentence outside make the corporal look better, it would mean that he and his wife would be relieved of the responsibility of caring for and feeding Charley for the thirty days he would spend in incarceration at Discha.

12. See, for example, Ernest Thompson Seton's characterization of them: "These Chipewyans are dirty, shiftless, improvident, and absolutely honest" (Seton 1981: 147)

13. Later in the same court session a man came to trial on charges relating to his child's death. After months of investigation, that case weighed heavily upon the RCMP officer's reputation with the court and his superiors in the RCMP. He lost that case, so Charley's conviction was a fortuitous face-saving.

18. FUTURE MEMORY

1. The Dene utilize residence and economic cooperation to form small restricted cognatic descent groups that are the effective subsistence and production groups in bush life. These groups are normally focused through parental attempts to keep their sons' families with them while drawing in their sons-in-law and their families. The membership of these groups often changes from season to season (Sharp 1977, 1988a; J. G. E. Smith 1975, 1976; Jarvenpa 1976, 1980; Irimoto 1981).

2. The context of their relationship and the events of the spring of 1975 are discussed in detail in *The Transformation of Bigfoot* (Sharp 1988a). After the separation between George and Wellington in the summer of 1975, relations between the two brothers remained somewhat distant. As George established his autonomy as the head of a household, the normal pattern of sharing possessions and joint economic cooperation diminished. When Paul died some dozen years later, Wellington shifted the locus of his bush life to just a few miles north of his father's old camp on Adeker Lake. George remained based at Foxholm Lake. As both men matured and developed their individual approaches to living in the bush, each accumulated an astonishing amount (by 1970s standards) of equipment, buildings, and material goods at their respective bush camps.

With the maturation of their children and the brothers' progression to grandparenthood, the ties between them largely became ones of casual socialization at Mission devoid of any real cooperative or joint activities. With May's death in 1999 and the maturation of so many of her grandchildren and great-grandchildren, the fission of the bonds between Wellington and George (and their descendants) should progress to the casual ties of those only distantly related.

3. This had begun to change by the early 1990s as the Mission Band gained sophistication in its own governance within the Canadian bureaucracy. The band began to use the missionary script in its publications, and there were signs of an increase in literacy in the Chipewyan language.

4. To the best of my knowledge, the patterns of behavior and the choices these men made were not the result of a deliberate or conscious decision-making process. The forms of their culture were being played out through them at an unconscious level. I doubt that they were consciously aware of the dynamics of their behavior. Prof. D. Trigger raised this point during my October 1995 presentation of this chapter before a seminar at the Department of Anthropology of the University of Western Australia: If it is possible to present these events by ordinary means, by assuming that the Dene calculate outcomes and plan events, why not do so? His point neatly encapsulates many of the current concerns in ethnographic writing. These events could be explained in conventional terms, but to do so would require me to distort the ways in which the Dene behave and think. Faced with the choice of distorting our cultural sense of reality and causality or that of Dene behavior, I have opted to preserve the latter at the cost of the former.

5. These connections can sometimes be felt. I have discussed my experience of this in "Experiencing Meaning" (Sharp 1996).

6. I make the analogy with some trepidation. In the mid-1960s, when the computer was first making an impact in psychology, all the graduate students I knew were using the working of the mind as a metaphor to explain the working of the computer. I am not quite sure what it says about us and the state of our knowledge that it has become so easy to use the workings of the computer as a metaphor to explain the workings of the mind.

7. Even memories of smell, pain, and physical sensation are culturally determined. One might argue about whether or not the sensations and perceptions themselves are culturally determined, but not about the memory of them.

19. LOON V

1. The Dene still believe that the black flies and mosquitoes fly away to the caribou herds when they approach. This is an accurate description of what happens in late

summer along the tundra fringes. The insects there vanish within a few days of the arrival of the caribou, whereas in the forest the insects can remain into October and often survive the first heavy snows of September only to reemerge when those snows melt off. The most probable explanation for the relationship in Western terms lies in the coolness of the nights that begin to come in late July. Insects, which may not seem like much of an issue, are a dominating factor in the lives of every human and animal in the North.

BIBLIOGRAPHY

Achenbach, J. 1994. "Why Things Are." *Washington Post,* 13 May: D5.

Asch, M. I. 1981. "Slavey." In *Handbook of North American Indians.* Vol. 6, *Subarctic,* edited by J. Helm. Washington DC: Smithsonian Institution Press: 338–49.

Ascher, R. 1968. "Time's Arrow and the Archaeology of a Contemporary Community." In *Settlement Archaeology,* edited by K. C. Chang. Palo Alto CA: National Press Books: 43–52.

Atwood, M. 1972. *Survival: A Thematic Guide to Canadian Literature.* Toronto: McClelland and Stewart.

———. 1995. *Strange Things: The Malevolent North in Canadian Literature.* Oxford: Clarendon Press.

Banfield, A. W. F. 1961. *A Revision of the Reindeer and Caribou, Genus Rangifer.* National Museum of Canada Bulletin No. 177, Biological Series, no. 66. Ottawa: Department of Northern Affairs and Natural Resources.

Basso, E. 1978. "The Enemy of Every Tribe: 'Bushman' Images in Northern Athapaskan Narratives." *American Anthropologist* 5, no. 4: 690–709.

Basso, K. H. 1976. *The Cibecue Apache.* Prospect Heights IL: Waveland.

Bateson, G. 1958. *Naven: A Survey of the Problems Suggested by a Composite Picture of the Culture of a New Guinea Tribe Drawn from Three Points of View.* 2d ed. Stanford CA: Stanford University Press.

———. 1972. *Steps to an Ecology of Mind.* New York: Ballantine.

Beidleman, T. O. 1961. "Hyena and Rabbit: A Kaguru Representation of Matrilineal Relations." *Africa* 31:250–57.

———. 1963. "Further Adventures of Hyena and Rabbit: The Folktale as a Sociological Model." *Africa* 33:54–69.

———. 1968. "Some Nuer Notions of Nakedness, Nudity, and Sexuality." *Africa* 38:113–31.

——. 1973. "Kaguru Symbolic Classification." In *Right & Left: Essays in Dual Symbolic Classification,* edited by R. Needham. Chicago: University of Chicago Press: 128–66.

——. 1982. *Colonial Evangelism: A Socio-Historical Study of an East African Mission at the Grassroots.* Bloomington: University of Indiana Press.

——. 1989. Review of *The Predicament of Culture: Twentieth-Century Ethnography, Literature, and Art,* by James Clifford. *Anthropos* 84:263–67.

Bishop, C. A., and S. Kretch III. 1980. "Matriorganization: The Basis of Aboriginal Subarctic Social Organization." *Arctic Anthropology* 17, no. 2: 34–45.

Bone, R., E. Shannan, and S. Raby. 1973. *The Chipewyan of the Stony Rapids Region.* Mawdsley Memoir No. 1. Saskatoon: Institute for Northern Studies, University of Saskatchewan.

Brace, C. L. 1989. "Medieval Thinking and the Paradigms of Paleoanthropology." *American Anthropologist* 91:442–46.

Brody, H. 1983. *Maps and Dreams: Indians and the British Columbia Frontier.* Bungay, England: Pelican.

Burch, E. S., Jr. 1972. "The Caribou/Wild Reindeer as a Human Resource." *American Antiquity* 37, no. 3: 339–68.

——. 1977. "Muskox and Man in the Central Canadian Subarctic, 1689–1974." *Arctic* 30:135–54.

Cannon, W. B. 1942. "Voodoo Death." *American Anthropologist* 44:169–81.

Carter, R. M. 1974. "Chipewyan Semantics: Form and Meaning in the Language and Culture of an Athapaskan-Speaking People of Canada." Ph.D. dissertation, Duke University.

Chang, K. C. 1962. "A Typology of Settlement and Community Patterns in Some Circumpolar Societies." *Arctic Anthropology* 1:28–41.

Clark, A. M. 1981. "Koyukon." In *Handbook of North American Indians.* Vol. 6, *Subarctic,* edited by J. Helm. Washington DC: Smithsonian Institution Press: 585–601.

Clark, G. A. 1988. "Some Thoughts on the Black Skull: An Archeologist's Assessment of WT-17000 (*A. boisei*) and Systematics in Human Paleontology." *American Anthropologist* 90:357–71.

——. 1989. "Paradigms and Paradoxes in Paleoanthropology: A Response to C. Loring Brace." *American Anthropologist* 91:446–50.

Cohen, A. 1974. *Two-Dimensional Man: An Essay on the Anthropology of Power and Symbolism in Complex Society.* Berkeley: University of California Press.

Coles, T. L. 1980. "Stanner and Mutjingga: A Reinterpretation of Myth." M.A. thesis, Simon Fraser University.

Crocker, J. C. 1977. "The Mirrored Self: Identity and Ritual Inversion among the Eastern Bororo." *Ethnology* 16, no. 2: 129–45.

Crow, J., and P. Obley. 1981. "Han." In *Handbook of North American Indians.* Vol. 6, *Subarctic,* edited by J. Helm. Washington DC: Smithsonian Institution Press: 506–13.

Cruikshank, J. 1990. *Life Lived Like a Story: Life Stories of Three Yukon Native Elders.* Lincoln: University of Nebraska Press.

Curtis, E. S. 1928. *The North American Indian.* Vol. 18. New York: Johnson Reprint Corporation.

Davis, N. Y. 1981. "History of Research in Subarctic Alaska." In *Handbook of North American Indians.* Vol. 6, *Subarctic,* edited by J. Helm. Washington DC: Smithsonian Institution Press: 43–48.

Douglas, M. T. 1966. *Purity and Danger: An Analysis of the Concepts of Pollution and Taboo.* London: Routledge and Kegan Paul.

Duby, G. 1980. *The Three Orders: Feudal Society Imagined.* Chicago: University of Chicago Press.

Dumont, L. 1983. *Affinity as a Value: Marriage Alliance in South India, with Comparative Essays on Australia.* Chicago: University of Chicago Press.

Durkheim, E. 1951. *Suicide: A Study in Sociology.* Toronto: Free Press.

———. 1964. *The Rules of the Sociological Method.* New York: Free Press.

———. 1965. *The Elementary Forms of the Religious Life.* 1915. Reprint, New York: Free Press.

Durkheim, E., and M. Mauss. 1963. *Primitive Classification.* Chicago: University of Chicago Press.

Dyck, N. 1980. "Booze, Barrooms, and Scrapping: Masculinity and Violence in a Western Canadian Town." *Canadian Journal of Anthropology* 1, no. 2: 191–98.

———. 1991. *What Is the Indian "Problem": Tutelage and Resistance in Canadian Indian Administration.* St. John's NF: Institute of Social and Economic Research, Memorial University of Newfoundland.

———. 1993. *Anthropology, Public Policy, and Native Peoples in Canada.* Montreal: McGill-Queen's University Press.

Dyen, I., and D. Aberle. 1974. *Lexical Reconstruction: The Case of the Proto-Athapaskan Kinship System.* New York: Cambridge University Press.

Evans-Pritchard, E. E. 1940. *The Nuer.* Oxford: Clarendon Press.

———. 1952. "A Letter to E. E. Evans-Pritchard." *British Journal of Sociology* 3:117–23.

———. 1956. *Nuer Religion.* New York: Oxford University Press.

———. 1980. *Witchcraft Oracles and Magic among the Azande*. Abridged ed. Oxford: Oxford University Press.

Fabian, J. 1983. *Time and the Other: How Anthropology Makes Its Object*. New York: Columbia University Press.

Feeley-Harnik, G. 1981. *The Lord's Table: Eucharist and Passover in Early Christianity*. Philadelphia: University of Pennsylvania Press.

Fienup-Riordan, A. 1988. "Robert Redford, Apanuugpak, and the Invention of Tradition." *American Ethnologist* 15:442–55.

Firth, R. 1985. "Degrees of Intelligibility." In *Reason and Morality*, edited by J. Overing. New York: Tavistock: 29–46.

Flannery, T. 1994. *The Future Eaters*. Port Melbourne, Australia: Reed Books.

Fortes, M., and E. E. Evans-Pritchard. 1940. *African Political Systems*. Oxford: Oxford University Press.

Fortune, R. F. 1932. *Sorcerers of Dobu: The Social Anthropology of the Dobu Islanders of the Western Pacific*. New York: Dutton.

———. 1936. *Manus Religion: An Ethnological Study of the Manus Natives of the Admiralty Islands*. Lincoln: University of Nebraska Press.

Foucault, M. 1974. *The Archaeology of Knowledge*. London: Tavistock.

———. 1979. *Discipline and Punish: The Birth of the Prison*. New York: Vintage.

———. 1980. *The History of Sexuality*. Vol. 1. New York: Vintage.

Freud, S. 1983. *Totem and Taboo*. London: ARK Paperbacks.

Fustel de Coulanges, Numa Denis. 1956. *The Ancient City: A Study on the Religion, Laws, and Institutions of Greece and Rome*. 1864. Reprint, Garden City NY: Doubleday/Anchor Books.

Gazzaniga, M. S. 1985. *The Social Brain*. New York: Basic Books.

Gell, A. 1992. *The Anthropology of Time: Cultural Constructions of Temporal Maps and Images*. Oxford: Berg.

Gillespie, B. C. 1975. "Territorial Expansion of the Chipewyan in the 18th Century." In *Proceedings: Northern Athapaskan Conference, 1971*. Vol. 1, edited by A. M. Clark. National Museum of Man, Mercury Series. Canadian Ethnology Service Paper No. 27. Ottawa: National Museums of Canada: 350–88.

———. 1976. "Changes in Territory and Technology of the Chipewyan." *Arctic Anthropology* 13, no. 1: 6–11.

———. 1981. "Mountain Indians." In *Handbook of North American Indians*. Vol. 6, *Subarctic*, edited by J. Helm. Washington DC: Smithsonian Institution Press: 326–37.

Ginzburg, C. 1985. *Night Battles: Witchcraft and Agrarian Cults in the Sixteenth and Seventeenth Centuries*. New York: Penguin.

Givens, D., and J. Jablonski. 1995. "1995 Survey of Anthropology PhDs." *Anthropology Newsletter* 36, no. 6: 11.

Gleick, J. 1987. *Chaos: Making a New Science*. New York: Viking.

Gluckman, M. 1954. *Rituals of Rebellion in South-East Africa*. Manchester, England: Manchester University Press.

Goffman, E. 1963. *Stigma: Notes on the Management of Spoiled Identity*. Englewood Cliffs NJ: Prentice-Hall.

Gordon, B. 1977. "Chipewyan Prehistory." In *Problems in the Prehistory of the North American Subarctic: The Athapaskan Question*, edited by J. Helmer, S. Van Dyke, F. Kense. Calgary AB: Archaeological Association of the University of Calgary: 72–77.

Gould, S. J. 1977. *Ever since Darwin: Reflections in Natural History*. New York: Norton.

——. 1987. *Time's Arrow, Time's Cycle: Myth and Metaphor in the Discovery of Geological Time*. Cambridge, Mass.: Harvard University Press.

Goulet, J. 1982. "Religious Dualism among Athapaskan Catholics." *Canadian Journal of Anthropology* 3, no. 1: 1–17.

——. 1992. "Gold In, Gold Out: The Objectification of Dene Tha Accounts of Dreams and Visions." *Journal of Anthropological Research* 48, no. 3: 215–30.

——. 1993. "Reincarnation as a Fact of Life among Contemporary Dene Tha." In *Amerindian Rebirth: Reincarnation Belief among North American Indians and Inuit*, edited by A. Mills and R. Slobodin. Toronto: University of Toronto Press: 156–76.

——. 1998. *Ways of Knowing: Experience, Knowledge, and Power among the Dene Tha*. Lincoln: University of Nebraska Press.

Gribbin, J. 1984. *In Search of Schrödinger's Cat: Quantum Physics and Reality*. New York: Bantam.

Hall, R., and H. S. Sharp. 1978. *Wolf and Man: Evolution in Parallel*. New York: Academic Press.

Hara, H. S. 1980. *The Hare Indians and Their World*. National Museum of Man, Mercury Series. Canadian Ethnology Service Paper No. 63. Ottawa: National Museums of Canada.

Harkin, M. 1988. "History, Narrative, and Temporality: Examples from the Northwest Coast." *Ethnohistory* 35:99–130.

Hawking, S. W. 1988. *A Brief History of Time: From the Big Bang to Black Holes*. New York: Bantam.

Hearne, S. 1971. *A Journey from Prince of Wales Fort in Hudson's Bay to the Northern Ocean*. Edmonton AB: M. G. Hurtig.

Heider, F. 1958. *The Psychology of Interpersonal Relations*. New York: Wiley.

Helm, J. 1961. *The Lynx Point People: The Dynamics of a Northern Athapaskan Band.* National Museum of Canada Bulletin No. 176, Anthropological Series, no. 53. Ottawa: Northern Affairs And National Resources.

——. 1965. "Bilaterality in the Socio-Territorial Organization of the Arctic Drainage Dene." *Ethnology* 4, no. 4: 361–85.

——. 1968. "The Nature of Dogrib Socio-Territorial Groups." In *Man the Hunter,* edited by R. Lee and I. Devore. Chicago: Aldine: 118–25.

——. 1972. "The Dogrib Indians." In *Hunters and Gatherers Today: A Socioeconomic Study of Eleven Such Cultures in the Twentieth Century,* edited by M. G. Bicchieri. New York: Holt, Rinehart, and Winston: 51–89.

——. n.d. "On Responsible Scholarship on Culture Contact in the Mackenzie Basin." Unpublished manuscript in the author's possession.

——. 1978. "On Responsible Scholarship on Culture Contact in the Mackenzie Basin." *Current Anthropology* 19:160–62.

——. 1980. "Female Infanticide, European Diseases, and Population Levels among the Mackenzie Dene." *American Ethnologist* 7, no. 2: 259–85.

——. 1993. "Always with Them Either a Feast or a Famine: Living Off the Land with Chipewyan Indians, 1791–1792." *Arctic Anthropology* 30, no. 2: 46–60.

——. n.d. "Horde, Band, and Tribe: Northern Approaches." Third Annual Presidential Lecture. University of Iowa, Iowa City.

——. 1994. *Prophecy and Power among the Dogrib Indians.* Lincoln: University of Nebraska Press.

Helm, J., and D. Damas. 1963. "The Contact-Traditional All-Native Community of the Canadian North: The Upper Mackenzie 'Bush' Athapaskans and the Igluligmiut." *Anthropologica* n.s., 5:9–22.

Helm, J., et al. 1975. "The Contact History of the Subarctic Athapaskans: An Overview." In *Proceedings: Northern Athapaskan Conference, 1971.* Vol. 1, edited by A. M. Clark. National Museum of Man, Mercury Series. Canadian Ethnology Service Paper No. 27. Ottawa: National Museums of Canada: 302–49.

Heusch, L. de. 1985. *Sacrifice in Africa: A Structuralist Approach.* Bloomington: Indiana University Press.

Hobart, M. 1985. "Anthropos through the Looking-Glass: Or How to Teach the Balinese to Bark." In *Reason and Morality,* edited by J. Overing. New York: Tavistock: 104–34.

Honnigmann, J. 1981. "Kaska." In *Handbook of North American Indians.* Vol. 6, *Subarctic,* edited by J. Helm. Washington DC: Smithsonian Institution Press: 442–50.

Huber, P. B. 1980. "The Anggor Bowman: Ritual and Society in Melanesia." *American Ethnologist* 7, no. 1: 43–57.

Hubert, H., and M. Mauss. 1964. *Sacrifice: Its Nature and Function.* Translation of "Essai sur la nature et la fonction du sacrifice," 1898. Chicago: University of Chicago Press.

Ingold, T. 1983. "The Significance of Storage in Hunting Societies." *Man* n.s., 18, no. 3: 553–71.

Irimoto, T. 1981. *Chipewyan Ecology.* Senri Ethnological Studies No. 8. Osaka, Japan: National Museum of Ethnology.

Irimoto, T., and T. Yamada. 1994. *Circumpolar Religion and Ecology: An Anthropology of the North.* Tokyo: University of Tokyo Press.

Janes, R. R. 1976. "Culture Contact in the 19th Century Mackenzie Basin." *Current Anthropology* 17, no. 2: 344–45.

———. 1977. "More on Culture Contact in the Mackenzie Basin." *Current Anthropology* 18, no. 3: 554–56.

———. 1983. *Archaeological Ethnography among Mackenzie Basin Dene, Canada.* Technical Paper No. 28. Calgary AB: Arctic Institute of North America.

Janes, R. R., and J. H. Kelley. 1977. "Observations on Crisis Cult Activities in the Mackenzie Basin." In *Problems in the Prehistory of the North American Subarctic: The Athapaskan Question,* edited by J. Helmer, S. Van Dyke, and F. Kense. Calgary AB: Archaeological Association of the University of Calgary: 153–64.

Jarvenpa, R. 1976. "Spatial and Ecological Factors in the Annual Economic Cycle of the English River Band of Chipewyan." *Arctic Anthropology* n.s., 18, no. 1: 45–60.

———. 1977. "The Ubiquitous Bushman: Chipewyan-White Trapper Relations of the 1930's." In *Problems in the Prehistory of the North American Subarctic: The Athapaskan Question,* edited by J. Helmer, S. Van Dyke, and F. Kense. Calgary AB: Archaeological Association of the University of Calgary: 165–83.

———. 1980. *The Trappers of Patuanak: Toward a Spatial Ecology of Modern Hunters.* National Museum of Man, Mercury Series, Canadian Ethnology Service Paper No. 67. Ottawa: National Museums of Canada.

———. 1982. "Intergroup Behavior and Imagery: The Case of Chipewyan and Cree." *Ethnology* 31, no. 4: 283–99.

———. 1998. *Northern Apprenticeship.* Prospect Heights IL: Waveland.

Keegan, J. 1994. *A History of Warfare.* New York: Vintage.

Kenny, M. G. 1981. "Mirror in the Forest: The Dorobo Hunter-Gatherers as an Image of the Other." *Africa* 51, no. 1: 477–95.

——. 1982. "The Stranger from the Lake: A Theme in the History of the Lake Victoria Shorelands." *Azania* 17:1–26.

Koolage, W. W. 1975. "Conceptual Negativism in Chipewyan Ethnology." *Anthropologica* n.s., 18, no. 1: 45–60.

Kuchler, S. 1988. "Malangan: Objects, Sacrifice, and the Production of Memory." *American Ethnologist* 15:625–37.

Laguna, F. de, and C. McClellan. 1981. "Ahtna." In *Handbook of North American Indians*. Vol. 6, *Subarctic,* edited by J. Helm. Washington DC: Smithsonian Institution Press: 641–63.

Layton, R. 1986. "Political and Territorial Structures among Hunter-Gatherers." *Man* n.s., 2, no. 1: 18–33.

Leach, E. 1966. *Rethinking Anthropology.* London: Athlone Press.

Levi-Strauss, C. 1955. *Structural Anthropology.* Garden City NY: Anchor.

——. 1963. *Totemism.* Boston: Beacon Press.

——. 1967. "The Story of Asdiwal." In *The Structural Study of Myth and Totemism,* edited by E. Leach. London: Tavistock.

——. 1969a. *The Elementary Structures of Kinship.* London: Eyre and Spottiswoode.

——. 1969b. *The Raw and the Cooked.* New York: Harper and Row.

——. 1981. *The Naked Man.* New York: Harper and Row.

Levy-Bruhl, L. 1967. *Primitive Mentality.* 1923. Reprint, Boston: Beacon Press.

——. 1979. *How Natives Think.* 1926. Reprint, New York: Arno Press.

Li, Fang-Kwei. 1933. "A List of Chipewyan Stems." *International Journal of American Linguistics* 7:122–51.

Lowie, R. 1912. "Chipewyan Tales." *Anthropological Papers of the American Museum of Natural History.* 10:171–200.

——. 1925. "Windigo, a Chipewyan Story." In *American Indian Life,* edited by E. C. Parsons. New York: Viking: 325–36.

MacLachlan, B. 1981. "Tahltan." In *Handbook of North American Indians.* Vol. 6, *Subarctic,* edited by J. Helm. Washington DC: Smithsonian Institution Press: 458–68.

MacNeish, J. H. 1954. "Contemporary Folk Beliefs of a Slave Indian Band." *Journal of American Folklore* 67:185–98.

——. 1956. "Leadership among the Northeastern Athabascans." *Anthropologica* 2:131–63.

——. 1960. "Kin Terms of Arctic Drainage Dene: Hare, Slavey, Chipewyan." *American Anthropologist* 62:279–95.

McClellan, C. 1981a. "History of Research in the Subarctic Cordillera." In *Handbook of North American Indians.* Vol. 6, *Subarctic,* edited by J. Helm. Washington DC: Smithsonian Institution Press: 35–42.

——. 1981b. "Tutchone." In *Handbook of North American Indians.* Vol. 6, *Subarctic,* edited by J. Helm. Washington DC: Smithsonian Institution Press: 493–505.

McDonnell, R. F. 1984. "Symbolic Orientations and Systematic Turmoil: Centering on the Kaska Symbol of Dene." *Canadian Journal of Anthropology* 4, no. 1: 39–56.

Marcus, G., and M. Fischer. 1968. *Anthropology as Cultural Critique: An Experimental Moment in the Human Sciences.* Chicago: University of Chicago Press.

Martin, C. 1978. *Keepers of the Game: Indian-Animal Relationships and the Fur Trade.* Berkeley: University of California Press.

Mauss, M. 1967. *The Gift: Forms and Functions of Exchange in Archaic Societies.* 1954. Reprint, New York: Norton.

Mills, A., and R. Slobodin. 1993. *American Rebirth: Reincarnation Belief among North American Indians.* Toronto: University of Toronto Press.

Moore, P., and A. Wheelock. 1991. *Wolverine Myths and Visions: Dene Traditions from Northern Alberta.* Lincoln: University of Nebraska Press.

Moran, N. 1992. "Quantum Leapers." *Natural History* 101, no. 4: 35–38.

Morgan, L. H. 1964. *Ancient Society,* edited by L. A. White. 1878. Reprint, Cambridge MA: Belknap, Harvard University Press (contains the note in response to J. F. MacLennan: 430–42).

Murie, A. 1944. *The Wolves of Mount McKinley.* Fauna of the National Parks of the United States, Fauna Series No. 5. Washington DC: U.S. National Park Service.

Needham, R. 1962. *Structure and Sentiment: A Test Case in Social Anthropology.* Chicago: University of Chicago Press.

——. 1966. "Age, Category, and Descent." dragen tot de taal-, land- en volkenkunde 2:1–35.

——. 1972. *Belief, Language, and Experience.* Oxford: Blackwell.

——. 1974. *Remarks and Inventions: Skeptical Essays about Kinship.* London: Tavistock.

——. 1975. "Polythetic Classification: Convergence and Consequences." *Man* n.s., 10:349–69.

——. 1978. *Primordial Characters.* Charlottesville: University of Virginia Press.

——. 1979. *Symbolic Classification.* Santa Monica CA: Goodyear Publishing.

——. 1980. *Reconnaissances.* Toronto: University of Toronto Press.

Nelson, R. K. 1983. *Make Prayers to the Raven: A Koyukon View of the Northern Forest.* Chicago: University of Chicago Press.

O'Keefe, D. L. 1983. *Stolen Lightning: The Social Theory of Magic.* New York: Random House.

Osgood, C. B. 1933. *The Ethnography of the Great Bear Lake Indians.* Annual Report, 1931, National Museum of Canada. Ottawa: F. A. Acland, King's Printer.

——. 1953. *Winter.* New York: Norton.

Oswalt, W. 1967. *This Land Was Theirs: A Study of North American Indians.* San Francisco: Chandler.

Overing, J., ed. 1985. *Reason and Morality.* New York: Tavistock.

Parkin, D. 1985. "Reason, Emotion, and the Embodiment of Power." In *Reason and Morality,* edited by J. Overing. New York: Tavistock: 135–51.

Pelto, P. 1973. *The Snowmobile Revolution: Technology and Social Change in the Arctic.* Menlo Park CA: Cummins.

Pielou, E. C. 1991. *After the Ice Age: The Return of Life to Glaciated North America.* Chicago: University of Chicago Press.

Radin, P. 1972. *The Trickster: A Study in American Indian Mythology.* New York: Schocken.

——. 1990. *The Winnebago Tribe.* Lincoln: University of Nebraska Press.

Ridington, R. 1968. "The Medicine Fight: An Instrument of Political Process among the Beaver Indians." *American Anthropologist* 70, no. 6: 1152–60.

——. 1981. "Beaver." In *Handbook of North American Indians.* Vol. 6, *Subarctic,* edited by J. Helm. Washington DC: Smithsonian Institution Press: 350–60.

——. 1988. *Trail to Heaven: Knowledge and Narrative in a Northern Native Community.* Iowa City: University of Iowa Press.

——. 1990. *Little Bit Know Something: Stories in a Language of Anthropology.* Iowa City: University of Iowa Press.

Robertson-Smith, W. 1901. *Lectures on the Religion of the Semites.* London: Adam and Charles Black.

Rogers, E. S. 1981. "History of Ethnological Research in the Subarctic Shield and Mackenzie Valley." In *Handbook of North American Indians.* Vol. 6, *Subarctic,* edited by J. Helm. Washington DC: Smithsonian Institution Press: 19–29.

Roscoe, P. 1995. "The Perils of 'Positivism' in Cultural Anthropology." *American Anthropologist* 97, no. 3: 492–504.

Ross, R. 1992. "Being Indian Is a State of Mind." In *Dancing with a Ghost: Exploring Indian Reality.* Markham ON: Octopus Publishing Group.

Rushforth, S. 1992. "The Legitimization of Belief in a Hunter-Gatherer Society: Bearlake Athapaskan Knowledge and Authority." *American Ethnologist* 19:483–500.

Sahlins, M. 1985. *Islands of History.* Chicago: University of Chicago Press.

Sansom, B. 1980. *The Camp at Wallaby Cross: Aboriginal Fringe Dwellers in Darwin.* Canberra: Australian Institute of Aboriginal Studies.

Savishinsky, J. 1974. *The Trail of the Hare: Life and Stress in an Arctic Community.* New York: Gordon and Breach.

——. 1975. "The Dog and the Hare: Canine Culture in an Athapaskan Band." In *Proceedings: Northern Athapaskan Conference, 1971.* Vol. 2, edited by A. M. Clark. National Museum of Man, Mercury Series. Canadian Ethnology Service Paper No. 27. Ottawa: National Museums of Canada: 462–515.

Savishinsky, J., and H. Hara. 1981. "Hare." In *Handbook of North American Indians.* Vol. 6, *Subarctic,* edited by J. Helm. Washington DC: Smithsonian Institution Press: 314–25.

Service, E. 1962. *Primitive Social Organization: An Evolutionary Perspective.* New York: Random House.

Seton, E. T. 1981. *The Arctic Prairies.* 1911. Reprint, Toronto: Fitzhenry and Whiteside.

Sharp, H. S. 1975. "Introducing the Sororate to a Northern Saskatchewan Chipewyan Village." *Ethnology* 14, no. 1: 71–82.

——. 1976. "Man:Wolf::Woman:Dog." *Arctic Anthropology* 13, no. 1: 25–34.

——. 1977. "The Chipewyan Hunting Unit." *American Ethnologist* 4, no. 2: 377–93.

——. 1978. "Comparative Ethnology of the Wolf and the Chipewyan." In *Wolf and Man: Evolution in Parallel,* edited by R. Hall and H. Sharp. New York: Academic Press: 55–79.

——. 1979. *Chipewyan Marriage.* National Museum of Man, Mercury Series. Canadian Ethnology Series Paper No. 58. Ottawa: National Museums of Canada.

——. 1981a. "Old Age among the Chipewyan." In *Other Ways of Growing Old,* edited by P. Amoss and S. Harrell. Stanford CA: Stanford University Press: 99–109.

——. 1981b. "The Null Case: The Chipewyan." In *Woman the Gatherer,* edited by F. Dahlberg. New Haven CT: Yale University Press: 221–44.

——. 1986. "Shared Experience and Magical Death: Chipewyan Explanations of a Prophet's Decline." *Ethnology* 25, no. 4: 257–70.

——. 1987. "Giant Fish, Giant Otters, and Dinosaurs: 'Apparently Irrational' Beliefs in a Chipewyan Community." *American Ethnologist* 14, no. 2: 226–35.

——. 1988a. *The Transformation of Bigfoot: Maleness, Power, and Belief among the Chipewyan.* Washington DC: Smithsonian Institution Press.

——. 1988b. "Dry Meat and Gender: The Absence of Ritual for the Regulation of Animal Numbers and Hunting in Chipewyan Society." In *Hunters and Gatherers.* Vol. 2, *Property, Power and Ideology,* edited by T. Ingold, D. Riches, and J. Woodburn. London: Berg: 183–91.

——. 1991. "Memory, Meaning, and Imaginary Time: The Construction of Knowledge in White and Chipewyan Cultures." *Ethnohistory* 38, no. 2: 149–75.

——. 1994a. "The Power of Weakness." In *Key Issues in Hunter-Gatherer Research,* edited by E. S. Burch Jr. and L. Ellana. London: Berg: 35–58.

——. 1994b. "Inverted Sacrifice." In *Circumpolar Religion and Ecology: An Anthropology of the North,* edited by T. Irimoto and T. Yamada. Tokyo: University of Tokyo Press: 253–71.

——. 1996. "Experiencing Meaning." *Anthropology and Humanism* 21, no. 2: 171–86.

——. 1997. "Non-directional Time and the Dene Life-cycle." In *Circumpolar Animism and Shamanism,* edited by T. Yamada and T. Irimoto. Sapporo, Japan: Hokkaido University Press: 93–104.

——. 1998. "À la recherche du caribou." *Recherches amérindiennes au Québec* 38, no. 3: 63–70.

Slobodin, R. 1960. "Some Social Functions of Kutchin Anxiety." *American Anthropologist* 62, no. 1: 122–33.

——. 1962. *Band Organization of the Peel River Kutchin.* National Museum of Canada Bulletin No. 179. Ottawa: Northern Affairs and National Resources.

——. 1969. "Leadership and Participation in a Kutchin Trapping Party." In *Contributions to Anthropology: Band Societies.* National Museum of Canada Bulletin No. 228, Paper no. 3. Ottawa: National Museums of Canada: 93–115.

——. 1970. "Kutchin Concepts of Reincarnation." *Western Canadian Journal of Anthropology* 2, no. 1: 67–79.

——. 1975. "Without Fire: A Kutchin Tale of Warfare, Survival, and Vengeance." In *Proceedings: Northern Athapaskan Conference, 1971.* Vol. 1, edited by A. M. Clark. National Museum of Man, Mercury Series. Canadian Ethnology Service Paper No. 27. Ottawa: National Museums of Canada: 259–301.

Smith, D. M. 1973. *I^{n}KO^{n}ZE: Magico-Religious Beliefs of Contact-Traditional Chipewyan Trading at Fort Resolution,* NWT, Canada. Mercury Series, Ethnology Division Paper No. 6. Ottawa: National Museums of Man.

——. 1982. *Moose-Deer Island House People: A History of the Native People of Fort Resolution.* Mercury Series, Canadian Ethnology Service Paper No. 81. Ottawa: National Museums of Canada.

——. 1985. "Big Stone Foundations: Manifest Meaning in Chipewyan Myths." *Journal of American Culture* 18, no. 1: 73–77.

——. 1990. "The Chipewyan Medicine-Fight in Cultural and Ecological Perspective." In *Culture and the Anthropological Tradition: Essays in Honor of Robert F. Spencer,* edited by T. Winthrop. Lanham MD: University Press of America: 153–75.

——. 1992. "The Dynamics of a Dene Struggle for Self- Determination." *Anthropologica* 34, no. 1: 21–49.

——. 1993. "Albert's Power: A Fiction Narrative." *Anthropology and Humanism* 18, no. 2: 67–73.

——. 1994. "Death of a Patriarch." *Anthropology and Humanism* 20, no. 2: 124–32.

——. 1997. "World as Event: Aspects of Chipewyan Ontology." In *Circumpolar Animism and Shamanism,* edited by T. Yamada and T. Irimoto. Sapporo, Japan: Hokkaido University Press: 67–91.

——. 1998. "An Athapaskan Way of Knowing: Chipewyan Ontology." *American Ethnologist* 24, no. 30: 412–32.

Smith, J. G. E. 1970. "The Chipewyan Hunting Group in a Village Context." *Western Canadian Journal of Anthropology* 2, no. 1: 60–66.

——. 1975. "The Ecological Basis of Chipewyan Socio-Territorial Organization." In *Proceedings: Northern Athapaskan Conference, 1971.* Vol. 1, edited by A. M. Clark. National Museum of Man, Mercury Series. Canadian Ethnology Service Paper No. 27. Ottawa: National Museums of Canada: 389–461.

——. 1976. "Local Band Organization of the Caribou-Eater Chipewyan." *Arctic Anthropology* 13, no. 1: 12–24.

——. 1978. "The Emergence of the Micro-Urban Village among the Caribou-Eater Chipewyan." *Human Organization* 37, no. 1: 38–49.

——. 1981. "Chipewyan." In *Handbook of North American Indians.* Vol. 6, *Subarctic,* edited by J. Helm. Washington DC: Smithsonian Institution Press: 271–284.

Smith, J. G. E., and E. S. Burch Jr. 1979. "Chipewyan and Inuit in the Central Canadian Subarctic, 1613–1977." *Arctic Anthropology* 16, no. 2: 76–101.

Sperber, D. 1985. "Apparently Irrational Beliefs." In *On Anthropological Knowledge: Three Essays.* Cambridge: Cambridge University Press: 35–63.

Stanner, W. E. H. 1960. "Durmugan, a Nangiomeri." In *In the Company of Man: Twenty Portraits by Anthropologists,* edited by J. Casagrande. New York: Harper.

——. 1963. *On Aboriginal Religion.* Oceania Monograph Series No. 11. Sydney, Australia: University of Sydney.

——. 1965. "The Dreaming." In *Reader in Comparative Religion: An Anthropological Approach,* edited by W. Lessa and E. Vogt. 2d ed. New York: Harper and Row: 158–67.

Steiner, F. 1967. *Taboo.* London: Pelican.

Steward, J. 1955. *Theory of Culture Change: The Methodology of Multilinear Evolution.* Urbana: University of Illinois Press.

Swartz, M., V. Turner, and A. Tuden. 1966. *Political Anthropology.* Chicago: Aldine.

Tanner, A. 1979. *Bringing Home Animals: Religious Ideology and Mode of Production of the Mistassini Cree Hunters.* New York: St. Martin's Press.

Toren, C. 1983. "Thinking Symbols: A Critique of Sperber (1979)." *Man* n.s., 18:260–68.

Townsend, J. 1983. "Firearms against Native Arms: A Study in Comparative Efficiencies with an Alaskan Example." *Arctic Anthropology* 20, no. 2: 1–33.

Turner, E. 1987. *The Spirit and the Drum: A Memoir of Africa.* Tucson: University of Arizona Press.

———. 1992. *Experiencing Ritual: A New Interpretation of African Healing.* Philadelphia: University of Pennsylvania Press.

———. 1994. "The Effects of Contact on the Religion of the Inupiat Eskimos." In *Circumpolar Religion and Ecology: An Anthropology of the North,* edited by T. Irimoto and T. Yamada. Tokyo: University of Tokyo Press: 143–62.

———. 1996. *The Hands Feel It: Healing and Spirit Presence among a Northern Alaskan People.* Dekalb: Northern Illinois University Press.

Turner, V. 1957. *Schism and Continuity.* Manchester, England: Manchester University Press.

———. 1967. *The Forest of Symbols: Aspects of Ndembu Ritual.* Ithaca NY: Cornell University Press.

———. 1969. *The Ritual Process: Structure and Anti-Structure.* Chicago: Aldine.

———. 1974. *Dramas, Fields, and Metaphors: Symbolic Action in Human Society.* Ithaca NY: Cornell University Press.

Tylor, E. B. 1958. *Primitive Culture.* 1871. Reprint, New York: Harper and Row.

Vansina, J. 1985. *Oral Tradition as History.* London: Currey.

VanStone, J. W. 1965. *The Changing Culture of the Snowdrift Chipewyan.* National Museum of Canada Bulletin No. 209, Anthropological Series 74. Ottawa: National Museum of Canada.

———. 1974. *Athapaskan Adaptations: Hunters and Fishermen of the Subarctic Forests.* Arlington Heights IL: AHM Publishing.

———. 1985. *Material Culture of the Davis Inlet and Barren Ground Naskapi: The William Duncan Strong Collection.* Fieldiana, Anthropology, n.s., no. 7. Chicago: Field Museum of Natural History.

Von Neumann, J., and O. Morgenstern. 1944. *Theory of Games and Economic Behavior.* Princeton NJ: Princeton University Press.

Wagner, R. 1981. *The Invention of Culture.* Rev. ed. Chicago: University of Chicago Press.

Warner, L. W. 1958. *A Black Civilization: A Study of an Australian Tribe.* New York: Harper and Row.

Whitten, N., Jr. 1988. "Toward a Critical Anthropology." *American Ethnologist* 15:732–42.

Wolf, E. 1982. *Europe and the People without History.* Berkeley: University of California Press.

Woodburn, J. 1982. "Egalitarian Societies." *Man* n.s., 17, no. 3: 431–541.

Yerbury, J. C. 1986. *The Subarctic Indians and the Fur Trade, 1680–1860.* Vancouver: University of British Columbia Press.

INDEX